I0119734

Robert Thomas Devlin

Report on Various Reformatory and Penal Institutions of the United States

Robert Thomas Devlin

Report on Various Reformatory and Penal Institutions of the United States

ISBN/EAN: 9783744718028

Printed in Europe, USA, Canada, Australia, Japan

Cover: Foto ©Suzi / pixelio.de

More available books at **www.hansebooks.com**

OF

ROBERT T. DEVLIN,

President of the State Board of Prison Directors of California,

ON VARIOUS

REFORMATORY AND PENAL INSTITUTIONS

OF THE

UNITED STATES.

SACRAMENTO:

STATE OFFICE, : : : : J. D. YOUNG, SUPT. STATE PRINTING.

1890.

CONTENTS.

PART I.

REFORM OR INDUSTRIAL SCHOOLS.

PART II.

REFORMATORIES OR INTERMEDIATE PRISONS.

PART III.

STATE PRISONS.

REPORT.

To the State Board of Prison Directors of California:

Having been authorized by you, for the purpose of maturing the system of government, instruction, and discipline of the Preston School of Industry, to be located at or near Ione, Amador County, to visit similar institutions in practical operation and of the best repute, and by personal inspection and investigation to acquire an insight into the principles and workings thereof for the information and benefit of the Board, I now submit the following report.

I visited and carefully examined the management of the following named industrial, reformatory, and penal institutions: Connecticut State Reform School, at Meriden; Boys' Industrial School of Ohio, at Lancaster; Illinois State Reform School, at Pontiac; State Industrial School for Juvenile Offenders of Nebraska, at Kearney; House of Refuge, at Philadelphia; House of Correction, at Chicago; Pennsylvania Reform School, at Morganza; Lyman School for Boys, at Westborough, Massachusetts; Reform School of the District of Columbia, at Washington; Indiana Reform School for Boys, at Plainfield; Pennsylvania Industrial Reformatory, at Huntingdon; Cincinnati House of Refuge; Illinois State Penitentiary, at Joliet; Massachusetts State Prison, at Charlestown; Western Penitentiary of Pennsylvania, at Allegheny City; Ohio Penitentiary, at Columbus; New York State Reformatory, at Elmira; State Penitentiary for Eastern District of Pennsylvania, at Philadelphia; Indiana Reformatory Institution for Women and Girls, at Indianapolis; Minnesota State Reform School, at St. Paul; besides the City Prison of New York, known as the "Tombs;" the prison at Blackwell's Island, New York, and some other public institutions for the care of the insane.

I also conferred with such persons as I was able to meet who had given particular attention to reformatory institutions.

For the purpose of securing an orderly arrangement, I shall divide this report into three main heads, the first devoted to the consideration of industrial or reform schools; the second to the subject of reformatories; and the third to State Prisons.

PART I.
Reform or Industrial Schools.

GENERAL VIEW.

The Act creating the Preston School of Industry provides that "the Board shall cause to be organized and maintained a department of instruction for the inmates of said school, with a course of study corresponding as far as practicable with the course of study in the public schools of this State, but the course shall not be higher than the course prescribed in grammar schools. They shall adopt a system of government, embracing such laws and regulations as are necessary for the guidance of the officers and employés, for the regulation of the hours of study and labor, for the preservation of order, for the enforcement of discipline, for the preservation of health, and for the industrial training of the inmates. The ultimate purpose of all such instruction, discipline, and industries shall be to qualify the inmates for honorable and profitable employment, rather than to make the institution self-sustaining."

The Act also provides that the school "shall be conducted on such plan as to the Board may seem best calculated to carry out the intentions of this Act, and its inmates shall be subject to military discipline, including daily drill. They shall be clothed in military uniform of such pattern and material as may be prescribed by the Board, but under no circumstances shall such inmates be clothed in convict stripes while undergoing commitment in said school."

Boys between the ages of eight and eighteen may be committed to the school for a period not exceeding the time when they shall attain majority, and the Board may make rules reducing for good conduct the time for which a boy is committed. Whenever the Board may consider an inmate sufficiently reformed to justify his reward, they may give him an honorable dismissal. The Board has power to issue certificates of conditional dismissal and parole to any worthy boy, on the condition that it binds him by articles of indenture to some suitable person who will engage to educate him and instruct him in some useful art or trade. It also has power to return him to his parents or to place him under the care of a reputable citizen and resident of this State, bound to the Board with sufficient sureties for the proper care, education, and moral and industrial training of such boy. For a violation of the parole the boy may be returned to the school, or if received from a State Prison may be returned to the latter. But if the parole be properly observed he shall be entitled to the same immunities as if he had been discharged from the institution. If a boy be found to be incorrigible he may be returned to the Court by which he was committed, and the Court may enter such judgment as it had power to make at the time of the commitment. Any boy undergoing sentence for less than life, in either of the State Prisons, who may be deemed a fit subject for training in the school, may, upon recommendation of the Board, with the approval of the Governor, be transferred to the school for the unexpired period of his sentence, and when honorably discharged shall be entitled to the same immunities as any other inmate may have.

These are the main features of the school. ·

DIFFERENT PLANS OF MANAGEMENT.

The question as to best methods to be followed for the reformation of juvenile offenders, has provoked much discussion and differences of opinion. Formerly these schools were of a penal character, in which the guarding and custody of the inmates were considered to be the main objects desired. At an early day many of these institutions were located in the heart of growing cities, and it became necessary, in order to secure the inmates, that the buildings should be strongly built and surrounded by high walls to prevent escapes. Institutions managed in this way, on what we may call the congregate plan, offered some advantages, and at the same time were open to several objections. By placing a large number beneath one roof, the cost of maintenance was lessened.

But the main object of a reform school is to develop *character*, to train for a useful life, as well as to safely guard. These schools were found in some way to be defective in accomplishing all that was hoped from them in the way of reforming or improving a boy.

THE COTTAGE OR FAMILY PLAN.

The great defect in institutions managed on the congregate plan was that they lacked the influences of family life. This led to the adoption of what is known as the cottage plan. The inmates under this system are divided into classes, according to size and form, forty to fifty being placed in a cottage, although Mr. Chapin, Superintendent of the school at Westborough, Massachusetts, advised that to attain the best results not more than twenty-five should be placed in one building. Schools managed on this plan may be differently managed, as different private homes are managed. But the nearer an approach to home life is made, the more is perfection of management attained. In the words of a gentleman who has given much thought to the subject: "The internal system of the reformatory school should be, as nearly as practicable, that of the family, with its refining and elevating influences; while awakening of the conscience and the inculation of religious principles should be primary aims. Perhaps a boy enters the school feeling that the hand of every man is against him, and with revenge in his heart; but let him there find a corps of just but merciful guides ready to teach him and help him and love him, and it is reasonable to expect that he will soon be actuated by better feelings and nobler resolves. The school should be thorough in all its methods, and aim to impart a plain education, and also give instruction in mechanical drawing. Every boy should be instructed in some useful trade or occupation, and his wishes consulted in selecting it."

A better idea can be obtained, perhaps, of the plan of management that should prevail in these schools by examining some of those of recognized merit, individually, than by entering into an abstract discussion. Accordingly, I shall proceed to describe in detail those that I inspected.

BOYS' INDUSTRIAL SCHOOL OF OHIO.

The State of Ohio, in 1856, appointed a Commission to visit reform schools, and report a plan for the management of a reform school for that State. The Commission recommended the adoption of the family or cottage plan, and finally the school was located on a farm of twelve hundred acres, six miles south of the town of Lancaster. The ground is hilly in places, with fertile valleys between the ridges. In some places it breaks into high rocks.

The buildings consist of the main building, ten family buildings, printing office, shoe, brush, polytechnic, paint, blacksmith, carpenter, tailor, and bake shops, carriage, bath, meat, ware, engine, gas, ice, corn, and green houses, water tower, hospital, mending-room, knitting-room, and barns.

The family buildings are named after the State and its rivers, and are known as the Ohio, Hocking, Union, Muskingum, Cuyahoga, Scioto, Huron, Miami, Erie, and Maumee buildings. With the exception of a double building used for the very youngest boys, and separated from the other buildings by a distance of half a mile, all the buildings are arranged in the form of a segment of a circle about the main building.

The main building is one hundred and sixty-one feet in length, and consists of three stories and basement. The chapel has a seating capacity of six hundred, and is ninety-one feet in length by sixty in width.

The school receives boys between the ages of ten and sixteen. In 1885 a system of merits and demerits was introduced, which classifies the inmates, according to the offense, into three grades. If a boy is committed on the charge of murder, manslaughter, obstructing railroads, highway robbery, rape, or arson, he is debited with seven thousand demerits; if on the charge of assault and battery with intent, embezzlement exceeding $35, burglary, grand larceny, forgery, or perjury, he is debited with six thousand demerits; if on the charge of aiding prisoners to escape, embezzlement under $35, or petit larceny, he is debited with five thousand demerits.

For good deportment a boy receives ten merits a day, and if he has a perfect record for three successive months he is entitled to three hundred extra merits. Information given of an attempt to escape, if the information proves correct, entitles the informer to a reward of three hundred merits. When all the demerits have been canceled, the boy is entitled to a leave of absence for four months, and if he continues to conduct himself properly, he may have his "leave of absence" card renewed at the expiration of every four months, until he reaches his majority. If he is guilty of misbehavior while on leave of absence, he is returned to the institution and charged with one thousand demerits in addition to the number originally debited against him.

The discipline is that of the family, school, workshop, and farm, and not of the prison. The inmates are not considered as prisoners or criminals, but are watched over as pupils in a public school. The rules of the school provide that the food used shall be that approved by the common custom of the country, well prepared. Before each meal, grace is said. No officer or assistant is allowed at any time or place to make use of liquor as a beverage. All persons employed at the school are required to attend all religious services on the Sabbath, unless a special leave of absence is obtained from the Superintendent.

The salaries paid at this institution are as follows:

Superintendent _____$100 per month.
Matron _____$33⅓ per month.
Assistant Superintendent _____$70 per month.
Assistant Matron_____$25 per month.
Steward_____$1,150 per annum.
Elder Brother and wife__$45 for husband, $20 for wife, or $65 per month.
Engineer _____$55 per month.
Gardener and florist _____ _____$55 per month.
Shoemaker _____$50 per month.

In addition to these salaries, the officers are allowed board, lodging, stationery, and washing.

The Superintendent, Mr. Barrett, said, in conversation, that he aims to feed the inmates well, as nothing is made by any other course. Bean dinners are supplied three days in each week, and meat every day. Eggs twenty-five times during the year.

The average per capita cost of maintenance is $120 per year. The buildings are heated by steam and lighted by coal gas manufactured at the place; but the Superintendent informed me that he considered electric light preferable. The boys bathe every Saturday. There is no distinction among the boys as to the kind of clothing worn or food eaten. They are all, in these matters, on an equality.

CONNECTICUT STATE REFORM SCHOOL.

This school is situated at Meriden, Connecticut, and is under the superintendence of Mr. G. E. Howe. Mr. Howe had charge of the Lancaster School before he assumed control of the school at Meriden.

I explained to him fully what we hoped to do, what money we had available, and asked him to put himself in the place of the Board of Directors, and from that standpoint to give me his views.

In reply he said that he would recommend the erection of four cottages costing about $20,000 each, and one administration building, which ought to cost about $60,000. The cottages should be built so as to accommodate about fifty inmates each. The administration building should have a department for boys who had not earned their freedom, and the part of the building devoted to this purpose should be made secure.

In arrangement, the administration building should be central and the others should be erected in semi-circular form around, at distances apart from the main building of not less than one hundred and fifty feet. The chapel should be a separate building. The administration building should contain rooms for the Board of Directors and apartments for Superintendent and assistant, and also general bakery, general laundry, tailor shop, and other shops, if necessary or convenient.

With regard to trades and labor, Mr. Howe thought that preference should be given to farm labor, as such work was well adapted to effect a reformation of the inmates. He does not favor the use of machinery. Each cottage should have a separate workshop. The boys should be kept in school during three hours of each day, and the remainder of their time should be directed between labor and recreation. There should be no distinctions in the matter of dress or food. It is a sufficient reward that good conduct will shorten the term of the inmate.

Mr. Howe believes that flogging should not be altogether dispensed with, but all punishment should be under the charge of the Superintendent. He prefers, for sleeping purposes, dormitories, to separate rooms.

At Meriden, the Superintendent is the purchasing agent, only meat being bought by contract. Supplies are delivered to the persons in charge of the cottages every Saturday morning, and charged up to them. The cost of keeping the inmates is $150 per capita per year. And this sum covers also all ordinary repairs to the buildings.

The buildings of this school embrace the original main building and five additional separate buildings. Each of these separate buildings or cottages will conveniently house about fifty boys. Each building is a miniature institution in itself. The boys in each building constitute a separate family; they eat, sleep, and attend school in the same building. They have a separate recreation ground, and do not mingle with the boys in other families. Each family is under the supervision of three persons—a man and his wife who reside with the family, and a lady teacher, who also resides in the same building. The buildings have only the ordinary fastenings, and are surrounded by no fence or inclosure of any kind. These buildings are situate upon an eminence within the corporate limits of the city and within a short distance of some of its most attractive residences.

Throughout the institution there prevails the neatness and order of a well regulated family. A system of marks is used for the purpose of maintaining discipline, and the boys are relied upon as monitors.

The boys are allowed two suits of clothes. For daily use, they wear all-wool, indigo-blue jackets, lined with flannel, with heavy, all-wool gray cloth for vest and pants, hickory shirts, good shoes and stockings, and blue caps. On Sundays the pants worn are blue instead of gray.

Great care is exercised to have the utmost cleanliness. The inmates sleep in single beds supplied always with an abundance of clean bedding. Their food is prepared in the most approved manner, meats and bread are of the first quality, and vegetables, when in season, are bountifully supplied. Coffee is served every morning and evening; and the tables, covered with white oil-cloth, with the white porcelain crockery and the silver-plated knives, forks, spoons, casters, and soup tureens, give the dining-rooms the appearance of a well kept restaurant.

During every Sabbath afternoon the pulpit is filled by some minister from the churches of the city, and also instruction is given to a class of Catholic boys by the Sisters of Mercy.

Mr. Howe has devoted his life to this work, and is constantly appealed to for advice and information. He has kindly furnished me with the plans of buildings at Meriden, and explained in detail the operation and management of his school. The whole system is founded in simplicity, but he has prepared the following explanation of the open or family system, which contains in his own language his views and counsel on such matters as will arise in the organization of a school to be conducted on this system and an answer to the objections made to it:

The family system is that which has for its underlying and grand idea the family as a divine institution, and that the Creator has ordained that human beings shall receive, through it, greater and more lasting social and moral influence than through any sphere of life. In conformity with this great and fundamental principle the inmates are classified, and limited numbers are placed in modest but well built cottages, which are free from anything like the usual prison appliances, and furnished with all the necessaries and comforts of a well ordered home, presided over by a Christian gentleman and lady, who, as husband and wife, hold the relation of father and mother toward the youth of the household. Each family is distinct from the other families in all matters of its own particular management, but is united with all the others under one central head, every family having its own school-room, dining-room, dormitory, and playground; the government of each family to be thoroughly parental, and physical coercion never to be used until other means have failed, and when used, to be administered under the humanizing spirit and genius of the family.

Thus we claim for our system a foundation upon natural and fundamental principles, and upon that one best known and deepest felt in the universal mind and heart of men: that in the family and home are found the most impressive and lasting influences that shape the child into the man. It would appear that there could be no cavil against the self-evidence that this was the Creator's design in the founding and conservation of human society. It follows, then, that in removing a boy from an inadequate or bad home, into a better and good one, we are not acting in violation, but in harmony with natural law.

And the wisdom of harmonious procedure must be further apparent, when we consider the nature, the instincts, and necessities of child life. If, in the being of man and woman there is the implanted instinct, the cry of nature for offspring, for some creation from their own loins to love, there is also the corresponding implanted appeal in the child for the protection and tenderness of a father and mother and the broodings of a home. So that if we remove a child from parents who have virtually orphaned him by their inadequacy, neglect, or cruel usage, and from a home unnatural and hateful, and bring him into the adoption of a wiser and better parentage, and into the more natural home of comfort and benevolence, then, again, we are not going contrary to, but in unison with, natural principles.

Such, in brief, is the fundamental idea and theory of our plan for juvenile reformative government, in opposition to the genius and methods of the common and penal institution.

The prison principle is more or less hateful to the adult delinquent;

it is an abhorrence to the youthful offender. The prison principle in reform peculiarly outrages the nature of child life. The shock penetrates to the ends of his being, and body and soul rise up against it in the fiercest antagonism; for, as soon as born, the great law is upon the child, that he springs toward the development of a man. To this end his Creator has endowed him with the most intense activity and restlessness. The child loves and pants for freedom. His every contact with nature is but his communion with a second mother. To a boy the bolted door, the barred window, the walled yard, the shadowy cell, and the divers contrivances of brute force, are not so much terrors as enemies, that he is not afraid to fight, and with which every impulse of his nature does wage implacable conflict, though, for the time being, he may be rendered helpless against them. These barriers against the deep cravings of his child nature, instead of becoming factors in his reform, become like Carthaginian altars, and he, like a young Hannibal, swears upon them undying hatred to them, to the builders of them; and such is the desperate growth of his ferocious hate, that he fancies in every man the architect of some new prison and its penalties.

Behind them and under their despotic sway, the question, we believe, never enters his mind, "How shall I reform through these agencies?" but "How shall I get away from them?" The darkness of these things is so great to him, that never a ray of Christian and humanizing light can he see in such an economy of government and instruction. All of it is an unnatural home to him, no home—only a horde of criminals, more or less bad, and the star of hope, if it shines at all, flickers dim and sickly. His officers and teachers, however kind in intention, are, by the genius of such a system, never parental or fraternal, but suspicious constables and taskmasters; every movement of his life under a galling surveillance. And to add to the cloudy prospect of a child under this system, there is increase of whatever natural stigma comes to him by being "sent to a reform school," and it makes such opprobrium far greater and miserable. As the child enters, he knows by public opinion that he is thought only fit to have a prison for a home, policemen for parents, and bolts and dungeons for laws; and when he comes out he finds the "jail bird" estimate engraven so deeply that no sweat of any virtuous effort can rub it out, and finally, as a crowning disadvantage and demerit of the prison reformatory, we see the State, in placing her wayward children under such a system, committing herself to a most stultifying and suicidal policy, in that while her great aim is to bring such children into reformed men, she seeks to do this by training them as criminals.

Whatever may be said of the penal institution for the rectification of adult and matured depravity, as a system for the wayward child it is a barbarism, a worthy relic of the harsh and heartless ages past, when men were rated about in the percentage of cattle, and belongs not to this age, so irradiated by influences that prize degraded humanity at something of the value put upon it by the redeeming, loving Christ.

In contrast with the destructive nature and methods, and the abortive results of the congregate or prison policy, we urge with every instinct of our soul, and on literal knowledge of the actual, tangible, and glorious successes, the claims of the open or family system.

The man or the woman, through the wear and grind of life outside the prison, may, even for the scant hospitalities inside of it, sink into a degree of contentment; but the child and youth deprived of this degree of liberty, with life a perpetual shackle, is put into an unconquerable antagonism to all reformatory influences; for, again, see the operations of natural law! The growing child and youth is under the press of the animal nature, environed by the conditions of animalism, has the motive power of animal spirits within as the adult has not. In youth we see the warm and eruptive. In the adult they have greatly spent their force. Now, the prison and its methods are those barriers to the necessary, proper vent and outflow of the basilar forces. But the open, the freer, the home system, with its wide facilities for labor, for play, for wide communion with nature outside, and the social and moral facilities within the home, are the natural, healthful means, the aqueducts through which these inflammable and critical propensities may expend themselves safely.

The family plan gives time and most'convenient opportunities for close contact and confiding interview with each child; for he is a child in a home and not one of a promiscuous and repellant gang. In the heads of the family he has a father and a mother; in his teachers he has elder brothers and sisters. His life passes day by day in review before them; but this parental and fraternal watchfulness never excites his hostility, but in natural, healthful way tempers and disciplines his tendencies to waywardness. And here the way opens to the most ample opportunities for woman's transcendent influence. The universal heart of men will acknowledge the strange potency of the mother upon the growing character of a child, and especially in lasting influence upon a boy. Here, then, in this system we give the boy to be mothered, by giving him a home, such as the necessities of the penal plan know nothing about; and especially does this consideration rise into momentous importance as we know that many of the commitments are of children of tender age. Then if we can have a reformatory system that will give us woman's ear to listen to little ailments; woman's hand to soften the rigors of the young orphaned life, and the scepter of woman's soft and winning love to rule in that strange kingdom, the heart of a child, then it is immeasurable gain!

But while we have full confidence in the soundness of these mere fundamental considerations, we hasten on to others, which, of course, will have greater general acceptance, the proofs wrought out by actual experience.

And here, in referring as briefly as possible to the history and results of the Ohio Reform School for Boys, over which we had the honor of presiding for so many years, we can only mention that the institutions in Germany and France, the authors of the Ohio school principle, were noble successes, the hope of philanthropists there, and gave the most promising warrant for the adoption of the experiment in Ohio.

The first reformatory institution organized upon the open or family plan in this country was at Lancaster, Ohio, in the year 1858, founded essentially on the principle, and adopting the methods of the "*Rauhe Haus*," at Horn, Germany, founded by Dr. Wichern, and the military school at Mettray, France, organized by DeMetz. The first ten boys were received from the Cincinnati House of Refuge, January thirtieth of the first year. Two of the four original buildings for family purposes were of brick, and two of logs, and very plain. These soon made way for better ones, until the school became one of surprising and splendid proportions. In the establishment of this school, of course, there were no precedents that were at all well defined and practicable, by which its economy could be guided. All was new, and to so great extent novel that the people at large were utterly skeptical and scoffing toward the pretenses of a system that proposed to govern bad and criminal boys without the usual apparatus of the prison; and appropriations came sparingly and grudgingly, so that the whole pioneer history of this institution is largely the unwritten one of arduous and painful toil. And the tide of disbelief and opposition only began to flow back when there went out from the institution into different parts of the State, by twos and threes, the first companies of reformed boys. These gave such universal and marked credit to the place and work that had saved them, that immediately we began to receive the grateful interest and support which the fuller success of the institution so imperatively demanded; and, thanks to an all wise helping Providence, it was demonstrated, to us convincingly, overwhelmingly, in our nineteen years of superintendence of that institution, that this was a better way to bring into a true captivity the wayward body and spirit, than by their incarceration between frowning walls, and its all-hateful and abortive array of brutal power. We have seen, again and again, most signally vindicated that heavenly reminder to men, that there is still left in the nature of their most fallen fellows a craving for mercy and kindness, and the instinct to respond to any such benign exhibition. Such far penetrating and marvelous transformations of character have we seen, as the harvest of this policy, that we have said, "Indeed, it does run current with the charities of God," "It is the plan of God himself," "It is the true one, and there is no other."

Of the large number that passed out of the institution to care for themselves, a mass of wonderful and most gratifying statistics could be gathered. Among the number may be found eminent lawyers, doctors, and members of other honorable professions; some passed through college with high honors; some have become editors and proprietors of influential journals; others, skilled mechanics and tradesmen, while scores have become industrious farmers and horticulturists, acquiring their taste and knowledge of these noble industries at the school. Most affecting reminiscences of soldierly fidelity could be given of those who enlisted in the war of the rebellion. We do not believe that the same number of youths taken from the ordinary walks of life would furnish a better average record, and yet the majority of these boys who have made these good records were from the lower walks of society. But it may be possible that it will occur to some minds that such successes were isolated and phenomenal; then let us add to this testimony the wide and significant fact that the Ohio school has become the pioneer and pattern of similar institutions in several of the States, and that no State, since the successes of that school, has erected a reformatory on the prison plan; while, on the other hand, some, while not seeing their way clear to make radical changes, have modified their penal systems.

The following States have adopted the open, or family, institution, either fully or with slight modifications: New Jersey, Wisconsin, Indiana, Iowa, Minnesota, Michigan, Western Pennsylvania, and the District of Columbia. The States of Ohio, Massachusetts, and Connecticut have each a school on the open plan for girls and for boys; Massachusetts has her institution at Westborough as a "mixed" one. In addition to the "big" house, or prison portion, there are "trust" houses outside the walls. Connecticut is adopting essentially this modification, beginning to build outside of the walls this year, it being the best she can do for the present. We are confident that other States would wholly or partially adopt the family system, if it were not that large expenditures having been made, new outlays would come only by great effort, and with natural reluctance.

Objections have been advanced against the open or family system, that it is natural to suppose will, from time to time, be revived. It will be our attempt to reply to these; and first, in a more general way, by discussing the requisites favorable to the success of a reformatory on the family system, which it is hoped will meet at least the more trivial misgivings; and second, by a particular consideration of the more specific objections.

The primary requisite is a farm of thoroughly good land, and large enough to furnish all the necessaries and some of the luxuries, that the needs of the institution may be met, and to spare. Large and fertile, that it may never lack support for a sufficient herd of cows, and for the necessary equipment of the farm. All the fruit trees which will flourish in the region should be lavishly planted and assiduously cultivated. The greatest number of acres possible should be reserved for tillage, because these acres are to be such real factors in the boy's reformation. We have remarked, as a prime consideration, that the land should be thoroughly good. We wish to emphasize this so essential necessity, not only that the institution may have the highest opportunities to pay its way, but also in the moral effect upon the minds of the officers who superintend, and the boys who work it. That they shall not have to toil and sweat, and reap not, but to expect bloom and wealth, and get them. Indeed, all agricultural and horticultural matters are to have such generous attention paid them, that it shall be felt throughout the institution that the noble farming industry is the chief and central one. Another prime prerequisite is the location of the school near an abundance of sweet, pure water; and we hardly need add that the site of the reformatory should be first and foremost an healthful one. It should also be situated in an intelligent and moral community. The surroundings of such an institution are of great importance. There are many such institutions that are suffering through the inimical feeling of its neighbors; springing largely from ignorance, and the narrowness bred of it. We are reminded by these considerations of the hinderances with which the Ohio school had to contend, and which still, in great measure, hamper it. Its farm land is wretchedly poor, necessitating a vast amount of labor and discouraging hope; and at its inception, at least, the standard of intelligence in the surrounding inhabitants, and their prejudices, were anything but desirable.

The location of a reformatory should be made with wise reference to markets and transportation, and yet, to be too near a city or large village is detrimental; but, on the other hand, extreme isolation is to be avoided. All life and animation which indicate the honorable progress of the age are profitable as incitements to body and mind.

The buildings should be plain, but substantial and comfortable; the executive buildings to be the central ones, and the family cottages conveniently and pleasantly surrounding. The cottages to be appropriately named, and surrounded with the beauty of lawn, shrub, and flower.

Each to have its own family garden for the common interest of the household, and, if possible, each child to have a part in it as his own. This latter feature was at one time pursued with most gratifying results in the Ohio school.

The homes should be ones to which every boy can aspire by industry and prudence, and he should be so taught. Everything in and outside the homes should be made educative and pleasant. They should be provided with an abundance of wholesome food. If it is true that the "way to a man's heart is through his stomach," how much more is this the road of promise in the growing, vigorous child. No specified dietary should be allowed—children should never know beforehand such times as "bean day," "fish day," etc. All distinguishments in dress should be avoided. Let the boys dress as other boys do. Let all such arbitrary distinctions be put as far away as possible, that the child may live a simple, natural life, and going back into general society, the transition shall be an easy and natural one.

And now, if, in the ideas thus set forth, it is thought there is created too much of the mere pleasure home, with danger of engendered idle disposition, and character lacking thrift and sturdiness, we say, no! While it should be the sacred aim that the comforts and pleasures of a true home are to accompany all efforts, yet the aim equally sacred and sought is to make the reform institution a nursery of honorable industry, and the formation of energetic, sturdy habits of thrift, to train in manly and Christian purpose and action. In trades and occupations, to teach the boys perfectly what they essay to learn, whatever it is; that for their own sake, when they go forth, and for the sake of the State, they shall be found skilled and expert laborers. The great aim of this education should be to make the boy self-sustaining, himself to become a a wise and worthy head of a family.

As a second consideration in the prerequisites for a thorough and efficient reformatory on the family plan, we remark upon the required character of its officers and teachers.

It will be readily acknowledged that this matter is of first moment in endeavors to get what little good is possible from the prison plan of reform; but regarding it in its relation to our family system, it is the core, the marrow of our system. It is to it our life, paralysis, or death. The genius of our system is the home—the family. In the heads of it the father and mother; in the subordinate, officer and teacher—the elder brother. In methods, its fundamental aim is kindness, gentleness, forbearance, self-sacrifice, humanizing and Christian influences. Now, to have a weak king or magistrate is damaging; but to have fathers and mothers and brethren of the family inadequate and weak, is destruction.

The Superintendent to be sought for is to be one who has had actual practical experience in reformatory, or at least in some philanthropic labor—of course, the more the better; a man who believes his work to be the noblest on earth, who has enthusiasm for his profession; a man believing with all his soul in the fundamental idea of the family system, and expecting results from it with an assurance like that which looks for the sun's light and shining on to-morrow; a man of intelligence, good common sense, tact, and conciliatory spirit.

These same general requisites of character are to be sought for in all the subordinate officers and teachers; love and enthusiasm for the work

are ever the great requirements to be insisted upon in the choice of those
to be in authority and parentage over these children and youth, and
anything like the hireling spirit in the candidate for these places is to
be abhorred, and the mere seekers of place and salary to be rejected as
unworthy.

In the government of the reformatory we hardly dare say that any
one person may be less fitted for his place than another; but if any such
thing can be allowed, then again we wish to emphasize the prerequisites
of character in the heads of the cottage homes—the husbands and
wives, the fathers and mothers. Yes; we will even say that there may
be some lack permitted in the chief and head of the institution; provided such want is offset by thorough and sterling worth in the heads
of the different homes. For here are the fountains of influence, here
are the hearts, the throbbing life centers of the institution. These
homes are the suns from which are to irradiate the real light of the
reformatory, and if they suffer any eclipse the shadows are deeper than
from any other cause. These are as rudders to the ship, while all else
is but the crew; and even if the Captain fails somewhat as a navigator,
still great safety may be hoped for, if those at the helm are good and
true.

Then the men and women to be sought as the heads of these homes
are to be of first worth, Christian gentlemen and ladies—persons of first
rate common sense and intelligence—of natural refinement as well as
some acquired culture, and if they have had or have children of their
own, it is a matter of gain. If not, then those are to be sought who
have strong natural love for children, and sympathy with child life.
They are to be Christian, that in ample way they may be in God's stead
to the untrained and neglected child—qualified to lay the foundation
for moral character, and the efficient architects of its further developments—persons whose interest in the child relate not alone to time, but
to eternity.

We pass, now, to more specific notice of the more common and prominent objections.

The matter of expense has been urged. Yes, we cheerfully admit the
family to be more expensive pecuniarily than the prison system. But
let the first part of our answer be the considerations of the commonest
expediency and sense. The family system is worth more! It is worth
more in dollars and cents to the State, in that its reformatory efforts are
so full of hope that its graduates will become permanently self-supporting and good citizens, putting the State to no further expense by coming
back to the institution, either speedily or eventually; either as criminals
or paupers, or both; but on the other hand enriching the State by good
citizenship. Yes, it costs somewhat more than the prison reformatory,
but it is worth more even by the measurement of the lowest standard.
If the reform school means anything, it means physical, mental, and
moral reformation for this life, and redemption for the life to come; then
where is the man who will sully his Christian faith and name by figur-
ing the dollar and cent cost of any reformatory system that will in the
greatest degree secure these transcendent results? And we argue that
the family system will give these results in the greatest degree.

Yes, and we argue more. We claim that even if our system was still
one in tentative and experimental conditions, and was not yet, what it

is, a realized and noble triumph, still it would be worth all the money cost to fairly try the promise that lies it.

The chief and only noteworthy cost in our system over any other would, of course, come from the increased numbers and superior qualifications required in the officers and teachers of the school. And yet an economy here may be wisely practiced. It is not necessary for the heads of these cottage homes, or for teachers, to be persons encumbered with anything like large and expensive families of their own. This would be a positive detriment to their needed efficiency, and would be a useless cost to the State. Nothing like dead weights upon any institution should be for a moment allowed.

But if the State will drive anything like a bargain in this matter, then our system must go unpurchased, for there is a cheaper. The genius of brute power may be bought for even a very low price. A jail need not be an expensive edifice; and the men are plenty and cheap who will make good master jailers. A single turnkey may have charge of even one half the inmates of a school, and all the teachers under such an administration may consistently be of a lower grade.

The greatest objection brought against our system is the liability of "escapes." This is so readily presumed that the question most frequently is not "Will not the boys escape?" as "How many escape?" We reply by saying that right here around this supposed pivotal critical liability of our system center its finest triumphs. We would have supposed this very possible from the fundamental principles of our system; but we have seen the assurance in the actual facts.

Boys will run away sometimes from even natural homes. They will fly from walled homes as from horrors, if they can. The boy will naturally take the first opportunity to flee from the prison home, feeling that it may be his last chance; but why should he fly from the family restraint when the opportunity is ever before him? And we find it to be a most singular fact that he either puts his flight off to some more convenient season, or else his contented abiding must be explained on the pretty well substantiated principle in human nature, especially in the juvenile, that when told that "he shall not do a thing," then he sets himself at once to work to do it, but, on the other hand, when left to carry out his own free will in such a matter, he is either indifferent or decides he will not.

Thus a wise liberty becomes its own defender. With us a boy has large and generous freedom. Why should he crave more and uncertain liberty? If his home is the rendezvous of comforts, his food good, his clothes tidy, his guardians parental and kind; if benevolence to his animal and higher wants encircle him, his time wisely divided between work and play, will he want to exchange such possessions for the neglects, the poverty, the distastes of even the home of his birth, and for society aimed against him? We should presume not, even if we were contemplating this matter in the light of theory. But suppose that if even five or ten per cent of the worst boys should irretrievably run away, should the remaining percentage never be trusted to the beneficence of our freedom? Very little philanthropy, surely, would lie in a philosophy that would say "yes" to such a proposition.

But, as intimated, our experience at the Ohio school singularly proves the confidence of our foregoing ideas and presumptions. One of our cardinal principles in discipline was to place confidence in our boys, to

2D

trust them; and not in one single instance in nineteen years as Overseer of a number averaging four hundred yearly did we have cause to regret it. Hundreds of most interesting illustrations might be given to show the most happy results of putting the boys upon their honor, their manhood.

We have taken, unattended by any other officer, as many as two hundred boys in one company to the woods "a chestnutting," amid brush of thick, dark growth, the boys dipersing where they pleased for hours, but when the recognized signal was given, every one responded, returning home in good order. At one time the whole body of inmates, four hundred in number, went to Lancaster, six miles distant, to a Sabbath-school "concert." The boys made the whole trip on foot, coming back in the dark, so that no officer knew the whereabouts of his company, and yet every single one returned in good time to the institution, there being a good deal of friendly strife as to which family should reach it first; and yet woodland lined the road almost the entire distance. Hundreds of other instances could be given to show the power over the boy's heart by being trusted; of feeling that he is thought worthy of confidence and esteem.

During the many years of our connection with the Ohio school there was never a time that at least nine tenths of the boys could not be trusted to go at any time alone to distant parts of the farm on errands, or to town, six miles away. We have received boys from the State Prison, at Columbus, and in three weeks' time they have gone alone to Lancaster, six miles distant, coming back promptly, transacting faithfully the business intrusted to them; and never in a single case was this trust abused. Great and most gratifying was the evidence of the power over the heart of the boy of being trusted, of the expectation that he would be faithful and manly.

The boy or man in need of reformatory treatment is well nigh hopeless if he is to be continually suspected. Such policy of perpetual suspicion is irritative, hateful, and a bondage that blunts and blights whatever desire he may have to be worthy of confidence. As a general policy in the reform of humanity, let us, in the name of Heaven, at least hope that all is right until good evidence of the wrong appears. Under the prison system the boy is constantly suspected. In it, suspicion and spying are reduced to a science, and the child is never in a position to have his honor fairly tried.

Another objection that appears to be held as a grave one, is that of classification; this taking on the twofold form of classification as to numbers and character.

As to the size of each family, fifty or sixty boys may be efficiently cared for in one home presided over by a gentleman and wife and one assistant. True, a smaller number would be more in accordance with the size of the natural family, and, we have no doubt, better upon the whole for the inmates; still, from the pressures of State prudence, this large number can be efficiently cared for. This was the size of the family in Ohio, and we believe, also, is the average number in other States; still, if the additional expense can be met, we recommend a smaller number.

The second form of objection is classification as to character.

Some institutions make a great virture of such a division, and cry out: "Do not let the bad boys mingle with the good!" We answer, do not tell a boy that he is bad by putting him by himself or with any exclusive company of the bad. If you create any such pernicious distinction, you do not restrain the spirit of evil, you develop it. If the bad boy sees that he is as well treated as the boy of superior merit, he will endeavor to rise to that merit. If you have good boys you need their influence over the bad. The natural Christian family does not discard and thrust into exile its wayward members, but seeks their reformation in company with all its other members.

This principle as to classification was tried in the Ohio school with equally gratifying results, with all the others. No classification as to character was ever known there.

Thus we have endeavored by direct and indirect statement to meet objections. We will hope to still cover more of such ground by further remarks upon discipline in general.

Upon this matter there is wide diversity of opinion. The judicious mind will seek for the desirable mean between the extremes. Discipline may be too lax; it may be, and often is, far too severe and cruel.

There is so much of the spirit in society yet that demands an "eye for an eye," and a "tooth for a tooth," that even the criminal child must not be allowed to escape until there is meted to him a certain amount of punishment. Under the old system of treating physical diseases the patient must be well bled before the healing treatment could be begun; and with many even the wayward child cannot be treated for his badness until he is first punished. This is false in philosophy, and evidently wicked in morals. Every child, in the matter of reform, should be taken at his word the first time and every time in which lies a reasonable hope that he will perform his promises.

In the administration of a reform school, next to its foundation upon humane and Christian principles, the great aim should be simplicity in government. The fewest possible of simple rules. The simple, but all-inclusive standard of "do right" should be little seen, but should be felt to pervade the institution like an atmosphere.

In the Ohio reformatory, for some twelve years, and up to the time of our departure, blanks were furnished the heads of families to be filled with the weekly records of discipline in each family, detailing punishments of whatever kind inflicted during the week. These reports were read every Sabbath morning before the whole school, and any boy was allowed to make his personal statement as to the correctness of these reports; and with an average of about five hundred boys in the institution, the aggregate of punishments for one week would not ordinarily exceed twelve, and would sometimes be less than half that number, and frequently several weeks would pass without a single punishment in some of the families.

In the first years of the history of the Ohio institution a stone lock-up, with cells, was built for the confinement, at times, of the worst cases; but we soon saw its damaging influence and it was abandoned, being converted into a meat house.

Corporal punishments were resorted to only as a last resort, and the rule was that no blow should be inflicted above the hips. At one time the loss of a meal or more was resorted to, or the feeding upon crust and water, but was soon abandoned as unwise and detrimental. And there is, too, a wise philosophy, we think, in discarding such a punishment. The appetite of the growing boy is a passion, and to starve it is to goad it into fury and bring the mind into the worst condition possible for reformatory purposes. All ludicrous and highly artificial punishments are to be avoided. All punishments that bring raillery and ridicule upon the object of it are not to be tolerated.

No reform institution, of course, can be a success without some corporal penalties, for even these are inflicted in nearly every, perhaps every, natural home.' But these are to be inflicted only under a system which shall be administered upon humane and Christian principles, and only by the hands of persons of the highest character.

And now, in remainder, we purpose to still further meet objections and seeming difficulties by a few observations upon the question: "Why even more is not accomplished under the family system;" and will conclude a paper, whose expanded proportions we trust will be excused in the importance of the subject, by some fragments of thought that have incidentally arisen during the progress of the paper.

In the medical and other important professions, the student is expected to spend a year in diligent study and toil before he is fit for his diploma, and even then he is employed hesitatingly and cautiously; and especially in the case of the physician, the one eagerly sought for and most trusted is the one of skilled reputation, for "everything that a man hath will he give for his life." But if so anxious to give the dangers and crises of our bodies and perishable lives into the hands of the highest skill and ability, what shall be asked for, in the requirements of character, of those who are to have the training and care not only of the bodily and mental powers of neglected and depraved youth for this life, but for their moral welfare for this life and the next?

We demand that the teachers of our children shall be persons in whom we have the highest confidence. Shall we demand less for the children of our neighbors whom we are to "love as ourselves?"

The reform school teachers and officers are to be persons of not only efficient professional ability, but persons ranking in integrity, honor, and purity of character, with any other calling that can be named.

And yet mark what is still so prevalently the popular opinion. It is not an uncommon thing, in many of the reformatories of the land, for the Boards of Trustees and Managers to hold their offices solely on account of political services to the party in power. So often totally unfit to be permitted to hold these solemn trusts, and then in ignorance and favoritism farming out the subordinate places to timeservers and sycophants. The popular opinion is still most lamentably prevalent, that any passable novice is fit for Superintendent of a reform school, and most any one who can "read, write, and cipher," fit for teachers.

Now, because a man has been moderately successful as a lawyer, farmer, grocer, Constable, or even Sheriff, is it an argument that he is fit for these positions? Is it an argument that any reputable nobody is fit for these posts because he happens to be in want of a job of some kind and is servant to some small politician?

It is injury enough to our prison schools to be filled and officered by political timeservers; but for all expectancy of anything like the measure of good which is possible to the family system, it is hopelessness and death.

Partisan politics, in its ignorance and greed, lays a destructive hand upon a great deal in this country; but it does no such ghastly work as when it intermeddles with the high necessities of our reformatory institutions, making them the playthings of its greedy caprices.

Not until the people shall with solemn resolution say that, whatever else the ignorance and arbitrariness of partisan politics may effect, they shall never lay a disturbing hand upon the best interests of our reformatory and philanthropic institutions—not till then will the prison systems of reform be better than they are; and not till then will be realized the broad and magnificent promise that lies in the genius and methods of our family system.

In conclusion, and by way of recapitulation, we would say, while the spirit and practice under the open or family system tend so naturally to lessen the stigma of a boy's being "sent to the reform school," and which would grow still less as the system became still firmer established and improved, yet the form of commitment to the reformatory has much to do in the opprobrium attaching to the history of "reform school boys." Surely it is enough to have in the Judge, in the ostentatious constabulary, and necessary legal formalities, features dignified and august, without the brutal terrorism to a child of handcuffs and shackles. Is this remark thought an exaggerated one? We have seen, many times, small boys accompanied to the reformatory by two able-bodied policemen, and manacled at that.

Time sentences should never be authorized, and a system of merits should be used until the boy has reached a sufficient degree of honor to permit him to be released on probation, to be returned to the school if need be.

In government and instruction the officers and teachers should have the incentive of diplomas held out to them, that professional pride may be exalted and aroused. And a very prominent aim should be to bring into service as officers and teachers the boys themselves. This incentive will work wonders in effects to virtuous aspirations. In the Ohio school this policy was so happily pursued that many of the inmates were employed as elder brothers, and several have held and are now holding important positions as officers in other reformatories.

The voice of criticism will continue to be heard here and there against the family system. Some of it will be honest and sincere misgiving; other will be, as it often has been, the voice of prejudice, or the results of partial and inadequate investigation. But here again let us remind the objector of some very reasonable considerations. A theory and principle may be perfectly sound and practicable, and yet be singularly abortive by maladministration. No philanthropic institution can stand the freaks of partisan politics. It cannot stand to have its places of trust filled by inadequacy and mediocrity.

STATE INDUSTRIAL SCHOOL FOR JUVENILE OFFENDERS AT KEARNEY, NEBRASKA.

This school is also conducted on the family or cottage system, and receives both boys and girls. It is organized under a provision of the Constitution of the State of Nebraska delegating to the Legislature the power "to provide by law for the establishment of a school, or schools, for the safe-keeping, education, employment, and reformation of all children, under the age of sixteen years, who, for want of proper parental care, or other cause, are growing up in mendicancy or crime." The school is located on three hundred and twenty acres of land donated by the City of Kearney and adjoining the western limits of the city. The inventory shows an investment in all of $145,000. Incandescent electric lights of the Mather system illuminate the buildings and grounds. The cost of the plant was $3,500. The plant embraces a two hundred and fifty-lamp dynamo, equivalent to sixteen candle power, and a high speed engine having fifty-seven horse power. Water for the uses of the school is obtained by a system of drive wells at the bottom of a hill, and the water is forced up by a double-acting steam pump, through a four-inch main.

The buildings and cottages are heated by steam. The radiators are heated by one central system connecting by pipes with the different cottages. The inmates bathe every Saturday. Each cottage is provided with bathtubs, besides which there is a pond covering four acres, used by the boys for swimming in summer.

The Superintendent, Mr. John T. Mallalieu, recommends that in the arrangement of the buildings for the Preston School the kitchen and cooking-rooms should be in one building, separated from the administration and other buildings. In this building the cooking should be done on the lower floor and the upper floor should be used for dining-rooms. At Kearney this arrangement does not prevail. The kitchen and dining-rooms are a part of the administration building, but Mr. Mallalieu is opposed to this plan.

At the time I visited the school, the number of inmates was two hundred and fifty-six, of which number one hundred and eighty-four were boys and seventy-two were girls. Mr. Mallalieu strongly recommends that boys and girls should not be cared for in the same institution. The cost per capita is $3 64 per week, which sum includes all expenses. The cost for clothing and bedding is $25 per capita per year.

Mr. Mallalieu, in speaking of trades, recommended that all light trades should be taught, and remarked that when a boy became interested in his tools, something could be done with him. He said that the inmates of his institution are in demand from different parts of the State; that he had thirty applications on file at the time of my visit, and had no difficulty in finding employment for the boys when discharged.

Mr. Mallalieu said he would recommend that forty boys be placed in each cottage, although at his school the cottage buildings contain from forty-four to forty-eight. Various slight punishments are used to correct misbehavior, and in some cases resort is had to solitary confinement.

Escapes occur at times, but most frequently in the winter when the boys are restless from lack of outdoor employment. Mr. Mallalieu informs me that since May first, of last year, there were only three attempts at escape. If the boys are kept employed and allowed a reasonable time for play and recreation there is little disposition to run away. The head of a cottage is called the family manager. He has the entire control of the cottage under his charge, and the Superintendent does not deal with the boys except through him.

In reference to a site for such a school, Mr. Mallalieu stated that it should be within three miles of a city, and should embrace at least a section of land. The boys have a band of eighteen pieces, which has frequently played at the State Fair and on other public occasions. Letters are read before they are delivered to the inmates or sent to their friends. They are allowed to write once a month at the expense of the school, and once a month at their own expense. When parents visit children in the school no watch is kept over them. They may do as they please.

"The principal thing," said Mr. Mallalieu, "in running a school of this kind is to keep the boys contented without their knowing you are trying to do it."

No particular mode of feeding the inmates is prescribed, the object being to have as much variety as possible. Breakfast generally consists of potatoes, bread, coffee, syrup, and gravy; dinner, of meat and two or three kinds of vegetables, and supper of stewed fruit, bread, and tea.

The Superintendent thinks the cottages should be about one hundred feet apart. He aims to be personally familiar with the boys, and to know them, and still make them respect him. The cloth used for the boys' clothes costs $1 75 per yard, delivered at Kearney. In addition to the industries now carried on the Superintendent expects to put in machinery for making socks, to be operated in connection with the tailor shop, and also expects to make all the syrup needed for the institution.

A large tunnel, with branches, seven feet in height and four feet in width, runs to the various buildings. In this tunnel are placed the steam pipes and electric wires.

Mr. Mallalieu, speaking of bathing apparatus, says he prefers bathtubs to a tank, shower baths, or other arrangements. In each cottage there is a play-room, in which, during the winter months, the boys find amusement in such games as authors and dominoes. The daily routine may be said to be: At six o'clock in the morning, the boys are expected to arise, wash, and clothe themselves. At half-past six, they go to breakfast, and at seven o'clock one half of their number go to the work-shops, and the other half to school. They so remain until half-past eleven o'clock, when they assemble again for dinner and play. In the afternoon, those who have been working in the morning attend school, and those who have been attending school take up their respective tasks. At five o'clock, the boys return from work or school, and are allowed to play until six o'clock. Supper is then served, and a short time is allowed for recreation. In summer the boys are in bed at nine o'clock, and in winter at half-past eight. The boys disrobe, and march to their beds in the dormitory, by the side of which they kneel, and in unison recite a short prayer.

The beds are made of iron, three and a half feet in width, with wire mattresses. Mr. Mallalieu recommends that wooden beds should be used instead of those of iron, as the former, he says, have a more home-like appearance. But nearly all the Superintendents with whom I talked differed with him on this point, preferring iron beds, for the reason that it was easier to keep them clean. In the dormitory one boy acts as monitor, but there are no other guards.

No restriction is placed upon the right of a boy to see the Superintendent. He may see him at any time that he desires. Medical services are furnished by a visiting physician, who receives $80 per month for his services, and furnishes his own medicines.

When a boy is about to be discharged, if he is unable to find a home, the school will pay his expenses to any place in the State to which he may desire to go. He is given a suit of clothes costing from $9 to $12, and sometimes a small sum of money. If a boy is returning to his parents, he is generally allowed to go alone, but if to a strange place, he is accompanied by the Chaplain. If the boy enters the home of a stranger, and is not treated well, he is taken back to the institution, though Mr. Mallalieu frankly remarked that sometimes they do not want him back.

From May fifteenth to October fifteenth, of each year, all lights in the employés' rooms must be extinguished at half-past ten P. M.; and from October fifteenth to May fifteenth, at ten P. M., unless special permission is granted by the Superintendent for an extension beyond these hours.

Attendance at all religious services on the Sabbath, or whenever held, is compulsory on all persons employed at the institution, unless they are excused by the Superintendent. The bringing of intoxicating liquors to the school, except for medicinal purposes, is strictly forbidden, and no person employed at the school is allowed at any time, or in any place, to make use of liquors as a beverage. The inmates are not allowed to receive or use tobacco, and smoking in the boys' buildings, or on the premises in the presence of inmates, is, at all times, strictly forbidden. In the case of an escape, the Superintendent is empowered to offer a reward not exceeding $25, for the recapture of the escaped inmate. And if the escape occurred through carelessness, negligence, or violation of the rules, the person in charge is required to pay the reward and expenses.

An inmate, when received, is assigned by the Superintendent to one of three classes. The first class is composed of those committed for burglary, obstructing railroads, rape, prostitution, or perjury, and each inmate in this class receives six thousand demerits. In the second class are placed those committed for larceny, forgery, assault, and similar offenses, and they are each charged with five thousand demerits. The third class comprises those committed for vagrancy, disorderly conduct, and similar offenses, and each inmate in this class receives four thousand demerits.

The demerits are canceled by the merits earned by good behavior and industrious habits. For such behavior an inmate receives ten merits a day, and for a perfect record during the entire month receives twenty-five extra merits, and if the perfect record is continued for three successive months he is entitled to an additional reward of one hundred merits. The furnishing of correct information to an officer of an inmate planning to escape entitles the informer to one hundred merits. For an attempt to escape an inmate forfeits all merits earned by him, and may receive such additional punishment as the Superintendent may determine. When all the demerits have been canceled, the inmate is placed on "honor" for one month, and if he continues perfect during the honor month he is entitled to a leave of absence for four months, if a suitable home can be found for him. If he conducts himself properly this leave of absence is renewed for a year, and annually thereafter until he reaches his majority.

While all necessary clothing is furnished to each inmate, still relatives may send such articles as suspenders, handkerchiefs, slippers, mittens, scarfs, and neckties.

ILLINOIS STATE REFORM SCHOOL.

This school is located at Pontiac, Livingston County, and at the time at which I visited it, had three hundred and thirty-six inmates.

Its management is vested in a Board of three (formerly five) Trustees, appointed by the Governor, with the advice and consent of the Senate, for the term of· five years. The law prescribes that the Board of Trustees shall appoint a Superintendent, whose salary shall not exceed

$2,000 per annum, and shall also appoint such other officers and assistants as the wants of the institution may from time to time require, and shall prescribe their duties and fix their salaries at reasonable sums. In this school boys are received for a specified time, and not generally to be discharged when the officers think proper. Whenever a boy between the ages of ten and sixteen years is convicted before any Court of competent jurisdiction of a crime, punishable, if committed by an adult, in the county jail or State Prison, such boy may be committed, by order of the Court, to the reform school for a term of not less than one nor more than five years. The Board of Directors thenceforth become by law the guardian of his person, and are required to detain him during the term of his sentence, less such time as may be credited to him by law.

An inmate receives credits for good behavior, as prisoners do in our prisons. For good behavior he is allowed for each month in the first year, five days; for each month in the second year, six days; for each month in the third year, seven days; for each month in the fourth year, eight days; and for each month in the fifth year, nine days. If an inmate is degraded for misconduct or violation of the rules of the school, he forfeits for each degradation five days of his credited time. Upon the discharge of an inmate, he is provided by the Superintendent with a suit of suitable clothing and $5 in money, and a ticket to his home, if resident in the State, or to the county in which he may have been convicted, at his option.

It will be observed that the school cannot receive persons unless they have been committed to it upon a trial before a competent Court for some offense.

A recent amendment to the State Constitution of Illinois prevents the letting out of labor in penal and reformatory institutions by contract. The shoe shop, which constitutes the principal industry carried on at Pontiac, has, since this amendment became operative, been running on State account. The Legislature of that State appropriated $30,000 to enable the plant to be purchased from the contractors, and to furnish a working capital. The State paid $7,000 to the contractors for the plant, thus leaving a balance of $23,000 with which to carry on the work. But the Superintendent, Dr. J. D. Scouller, informed me that difficulty was encountered in disposing of the manufactured product, and not as much profit was realized from this mode of working the shop as had been anticipated. Under this plan the profits amounted to only about two thirds of what would have been realized under the old system. Dr. Scouller did not desire, however, in giving the financial results of the two systems of labor, to be understood as advocating a return to the contract system, as he was convinced that in a short time a greater number of industries would be introduced into the school.

For the ordinary expenses of the school the plan pursued is to draw one fourth of the yearly appropriation in advance at the beginning of the quarter and deposit the same with the Treasurer. Claims are then paid as they mature, and the vouchers and accounts are transmitted to the Secretary of the State Board of Charities at the Capital of the State. It costs, for the maintenance of the school, from $42,000 to $46,000 per annum. When I was there last year, the cost per capita for the nine months of that year, then past, was $123 69.

The buildings are lighted by gas made from gasoline, though the Superintendent strongly favors a system of electric illumination.

No particular form of dress is prescribed for the inmates. They are required to bathe twice a week. Their food is plain and substantial, and they are allowed meat once a day.

Dr. Scouller prefers for sleeping purposes separate rooms to large dormitories, and has one of the cottage buildings arranged on this plan, but considers that buildings so arranged are too expensive to permit the general adoption of this system. But the majority of Superintendents with whom I conversed on the subject preferred the large dormitories.

The branches taught are the same as those prescribed by the common school course of the State. The boys are drilled in military tactics, and have a brass band, which is in frequent demand on local occasions.

For bathing, Dr. Scouller prefers large tubs to separate bathtubs. He recommended that we should make our buildings large enough for all ultimate purposes, and that we should secure as much land as possible, and that the dining-hall should be in a separate building. For heating purposes, he said he knew of nothing better than steam.

Friends can visit the boys when they please, and boys are called from their work in order that they may receive the visits of their friends. Every inmate is allowed to write regularly the first Sunday of every month, and in case of sickness whenever he desires. No distinction is made between the inmates as to the amount or character of food to which they are entitled, with the exception that there is an "honor" table, at which only those who have earned their release by good behavior are entitled to sit.

Some of the salaries paid are:

Shopmen _____$40 per month.
Night Watchman_____$35 per month.
Teachers_____ _____$50 and $60 per month.
Assistant Superintendent_____$80 per month.
Lady teachers_____$25 per month.

The religious services are generally conducted by the Superintendent, but when a sermon is delivered by a minister a fee of $3 is allowed therefor.

Dr. Scouller has had long experience in his work. He believes in kindness and firmness, and does not take kindly to changing the names of schools from reform to industrial, as the name, he says, cannot change the character of the institution.

INDIANA REFORM SCHOOL FOR BOYS.

This school is situated on the Vandalia Railroad, about a mile southwest of the village of Plainfield. The school is managed by a Board of Control, consisting of three Commissioners, appointed by the Governor, holding office for four years, and receiving a salary of $500 per annum. The Board appoints the Superintendent and all the officers. The farm consists of two hundred and twenty-five acres of land, and the buildings, which are principally built of brick, number over thirty.

The school is conducted on the cottage or family system, there being twelve cottages in all. Each family is in charge of a teacher, who is known as a "House Father," and if he is married, his wife is also generally employed as an assistant. The boys of all the cottages eat in a general dining-room, but each family has its own playground. The general arrangement of the cottages is this: The lower, or basement, story is used for a play-room in bad weather; the second story consists of a sitting-room, wash-room, and officers' rooms; and the third story is used for dormitories. For the commission of a crime boys, in age from eight to sixteen years, may be committed to the school, and for incorrigibility, in age from ten to seventeen years. All boys are committed until they attain their majority, and none are ever discharged until that time. But if the authorities of the school consider it advisable, a boy may, for good conduct, be released on "furlough" or "tickets of leave," and these favors may be renewed or recalled, as the boy's conduct may determine.

The aim of the school is to teach every boy a trade, and among the different trades taught are plumbing, brickmaking, steamfitting, plastering, bricklaying, cooking, breadmaking, shoemaking, tailoring, gardening, farming, and floriculture; and in teaching a trade the primary aim is to *instruct* rather than to make the labor of the inmate productive. The management is strongly opposed to the use of machinery, or to teaching trades that must be followed in crowded shops. Each boy attends school one half the day, and works during the remaining half, and by this course one half of the inmates are attending school in the forenoon and the other half in the afternoon. The schools are conducted in the same manner as the public schools of cities, and no vacations are given save to the higher grades, and to them only when the teaching of trades in the busy season may require their labor. During the evening the dull hours are whiled away by music, recitations, and various amusements. The boys are provided with large playgrounds and an extensive gymnasium.

In selecting officers the rule that "the blind cannot lead the blind" is applied, and hence no person is employed at the institution whose life is not suitable as a model for the inmates. In securing discipline, in suppressing bad dispositions and cultivating obedience, in breaking up evil habits and forming good, the first object to be always kept in view, the officers say, is good treatment, and precept must be accompanied by example. A boy on his arrival expects harsh treatment, and is surprised when he finds that he is cordially welcomed, and that the labor that he is called upon to perform is not irksome, and that he is allowed reasonable time for play and amusement.

Every boy may report at any time any imposition on the part of an officer, and if an officer mistreats a boy he is discharged.

The cost for each inmate averages $120 per annum. The salaries paid are:

Superintendent _____$150 per month.
Matron _____$50 per month.
Clerk _____$70 per month.
House Fathers _____$30 to $55 per month.
Assistant Superintendent_____$70 per month.
Florist _____$35 per month.
Superintendent of Live Stock and Teams_____$25 per month.
Night Watchman_____$20 per month.
Lady Teachers _____$30 per month.
Lady having charge of boys' kitchen _____$25 per month.
Lady having charge of boys' dining-room _____$18 per month.
Lady having charge of officers' dining-room_____$20 per month.
Housekeeper of main building_____$20 per month.

CINCINNATI HOUSE OF REFUGE.

This institution was opened for the reception of inmates in 1850, and is situated about four miles from the Post Office in the city. It receives both boys and girls, and is arranged somewhat on the congregate plan, although the inmates are separated as much as possible into classes. The boys are divided into four classes or families, and the girls into two, each of the separate families having separate schools, dining and wash rooms, playgrounds, workshops, and dormitories. The site consists of nine and seven eighths acres of land, and five of these are inclosed on three sides by a stone wall, twenty feet in height, and on the fourth side by the main building.

The main building is two hundred and seventy-seven feet in length, four stories in height, besides the basement. One wing of the building is devoted to the boys' department, and contains one hundred and twelve dormitories. In the basement is a bathing or swimming tank, in size twelve by fifty feet, and deep enough for swimming purposes. Besides this, there are in the basement also twenty-six dressing-rooms.

The other wing, devoted to the girls' department, contains seventy-two dormitories, and also nursery, sewing-room, school-room, store-room, girls' hospital, and one large sleeping-room. The basement contains wash-rooms, bath-rooms, and playground.

The chapel building is connected with the main building by covered passage ways, and is situated in the rear of the main building. On the first floor of the chapel building are situated the bakery, kitchen, three dining-rooms, and four store-rooms; and on the second floor, the chapel, a school-room, and a reading-room. The chapel is fifty-six feet wide and sixty feet long. There are two shop buildings. The main one is one hundred and forty-two feet in length and thirty-seven feet in width, and contains on the first floor engine and fuel-rooms, covered playgrounds, wash-rooms, etc., and on the second and third floors, five workshops and reading-room, and a dormitory containing forty-six rooms. The other shop building is eighty feet in length and forty-four in width. The ground floor of this building contains two covered playgrounds, and two wash-rooms. The second floor contains a shop-room and a large sleeping-room. The third floor contains a school-room for the smaller boys, a dormitory for these boys, and two bed-rooms for officers. There is also a school building, eighty feet in length, forty in width, two stories in height, and built of stone and brick. The lower story is used as play-room and gymnasium. In the upper story are placed four school-rooms, provided with sliding partitions, so that the four rooms may be thrown into two rooms or into one.

Light is supplied by gas made upon the premises, and steam is used for heating purposes.

There is accommodation in the buildings for three hundred and fifty inmates, and the necessary number of officers.

Last year some of the Directors, with the Assistant Superintendent, made a visit to the House of Refuge at Rochester, New York, for the purpose of investigating its school of technology; and after a thorough investigation they recommended that system for adoption by the Board of the Cincinnati school. In the school at Rochester are taught black-smithing, carpentering, painting, wood-turning, foundry work, brick-laying, boot and shoemaking, and tailoring. But in the Cincinnati school it was not deemed expedient, owing to the smaller number of inmates, to introduce so many trades, the average number of inmates at the Cincinnati school being about three hundred. The first trade introduced in the industrial training school was carpentry.

Employment for the inmates is found in the domestic work of the institution. All the clothing, boots, and shoes used in the institution are made by the inmates. The girls have found employment in the laundry, kitchen, sewing-room, and in general housework.

PENNSYLVANIA REFORM SCHOOL.

This school was formerly known as the "House of Refuge of Western Pennsylvania," and was at first conducted on the congregate system, being opened in 1854. Its first location was in Allegheny City. But in time the managers were convinced that the school could be much improved by the adoption of the family system. The adoption of this system required a location where sufficient ground could be obtained, and in 1876 the institution was removed to Morganza, its present site. The school receives both boys and girls. The inmates are classified into eight families, each of which is under the control of a First and Second Officer, and a Matron.

A daily record book is kept by the First Officer, in which he notes all misconduct and punishment. This record is read every evening to the inmates in the school-room. The officer then asks if any desire to appeal from the record, and if so, the appellant raises his hand, and states his case. If the officer is satisfied with the record after such statement, but the offender still wishes to make an appeal to the Super-intendent, the word "appeal" must be written opposite the record. The Superintendent meets each family in its school-room as often, at least, as once a month, and determines the justice of the record. The appeal may be sustained, but if made improperly, and without any reasonable ground, it will subject the offender, if the Superintendent thinks the case justifies it, to a loss of a still larger number of demerits.

The management seeks to avoid every indication of prison life, and is successful in so doing.

Officers are not permitted to smoke during office hours, or in the presence of the inmates; and, unless ordered by the attending physician, spirituous liquors are not allowed to be kept or used by any employé. Gambling in any form is strictly prohibited.

The plan of giving merits and demerits is similar to that followed in other schools. An inmate is entitled to ten merits for each day of perfect conduct, and for continued good conduct during four successive months an inmate is entitled to a credit of two hundred additional merits. When an inmate has earned six thousand merits he is entitled to release on parole, as soon as he can be placed in a suitable home. Demerits are given for want of attention to study, uncleanly habits, and improper conduct, and for certain offenses the number of demerits that an inmate shall receive is prescribed. For instance, for absconding the punishment is one thousand demerits; for conniving at escape, five hundred demerits; for theft, eighty demerits; for profanity, obscene conduct or language, fifty demerits; for falsehood, thirty demerits; for fighting, or destruction of clothing, property, or tools, twenty demerits; and for disobedience, quarreling, use of tobacco, or talking while in line, ten demerits. For other offenses the Superintendent fixes the number of demerits to be given, and in aggravated cases inflicts corporal punishment. No officer, however, except in cases where delay might prove dangerous to the person or destructive of discipline, is allowed to inflict corporal punishment, without first consulting the Superintendent and obtaining his permission.

Great care is used to impress upon the offender's mind the justice of the punishment, and that it is not arbitrarily inflicted. Only light punishments are given for first offenses, but when they are repeated, and insubordination is marked, the punishment is prompt, and is intended to impress the offender with the conviction that no matter what the cost discipline and order must be preserved.

Among the different committees appointed by the Board of Managers is a Visiting Committee, composed of two members. When first appointed at the annual meeting, the member first named on the committee serves for one month, and acts as Chairman. The second named member serves for two months, and acts as Chairman for the second month. As a member retires from the committee monthly, the next member in alphabetical rotation takes his place, and each member of the committee is Chairman for the last month during which he serves. It is the duty of this committee to visit the school the first secular day of each month, and also on the fifteenth of each month, for the purpose of conferring with the Superintendent, examining all persons received by the school, and preparing the business for the next meeting of the Executive Committee.

One of the features of the school is a special book kept by the Superintendent, in which an account is opened with each officer of the school. On the debit side of the account is placed every item of inattention, want of promptness, absence without leave, or other irregularity. On the credit side is noted any specially commendable act. If the page is entirely blank, it indicates that the officer's duties have been satisfactorily discharged. Before the record is complete, an appeal may be taken to the Superintendent, and this record is accessible at all times to the Board of Managers.

Officers are not granted leave of absence for a longer period than ten days without deduction of salary; and without special permission no officer must be absent after ten o'clock P. M. Officers are directed not to converse about the affairs of the school when inmates are present or within hearing, and officers when on duty are directed not to converse with each other except on official business. They are expected to give their whole time and attention to their duties, and are not allowed to read books or papers while on duty or during business hours. On a matter of interest in the management of institutions it may be observed that the rule in this school is, that while the Superintendent does not attempt to interfere with the social relations of officers, or control in any way their personal affairs, yet if they allow such matters to interfere with the discipline of the institution, and do not settle them promptly, the Superintendent takes the responsibility of deciding them, and his decision must be adopted as a final settlement.

The salaries paid at this institution are:

Superintendent _____$2,400 per annum.
Clerk_____$900 per annum.
Steward _____$720 per annum.
Engineer _____$1,000 per annum.
Two assistants_____$600 each per annum.
Hospital Steward _____$360 per annum.
Watchman_____$420 per annum.
Carpenter_____$540 per annum.
Housekeepers (female) _____$200 per annum.
First Officer_____$45 87 to $52 50 per month.
Second Officer_____$30 00 to $33 34 per month.

HOUSE OF REFUGE, PHILADELPHIA, PENNSYLVANIA.

In 1826 a meeting was held in the City of Philadelphia by some of its benevolent citizens for the purpose of establishing a school for the vagrant, disobedient, and neglected children of that city. A committee

3D

was appointed to prepare a constitution and secure from the Legislature an Act of incorporation, and in that same year the House of Refuge was incorporated. The preamble to the Act of incorporation states that the object of the school is "for the humane and laudable purpose of reforming juvenile delinquents, and separating them from society and intercourse of old and experienced offenders."

This institution is supported by donations and bequests, life and annual subscriptions, by its earnings, and appropriations by the State of Pennsylvania and the City of Philadelphia. A majority of the Board of Managers are elected by the contributors, and three of their number are appointed by the Courts of Common Pleas, and two by the Mayor.

The daily routine is apportioned by devoting three hours to school, six hours to work, one and a half hours to meals, four hours to recreation, half an hour to morning and evening devotions, and nine hours to balmy sleep.

The average number of inmates is six hundred and upwards. Until recently the average time of detention has been about fifteen months, but now the term has been extended to about two years. The schools are under the charge of lady teachers selected not only for their knowledge, but also for their kind and gentle disposition. One evening in each week is devoted to instruction in vocal music.

When an inmate is received he is first bathed and dressed in clean garments, and then is taken down, from his statements, the history of his life. One reason for this latter step is to separate the depraved from those who have strayed but slightly from virtue's path. The children assemble every morning and evening in their class-rooms, and after a short portion of the Scriptures is read, a hymn is sung and a prayer offered. The children go to chapel service twice every Sunday.

One of the officers of the institution is the visiting agent, whose duty it is to acquaint himself with the children, find proper homes for them, and exercise subsequent care over all children that leave the house, whether they are indentured, put to service of any kind, simply discharged, or returned to parents or friends.

Among the industries carried on are brushmaking, wicker work, and tailoring. The institution receives both boys and girls.

No inmate is allowed to use tobacco, and no intoxicating liquors are permitted, upon any pretense whatever, unless ordered by the Physician, to be brought into any part of the buildings. The gates are closed at eleven o'clock P. M., and no officer or employé is allowed, without written permission of the Superintendent, to be absent after that hour. Such permission can be granted to only one officer at any one time, and the Superintendent is required to report the grant of such permission, with the reasons therefor, to the Board.

The time allowed for work, play, meals, attending school, and retiring for sleep, is divided into periods as follows:

From April First to November First—Seven Months.

			Time Occupied.
Time to rise	5.30 A. M.		
Washing and exercise	5.30 to	6.00	.30
Devotional exercises	6.00 to	6.15	.15
Breakfast	6.15 to	6.45	.30
Play	6.45 to	7.00	.15
Work, with intermission of ten minutes	7.00 to	12.00	5.00
Recess, washing for dinner	12.00 to	12.10	.10
Dinner	12.10 to	12.40	.30
Play	12.40 to	1.00	.20
Work	1.00 to	3.00	2.00
Play and washing for school	3.00 to	3.30	.30
School	3.30 to	6.30	3.00
Supper	6.30 to	7.00	.30
Play—Singing lessons, etc.	7.00 to	7.45	.45
Devotional exercises	7.45 to	8.00	.15
To bed	8.00 to	8.15	.15
Bed	8.15 to	5.30	9.15

School	3.00 hours.
Work	7.00 hours.
Meals	1.30 hours.
Devotions	.30 hour.
Play	2.45 hours.
Sleep	9.15 hours.
Total	24.00 hours.

From November First to April First—Five Months.

			Time Occupied.
Time to rise	6 A. M.		
Washing and exercise in yard	6.00 to	6.30	.30
Devotional services	6.30 to	6.45	.15
Breakfast	6.45 to	7.15	.30
Play in yards	7.15 to	7.30	.15
Work, with intermission of ten minutes	7.30 to	12.00	4.30
Recess, washing for dinner	12.00 to	12.10	.10
Dinner	12.10 to	12.40	.30
Play in yards	12.40 to	1.00	.20
Work	1.00 to	2.30	1.30
Play and washing for school	2.30 to	3.00	.30
School	3.00 to	6.00	3.00
Supper	6.00 to	6.30	.30
Play—Singing lessons, etc.	6.30 to	7.45	1.15
Devotional exercises	7.45 to	8.00	.15
Marching to dormitories, preparing for bed	8.00 to	8.15	.15
Bed	8.15 to	6.00	9.45

School	3.00 hours.
Work	6.00 hours.
Meals	1.30 hours.
Devotions	.30 hour.
Play	3.15 hours.
Sleep	9.45 hours.
Total	24.00 hours.

The·beginning of each of these periods is denoted by the ringing of a bell.

The Board of Managers have decided to change the system from the congregate to the family system, and for that purpose have purchased three hundred and eighty-five acres of land, distant about twenty miles from the center of the business portion of Philadelphia. A committee of the Board visited the leading schools in the United States conducted on the family plan, and a member of the Board visited the reform schools of England and France. When the new buildings are completed instruction will be given in agricultural and horticultural pursuits, and in the elements of such trades as bricklaying, carpentering, plastering, printing, and woodturning.

These new buildings are now in process of erection, and it is estimated that from two to three years more will be required for their completion. This institution has been richly endowed by the philanthropic citizens of Philadelphia, having received many donations of $100,000, and of even larger sums.

LYMAN SCHOOL FOR BOYS.

This school is located at Westborough, Massachusetts, and now is under the superintendence of Mr. T. F. Chapin. At the time that I visited the school it had one hundred and eighty-five inmates.

A school for manual training has been recently organized, and every boy in the institution receives instruction for one and one half hours each week in the manual training room. The system used is the Slojd, or Swedish, and is designed to teach the boy to think. In one of the schools a class has undertaken the study of algebra. Instruction is also given in modeling and music, and it is said that the boy who does not sing is an exception.

The salaries paid are as follows:

Theodore F. Chapin, Superintendent	$1,800
Mrs. T. F. Chapin, Matron	400
George F. Bullard, Assistant Superintendent	500
Mr. and Mrs. A. F. Howe, Charge of Family	700
Mr. and Mrs. J. A. Norton, Charge of Family	800

Mr. and Mrs. I. T. Swift, Charge of Family _____ $700
Mr. and Mrs. B. E. Robertson, Charge of Family _____ 700
Mr. and Mrs. E. J. Keith, Charge of Family _____ 750
Mr. and Mrs. L. C. Jones, Charge of Family _____ 700
F. E. Corey, M.D., Physician_____ 150
Miss Carrie Dana, Teacher_____ 300
Miss Emma F. Newton, Teacher_____ 300
Miss Bertha C. Leech, Teacher _____ 300
Miss Flora E. Strout, Teacher _____ 300
Miss Flora E. Loomis, Teacher_____ 300
Miss Ella E. Glover, Teacher_____ 300
M. E. Howard, Teacher of Printing _____ 400
Miss Mary E. Greeley, Seamstress _____ 250
Miss Mary E. Custer, Nurse_____ 250
Mrs. George F. Bullard, Housekeeper, Superintendent's house_ 300
Miss Mabel B. Mitchell, Assistant Matron _____ 250
Miss Mae E. Hartford, Assistant Matron _____ 250
Mrs. J. J. Donovan, Assistant Matron_____ 250
Miss Lizzie J. Parkhurst, Assistant Matron _____ 250
Mrs. B. F. McFarland, Assistant Matron _____ 200
Mrs. Edith Howard, Assistant Matron _____ 250
J. W. Clark, Engineer_____ 900
J. H. Cummings, Overseer _____ 500
J. T. Perkins, Steward_____ 400
J. J. Donovan, Farmer _____ 400
B. F. McFarland, Assistant Farmer_____ 250
Harlan M. Thompson, Watchman _____ 400

The two principal points that the Superintendent, Mr. Chapin, called
to my attention were the introduction of the manual training school,
and the guarding against placing too large a number of inmates in the
same building. He thought the proper number that should be cared
for in one cottage was twenty-five.

REFORM SCHOOL OF THE DISTRICT OF COLUMBIA.

This school was established some twenty-one years ago, and had from
the time of its organization up to the thirtieth of June, 1889, received
one thousand three hundred and eighty-six boys.

Boys are not discharged by the Trustees until proper homes can be
found for them; and if the boys are unable to find suitable homes
through their own efforts, or those of friends, the Trustees and Superintendent make every effort to find such a home.

The school has three family buildings, and the officers believe that
not more than fifty boys should be placed in the same building, although
they have been forced at times when overcrowded to place a larger number in a cottage. The small boys are now placed in the main building,
where they are under the immediate surveillance of the Superintendent

and Matron. From the organization of the school only nine deaths have occurred, and not a single death has been recorded for the last two years.

Among some of the salaries paid are those of Superintendent, $1,500 per annum; Assistant Superintendent, $900 per annum; Matron, $600 per annum; Matrons of families, $180 per annum; foremen, $660 per annum; farmer, $480 per annum; cook, shoemaker, and tailor, each $300 per annum; Secretary and Treasurer of Board of Trustees, $600 per annum.

Formerly the boilers in use at the institution were placed in the several buildings, but now they are situated in a boiler-house placed at some distance from the buildings, and steam is conveyed underground by connecting pipes to the various buildings where required. By this arrangement the possibility of danger from explosion of boilers is avoided.

During the past year the school received $3,143 40 from the labor of the inmates and other sources. Of this amount the sum of $1,702 47 was received from the chair shop; $443 73 from farm products; $667 50 from the greenhouse; $257 67 from the paper box account, and the balance, $72 03, from other sources.

Owing to the crowded condition of the school, the President of the Board has frequently during the past year been compelled to notify the Courts to refrain from committing boys to the institution. The school has no power to recall a discharged inmate during his minority, who should be returned for want of a proper home or other sufficient cause. A bill was introduced at the last session of Congress to secure this result, but failed to become a law.

It is expected that each boy, when free from sickness, will spend a portion of each school day in study, and without the permission of the Superintendent none are excused from attendance upon one daily session. The books in use are those provided for the common schools of the district, but several classes in the higher grades are taught algebra, geometry, and history. The routine of daily study adopted in the public schools is followed as nearly as practicable, and boys can only be discharged on their "Honor Badge," and after having gained some knowledge of arithmetic, and possessing the ability to read and write and also recite the tables of multiplication.

A committee was appointed from the Board of Trustees, on August 29, 1889, to visit the House of Refuge, at Philadelphia, and at Randall's Island, New York, and as it may prove interesting I cull from their report the following:

At the House of Refuge, Philadelphia, the principal industries are brushmaking, tailoring, shoemaking, and caning chairs.

The population of this institution on the day we were there was six hundred and fifty boys and one hundred and seventy girls.

The salaries paid amount to $32,000 per annum.

The salary of the Superintendent is $3,000 per annum, and the Superintendents of the Shops, from $1,000 to $1,200 per annum.

The teachers receive on an average $30 per month, but are not employed in any other capacity, and teach three hours per day five days during the week.

An officer is employed in this institution, designated as an agent, who receives a salary of $1,500 per annum, whose duty it is to find homes for discharged boys, and to visit them at their homes at least once a month.

Under the laws of the State of Pennsylvania, the institution has control over its inmates until they are twenty-one years of age, and if their homes are found at any time to be improper, or if they are liable to be led astray or are not doing well, they can at any time be recalled to the institution.

A similar law, we are informed, applies to nearly every institution of a like character throughout the United States, with the exception of the Reform School of the District of Columbia, and although the attention of Congress was called to this matter, and a bill introduced at its last session, giving our school this authority, it failed to become a law.

After leaving Philadelphia, your committee proceeded to the House of Refuge at Randall's Island, New York.

The population of this institution on the day your committee arrived there was five hundred and seventy-nine boys and eighty-five girls.

This institution employs seventy-two officers and employés, including twenty teachers.

The salary of the Superintendent is $3,500, and the salary of the principal teacher is $2,000 per annum, and the salaries of the assistant teachers average from $600 to $800 per annum. They are employed, in teaching and other occupations, from seven to eight hours per day.

The State appropriates about $120,000 per annum, and the proceeds from the work of the inmates average $20,000 per annum; making a total of about $140,000 per annum, to be expended for the current expenses of the institution.

Each of the institutions that we visited had a fine band, made up from the inmates, which was not only a great addition to the institution, but a great advantage to the boys composing the band, as the committee was informed that these boys had no difficulty in obtaining lucrative employment in the line of their calling after leaving the institution. We respectfully recommend that a band be also attached to our school. The instruments can be purchased at an expense not to exceed $400, and an instructor can be obtained at a compensation of $600 per annum.

The House of Refuge at Philadelphia, after an experience of many years, has finally come to the conclusion that bars and bolts, high fences, stone walls, and cells are things that belong to the past and have no part in the reformation of juveniles.

They are about to abandon their present location, and have purchased a farm of four hundred acres about twenty miles from the City of Philadelphia, paying therefor $52,000, and there has been appropriated for the erection of the necessary buildings the sum of $750,000, making a total of over $800,000 expended or to be expended by the State of Pennsylvania upon this one institution for the reformation of boys and girls.

After careful examination we find the industries of these schools to be similar to those of our own.

In conferring with the Superintendents of these institutions, they strongly advised that as little machinery as possible be used and that no trades be taught which require the use of much machinery, for the reason that when the inmates leave the institution they have no machinery of their own and must depend upon their own hands. Therefore, they should be taught to work with their hands, without the aid of machinery. Of course some machinery is necessary.

In some institutions bricklaying, plastering, and carpentering are taught to a large extent. Practical mechanics are employed in daily teaching boys by building temporary houses and structures, and then tearing them down and rebuilding others of a different character, using the same material over and over.

It is true that in this work there is no pecuniary profit, but reform schools are not established for the purpose of making money, but for the education and benefit of the inmates, to enable them to be self-supporting when they go out into the world.

After giving the matter careful consideration, your committee respectfully recommends that as large a class of boys as possible be employed in making shoes and clothing for the school. It is thought possible that the school can obtain work from large clothing establishments in this city and in Baltimore, and it might be worth trying.

All the shoes needed at the school can be and should be made upon the premises.

Caning chairs is an occupation only, and not a trade. The boys can be employed at it, and a small revenue derived from it, but it is of little use to the boys when they leave the school.

In addition to these, the most inexpensive industries that can be established would be bricklaying, plastering, and carpentering. These trades could be readily taught in the manner above suggested, and would be most useful callings for the boys.

The carpentering would also be of great advantage to the school, as the boys engaged in this work, being proficient in it, could do all the carpentering which will be required at the school, which would in the end amount to a great deal and save a large sum of money which is now expended.

The boys engaged in bricklaying could also be of use in making culverts, drains, and other work upon the premises, and the boys learning the trade of plastering could also be made useful.

MINNESOTA STATE REFORM SCHOOL.

This school is at present situated in St. Paul, but it has been found desirable to move away from the city, and a site has been secured at Red Wing. This school is conducted on the family system, and in discipline and management is similar to the other institutions of this character previously described.

In building their new school at Red Wing the management have been able to profit by observation of other institutions and all that experience has taught to be necessary in their own. The Superintendent, Mr. Brown, and the architect of the school, Mr. Warren B. Dunnell, made a tour of the Eastern States for the purpose of adopting such improvements as might be found desirable in buildings of the most approved construction.

The architect resides at Minneapolis, and the Superintendent kindly offered to accompany me to his office and allow me to inspect their plans. I spent most of the time in conversation with the Superintendent and architect in talking of the plan best adapted for the purposes of such an institution, and have brought with me tracings of their plans, which I herewith submit to the Board.

While theoretically each cottage building should be separate and distinct by itself, and should provide within itself for all its wants, yet there are practical considerations that may require a departure from this plan without in any manner impairing the efficiency of the family plan of management.

According to the plans for the new school in Minnesota, the main building will be a large structure in the form of a cross. The basement will be devoted to storage-rooms, lavatories, and play-rooms, and the rear wing will be used for a kitchen. The floor above the kitchen will be used as a dining-room, and the other stories of the building will be used for offices, dining-room for the officers and employés, library, and reception and bed-rooms. There will be also a number of cottages of modern design. The reason that this course of arranging the buildings has been adopted is, that a general kitchen and dining-room will prove less expensive than separate kitchens and dining-rooms in each cottage, and will not interfere with the plan of segregation of the inmates into families; besides, it allows a main building of imposing appearance to be erected, which is to some extent an ornament to the place in which the school is located.

BUILDINGS.

From what I have seen of these institutions in the East, I would recommend the cottage or family system of management. I think, however, that provision should be made for those whom it would be at first unsafe to trust with the liberty accorded to inmates of cottages. For such persons, it would be advisable to preserve many of the features of the congregate system. Hence, I think that the schools should be partly congregate and partly on the cottage plan, although these terms scarcely express the idea I have in mind. The main building should be large and commodious, providing suitable quarters for the necessary officers of the institution, and one or more wings should be utilized for housing the inmates. This plan will be all the more necessary, because in a new institution there will for some time be a lack of that popular opinion in favor of the management that would prevail in an institution conducted on the cottage system for years. For economic reasons a portion of the main building could be used as a dining-room, while the kitchen could conveniently be placed in one wing or in a separate building.

I submit with this report plans of some of the Eastern schools for the information of the Board.

SUPERINTENDENT.

The success of the school will depend upon the Superintendent. A good Superintendent can maintain a well managed school, no matter what system of rules may be adopted, while one who does not possess the necessary qualifications can derive no support from the best plan of management ever devised. One who has had some experience in these schools should, in my judgment, be selected. It does not, perhaps, require any high order of talent to conduct one of these schools, yet, as a book agent who has had long followed the business can probably sell more books than one who has not, so a Superintendent who has had experience can avoid the errors that a novice would make. Still, it is not to be considered that only a few such persons can be found. It does not require as much genius to conduct a public institution as it does to command a victorious army. The simple truth is that an institution when well conducted runs itself. The Superintendent should be a person who knows what is necessary in the management, selects proper subordinates to attend to the details, and gently but firmly and unmercifully corrects any deviation from the straight path of duty. Nevertheless, it does not follow that every man who is out of a position or unable to earn a living in a regular occupation, possesses these qualities. One who has undertaken this work as a business will probably be better qualified than one who has not. To him must be left, in a great measure, the question of what trades should be taught; but I would recommend that such trades should be adopted as require little or no machinery for their practice, so that an inmate can, on his discharge, earn his living by his hands, without the aid of costly tools.

PART II.

Reformatories, or Intermediate Prisons.

I had the opportunity of visiting some of the reformatories, or intermediate prisons, which receive criminals under a certain age, and by a system of labor, education, and discipline seek to secure their reformation, so that when they have earned their discharge they may enter the world again, prepared to withstand its temptations and to follow some legitimate kind of labor.

I submit a brief account of those visited.

PENNSYLVANIA INDUSTRIAL REFORMATORY.

This institution is located at Huntingdon, Pennsylvania, and is under the superintendence of R. W. McClaughrey, who, for many years, was Warden of the Illinois Penitentiary at Joliet. It is under the management of a Board of five Directors appointed by the Governor, who hold meetings once a month and oftener if necessary, and are paid 10 cents per mile, computed circular, for traveling expenses. The term of office is ten years, one Director going out every two years. For misconduct, incompetency, or neglect of duty the Governor may remove any of the managers, after an opportunity has been given to be heard upon written charges. The Board have the charge and management of the reformatory and appoint a General Superintendent, Chaplain, and Physician, and may remove any of these for any cause impairing the proper administration of their office, after an opportunity to be heard upon written charges has been given. The General Superintendent has power to appoint all the other officers and employés, and to remove them at his pleasure; but such subordinate officers are appointed only after a strict examination as to their education, trade, moral character, knowledge, and fitness for the performance of their duties.

The undeterminate sentence is applied to persons committed to the reformatory, which receives any male criminal between the ages of fifteen and twenty-five years, convicted of an offense punishable by imprisonment in the State Prison, and who is not known to have previously been sentenced to a State Prison in Pennsylvania or any other State or country. The sentence is generally to the reformatory, the duration of the term of imprisonment not being fixed or limited by the Court in passing sentence.

The object of the reformatory is to prevent young first offenders from becoming habitual criminals, and to train them so as to make them honest, law-abiding citizens. For this purpose the law confers authority upon the Board of Managers to provide such a system of discipline for the inmates as will obtain for each instruction in the rudiments of an English education and in a trade that will be useful to him in securing after discharge some employment by which he may support himself. The law directs that when a prisoner is received there shall be entered in a register the date of his admission, his name, age, and nativity, with such facts as can be learned of his parentage, and of such social influences as would bear upon his constitutional and acquired defects and tendencies. An estimate, based upon these facts, is then made of the prisoner, and of the plan of treatment that appears to be best. At stated times are entered in this register minutes of improvement or deterioration of character. The prisoners are employed on public account, and the contract system of labor is inhibited by statute.

Each prisoner is credited for good personal demeanor, diligence in labor and study, and for all results accomplished, and is debited for all derelictions, negligence, and offenses. An abstract of the record of each prisoner under the control of the Board, showing the date of his admission, his age, and present condition, whether in the reformatory, State Prison, asylum, or elsewhere, the improvement if any, and reason for release or continued custody, is made up semi-annually, considered by the Board at a regular meeting, and filed with the Secretary of the Commonwealth.

If after proper investigation and obtaining the opinion of the Physician and Moral Instructor, any person has given evidence, in the opinion of the Superintendent, that he may be deemed reliable and worthy, and may with safety be liberated, a certificate of this fact, and the opinion of the Superintendent, Physician, and Moral Instructor, are then submitted to the Board of Managers, who, after due notice to all the Managers, consider at the next meeting of the Board the case so presented. If the Board believe that he is entitled to his discharge, a record stating the material facts is made and transmitted to the Judge of the Court that pronounced sentence, who if he sees, after consulting the District Attorney, no further reason for the detention of the prisoner, sends an order for his discharge.

Officers and employés are not permitted to hold unnecessary communication with one another while on duty, nor with visitors or the persons escorting visitors. Officers are strictly forbidden, either at the reformatory or elsewhere, to make as topics of conversation either the institution, the officers, the inmates, or their duties. They are required to wear such uniform as the Superintendent may direct and to maintain always a tidy appearance. They are not allowed to use or bring upon the premises any ardent spirits or malt liquors, nor to smoke or chew tobacco while on duty.

All officers and employés are required to assemble on the guard-room floor at six o'clock A. M. of each day, unless the Superintendent or deputy for special reasons has granted an excuse, and those excused from the six o'clock assemblage are required to report at or before half-past six. Each officer and employé, when he first enters the guard-room in the morning, reports to the Turnkey, who enters the exact time in a book. The institution is closed to visitors at five o'clock P. M., and to officers at eleven o'clock P. M. When officers and employés desire to absent themselves from the reformatory at any time, they must procure permission of the Superintendent or his deputy, and are required personally to place their names on the register, stating by whom the permit has been granted, and the exact time of day of departure and return. They are forbidden to receive or present a gift to any inmate, or to buy from or sell any article to him; nor are they allowed to give the prisoners any information nor hold any conversation with them except upon duties to be immediately performed, and then briefly and to the point.

Leave of absence without deduction of salary, whether required on account of sickness, for business purposes, or for vacation, is limited to ten days in each year. If the absence continues for a longer period than ten days, the salary of the officer or employé ceases, unless the Board of Managers for exceptional reasons shall otherwise order. Unless for special reasons permission is granted by the Superintendent, officers are not allowed to sit while on duty, and they are not permitted to read papers, books, or periodicals of any kind while on duty, or perform any act that would divert or relax their attention from strict vigilance.

NEW YORK STATE REFORMATORY AT ELMIRA.

This institution is well known throughout the United States. It is under the management of Z. R. Brockway, who kindly explained to me the plan of management, and showed me all the various modes of instruction and discipline followed.

Every sentence to this reformatory is a general sentence of imprisonment; in other words, an indeterminate sentence. The Courts do not fix or limit the duration of the sentence. The Board of Managers have

power to transfer, temporarily, with the written consent of the Superintendent of Prisons, to either of the State Prisons, any prisoner who
subsequently to his committal shall be shown to have been at the time of
his conviction over thirty years of age, or to have been previously convicted of crime. They also have power to transfer to the State Prison
any apparently incorrigible prisoner whose presence in the reformatory
seems to be injurious to the welfare of the institution, and by written
requisition may require the return of any prisoner so transferred.

The indeterminate sentence and the plan of treating prisoners on this
fundamental idea has many warm supporters, and there is much that
can be said in its favor. This system, however, has equally strong
opponents.

Mr. M. J. Cassidy, Warden of the Eastern Penitentiary at Pennsylvania, who attended a meeting of the Prison Association of the United
States at Boston, by direction of the Board of Inspectors of his prison,
in a report to the Board, says:

The Convention continued in session five days. During that time
many papers were presented and read on the subject of crime, its causes,
and the very many remedies proposed for its cure. There was not
much discussion of the topics contained in the various well prepared
papers, as the reasoning of the able men who prepared them exhausted
the subject of the methods of treating persons convicted of crime. Not
much was said for any known system. Most of the experts on theoret-
ical criminal treatment, and some of the practical prison officers were
caught in the new contagion now prevailing, known as indeterminate
sentence and parole, that has been transmitted from England, where it
has been tried and failed of accomplishing the results desired. The
most successful test of "ticket of leave system" in this country is being
directed by Z. R. Brockway, who is managing the Elmira Reformatory,
in the State of New York, at Elmira. He is doing more with it than
has ever been done elsewhere. But he is an exceptional man, and has
given his life to this subject, and can make anything go that will go.

There is so much plausible theory about the method that is alluring,
as in all things that are indefinite. The injustice that must be done in
the application of the scheme, the dangerous proceeding of making the
decisions of properly constituted Courts indefinite, should be well considered in all its features before it is adopted.

The paper read by Superintendent Brockway, Chairman of the Committee on Discipline, was prepared by him. It was an indorsement of
the indeterminate sentence and parole system, which Superintendent
Pillsbury, of New York, did not fully indorse, but signed the report,
stating in substance that in his opinion it was not practicable for State
Prisons. Mr. Pillsbury not being present, and I being the third member
of the Committee of Three on Discipline, could not agree to the Chairman's report, and gave the following reasons:

"I have no doubt you will think it is great presumption in me to
dissent from anything that the pioneer of the indeterminate sentence
and of the new method of reformation may present. There are many

things in this report that I heartily agree with. Much of it is good. But I cannot agree with it all, and there was not sufficient time given to admit of my making suggestions which would not so materially have altered the report that it would have failed to express what Mr. Brockway intended; therefore I did not sign it.

"The indeterminate sentence and parole I do not approve. I know you will think me egotistical in setting up my opinion against the prevailing tide now setting in that direction. But life is too short for any one individual to have three or five or ten years taken out of it. Human judgment is the only lever that can be used in determining whether a person's time shall be lengthened or shortened. Human judgment is very fallible. Courts with juries and with able counsel are unable to determine the exact amount of guilt or innocence of the person tried. Many times the offense does not warrant the sentence imposed.

"What Macaulay says is true, that there are several undefined lines that verge so close upon each other that we cannot determine the lines which separate courage from rashness, prudence from cowardice, frugality from prodigality. So there are lines that no jury has ever been able to determine, the line of the amount of violence necessary to justify a killing, and the line where mercy to offenders ceases to be a mercy and becomes a pernicious weakness. I would not act as a Prison Warden where I had to determine the time that any person should serve in prison.

"Boards of Pardon, which are constituted of gentlemen versed in the law, who have facilities for procuring all the evidence in the case and weighing all the pleas that may be offered, in very many cases err in their judgment in granting pardon, not from a want of a disposition to do what is exactly right, but from the fallacy of human judgment. We cannot foresee and determine what is to become of a prisoner after his term expires. Once a criminal always a criminal, is not true. There are many men serving time in prisons, who recover after three, four, and five falls. I would not like to go to the grave with the consciousness that I had deprived any individual of any portion of his life. That part of the report I disagree with, and these are my reasons.

"Mr. Brockway has launched a very elegant ship, well built and secure in every way. No doubt he will make a successful voyage, but the most important need for the safety of the ship he has not provided, that is, a master and crew that understand sailing the ship. The most important thing for the people who are interested in the reclamation of prisoners, is to provide some means for the training of prison officers to render them efficient in the discharge of their duty. It is very well to go over the old ground of discipline for prisoners, and 'go as you please' for officers, but it is just as absurd to place inexperienced men who have had no training at all, to control these men in prison, as it is to place a shoemaker or tailor on board a Government vessel carrying a thousand or fifteen hundred men. Railroads are controlled and managed by people who begin at the beginning. A railroad man begins as a yardman, then he may become a train hand, then brakeman, and perhaps, after a time, an engineer; but to go out into the street, take a man who has never been in a prison before, and place him in control, that is not right.

"Mr. Brockway, no doubt, will agree with me in some of my notions. As I declined to sign this report, I deem it proper to give some explanation for doing so. I hope you will forgive me for not advocating the prevailing epidemic of indeterminate sentence and parole."

The institution at Huntingdon is now completed and is ready to receive inmates. Young first offenders are to be there treated for their reclamation from the influences by which they had been surrounded and made criminals, and taught habits of industry, preparing them to become good and reputable citizens. The management of this training school for the wayward youth of the State has been fortunate in securing the services of a man for Superintendent, R. W. McClaughrey, who of all men with any knowledge of the business required of him is one of the few men in the country that is fully adapted for the management of such an institution. If success can be attained, he is the one who can make it. I make this statement from a knowledge of the man for some years as one of the most successful prison managers of much experience. In my opinion the results will justify his selection.

A better description of this institution, and the system there followed, than perhaps I am able to give, is furnished by Charles Dudley Warner, who remarks:

The Elmira Penitentiary is in its outward appearance a handsome edifice, built not very well, but with some little pretensions to architecture, for the accommodation of about six hundred people. It is well ventilated. The cells are of two or three sizes, fitted for a graded prison in that respect. The reformatory receives convicts from any part of the State, in the discretion of the Judge, who are between the ages of sixteen and thirty, and who are then convicted of the first penitentiary offense. It is called technically a juvenile reformatory, but in all the prisons there are very many prisoners between the ages of sixteen and thirty. A very large proportion of all the convicts who are there for the second and third time are under thirty. In all the prisons that you visit, you are struck with the youthfulness of the occupants. So that, while this is a prison for first offenders, yet ranging up to the age of thirty there is there a very large number of men just as fully furnished for criminal life, just as determinedly set on it, as you will find anywhere else. The accident that they have not been before caught and convicted, is an accident, very likely. They are, for the most part, men who have been brought up from boyhood to a criminal life. They belong in any philosophical classification to the criminal class, so that the experiment there is really with difficult and hardened criminals.

Before I go farther I want to say another thing about education. The notion very largely prevails that it is not a proper thing to educate a criminal; that it may not only make him a greater adept in crime, and that he will become an accomplished rascal. It is my observation that the criminal is not an intellectual being; that the criminal class and the class that will be criminal are low in physical as well as mental and moral condition. They are men usually given to vices through inheritance or by carnal and vicious tastes. They are not intellectually capable in any way; their will is gone, their motive power is lost. They are, therefore, men who must be approached, if approached at all in any reformatory, on the intellectual side. I do not believe at all in the rose-water treatment of many prisoners. I have an entire disbelief in holidays, in flowers, in tracts, in the little dabbling of sentiment that would make a prison a pleasant place to visit. You must go more radically at the man himself, and come at him physically, intellectually, and morally, in order to effect anything at all.

The prison at Elmira is in charge of Mr. Brockway, who has organized and originated this, to me, entirely novel treatment of prisoners. When the prisoner is brought in he is submitted to a very thorough personal examination by the Superintendent. There is a large ledger kept, in which a page or pages are devoted to his case. The examination goes into his heredity—who was his father, who was his mother, and even who were his grandparents, if it is possible to ascertain. What sort of lives did they all lead. Where was he born. Had he any home life. How long did he stay at home. Had he any education. The ancestry of the boy as showing the tendency of the man. An examination is also made of him physically; and this interested me very much, because it is not a mere examination of whether he is fat or lean, or consumptive, or with tendency to some other disease, but of the quality of the man's flesh, is there any fineness in him, or is he coarse in his physical fiber. Next, a careful examination is made of him mentally. What intellect has he. What quickness, what solidity. Has he any training. Is he bright or dull. Then a thorough diagnosis of his past life is made, relating not to crime, but to his capacity for good. After that is prognosticated with increasing certainty, the sort of treatment that is best for him. Before that, he is, of course, washed and clad, and made fit for association in a decent prison. At first he is put into the second grade.

In the institution there are three grades—first, intermediate, and third. The newcomers go into the second grade. From that, they may go up or down, according to their behavior. When a man is put into the second grade he is told the length of his sentence, the maximum length. He is also told what he has to do to free himself from the institution. That is, he has to make so many marks in order to get out. He is informed what is expected of him in a disciplinary way. Before going there, I could never understand how an indeterminate sentence could be best for criminals and for society. I never before saw any tribunal that could ascertain when a man was fit to go out of prison. The easiest thing in the world is to be religious and be a hypocrite, and not be a bit changed. How are you going to know when a man is to go out? that was always the sticker with me. A prisoner may be kept for the maximum time for which he may be sentenced, or under the discipline of this prison he may leave within a year. In all the grades there are distinctions of dress and treatment. In the second grade he is not much removed from the citizen in appearance—he wears clothes of a brown color, and a Scotch cap. In the first grade, which he may reach by good conduct, he wears a blue uniform, with a soldier's cap. In the third grade, to which he may descend by bad conduct, he is put into a red garment. He looks like a criminal in his apparel. It is a stigma on him. These three grades have different privileges. The first grade men occupy better cells and have better fare. They dine together, and in the dining-hall sit at little tables, eight or ten at a table, as at a hotel. When I visit the institution I always like to go into that dining-hall, it is so well conducted and the men are so polite to each other. When the first grade men march, they walk four abreast, in honorable ranks. They are officered by men chosen from their own grade. They are also the

4D

officers of the second grade. They have also certain disciplinary duties in the institution. All this is openly known. They are overlooked by the officers of the institution, who report any one guilty of dereliction of duty. The second grade men take their meals in their cells, and march in ranks of two. The third grade men march in the prison lock-step, and take their meals in their cells, which are not so comfortable as the other cells. The prisoners feel these distinctions the more keenly the longer they stay there.

The Superintendent has to decide for the newcomer what is the best sort of work for him to do, for there are several things taught there; next, into what school shall he go. The code of behavior is very strict. The discipline in little things that go to make up conduct in Elmira is exceedingly minute, so that it is impossible for a man to submit himself to it without feeling it very thoroughly. In the workshop he is marked, as well as for his progress and conduct in school. In the school he is marked for his attainment, his diligence, and his progress. He may be in the primary class or pursuing higher studies; but wherever he is, he is required to come to a certain standard, according to his capacity, and he is marked on that. He has to earn a certain number of marks before he can change his condition from the second grade to the first, and be on his way out of the prison. He has to earn these marks by a kind of discipline in all respects exceedingly repugnant to him. He has to earn them, not to-day, but day after day, for months. He has to behave himself perfectly, so that he gets his nine marks without any dereliction. After he has earned all his marks he is put into the first grade; and after six months more, if his marks are perfect and other things are favorable, he is entitled to a conditional release. The interest to me in that was this: that no man can submit himself to that threefold discipline, I do not care whether he does it willingly or unwillingly, for one or two years without being decidedly changed. I do not believe it is possible to put a man through a drill of that kind without changing him. At first, very likely, he may be a hypocrite; but that cannot last. It is sometimes a long time before they come down to business, but, in a majority of cases, they do come down. It is said that some men are incorrigible, that they cannot be touched and reformed. I am not certain that that is not true. There are some snarls that can not be straightened, and perhaps there are some men. I remember Mr. Brockway said at my first visit that about 20 per cent were incorrigible, and that the statistics of the institution show that 80 per cent of the men who went away remained beyond the law, or, as some one said, they were taught to "steal honestly." The second time I was there Mr. Brockway said he did not know about that incorrigible business; he did not feel so sure as a few weeks before about the per cent. He said that he made out a list of ten men that he had a right to send to Auburn who should be sent there if they were incorrigible, but he did not send them. In about a week from that time two of the men got a start, and were doing very well. When I was there later that list had disappeared. Those ten men were doing as well as any one, and likely to keep on doing well.

When a man has gone on his three-ply duty, and has come to the end of a year with a perfect record, then he must submit himself to the judgment of the Board of Directors, who are responsible to the State and not to the Superintendent. The case with all its aspects is submitted to them, and the question is asked whether the man shall go out. If he goes out, he is paroled for six months, but he is never sent out without a place being provided for him. That place is provided often by the man's friends, often by the men who have employed him before, for this seminary at Elmira is getting to have a good reputation for turning out honest boys. It is asked every month to place men from there. It is a very good diploma to graduate there. The number of its correspondents is increasing, so that it is easier and easier to place men. The men who are sent out are required to report every month as to their condition, and this must be certified to by some one known to the institution. When that has gone on for six months, and the man is earning his own living and behaving himself, the release is made absolute by a vote of the Board, and nothing more is heard of it. It seems a little absurd that criminals should be educated as college boys are, and yet education there is carried to as high a pitch in some respects as in some of our High Schools. It is carried on especially in the direction which will go to make a man a good and intelligent citizen, to make him fit to exercise the right of suffrage, and to do his duty to the State with understanding. Ordinary political economy, history, English and American literature, and branches of that sort are taught, and taught very thoroughly, because these young men are not studying as some other young men do, to satisfy some one's pride at home, but to get out, and they give their minds to it. They have to pass examinations, and are marked on their reports. They have among themselves a weekly newspaper. By the way, I recommend it as the most decent family paper I know in the country. It has nothing in it that would injure a prisoner, and you cannot afford to send some of our papers to the prisons. I was very much interested in a very high development that I found there. A lawyer of Elmira has, every Sunday morning, what is called a practical morality class. It is made up of a little more than two hundred of the six hundred in the institution, chosen from the three grades according to their ability. There came up in connection with this a very curious psychological fact bearing upon this relation of morality to education. I found that the very much larger proportion of these higher men were selected from the first grade. There were very few from the third grade. The Superintendent made out a table showing exactly how, from time to time, like an isothermal line, conduct went along with intelligence. The best behaved men were the best scholars; the moral training went along with the intellectual. It is an exceedingly interesting table. In this practical morality class they were finishing the reading of Socrates from Professor Jowett's translation. The class was as remarkable in its intellectual quickness, readiness, and ability to understand the problems of the Socratic teaching as any class I ever saw. I do not think that I ever heard among young men such apt and wonderfully intuitive discussions as they carried on there. What happened one morning? Here is an institution made up of perhaps one half Catholics, a good many Jews, and people of all denominations and no denomination. They had been studying and discussing Socrates, weighing all the abstract questions of right and wrong, and morality, and that morning they came to the conductor of the class, and said to him, "We would like to go on to the New Testament and study the character of Christ." I do not suppose that all the good clergymen of the State of New York could have drawn that class to the study of Christ in five hundred years. But they came nat-

urally to it as a study of morality, and the next term they were studying the New Testament, and studying it without prejudice.

I believe that a State Prison should pay. I do not believe that the
State ought to support any man, because he is a criminal, in idleness.
I asked about this place, and found that it did not pay. It cost the
State about $30,000 a year to carry it on; and as we were talking about
building a new prison in Connecticut, that seemed to me a lamentable
fact. After I went a second time, I thought it over more, and it came
to me in this light: At our Connecticut Prison we get back 60 per cent
of those whom we have educated there as criminals. They are very
accomplished. They come back a great many times. We get back, I
say, 60 per cent; that is about the average of all the State Prisons of the
country. Here is an institution that takes men of this character, and
80 per cent do not only not come back, but are made productive, decent,
and respectable citizens, while it only costs $30,000; all the rest the men
earn themselves. They earn it in various trades, besides thus fitting
themselves for their own occupation. Classes in stenography, in teleg-
raphy, in modeling, in drawing, are all taught, and the men are fitted
to work in the world, and it only costs $30,000. Why, it costs more
than that, under the old system, to catch the men, and try them, and
bring them back to us again. Thus, the State is making and saving
money by this institution. The first thing that struck me, after I became
familiar with the reformatory, was the absolute change in the faces of
the men. All the insensibility, the heaviness, had gone out of them,
physically as well as mentally, and moral energy was awakened. They
ran up and down stairs, and moved briskly, and the whole aspect of the
person was changed.

There is one very serious objection to any kind of institution life.
That is to say, it makes the men dependent. The more we can get rid
of institution life in every way, the better for us. The trouble at Elmira,
as everywhere else, is that the men are fed, lodged, and clothed, and
everything is done for them. This trouble of the dependence of the
men, of course, obtains there. They get good food, because the Superintendent says he gets better work out of the men when he gives them
good food; but he finds that they are to a certain degree dependent, and
he thinks of putting the whole thing on the "European plan." There
is a good deal of sense in that. Let a man go into a restaurant and
order what he chooses, knowing what he earns. He would very likely
over-eat at first, but the process would bring him down to the basis of
knowing how to spend his money as well as to earn it. I do not know
any one but Mr. Brockway who could carry out this plan; but I believe
that he can make that institution fully independent, earning its money,
buying its food and clothing, just as people are required to do outside.

Some time ago, owing to the operation of a law in New York on the
subject of the employment of criminals, most of the inmates were
thrown into idleness, and to secure exercise for them they were formed
into companies and drilled in military tactics. Although the necessity
that brought this result about has passed away, yet the advantages that
accrued from the system of military discipline enforced were considered
so numerous and important that this feature is still preserved.

At the time of my visit the spectacle of a military review was presented, the convicts carrying wooden guns and accompanied by a brass band. They drilled and marched with the utmost precision, and demonstrated the exact and severe drill to which they had been subjected. Aside from the beauty and splendor of the display, it is claimed that the practice of military tactics exercises an important influence in the work of reformation.

The inmates are drilled in different trades, and exhibit a high state of proficiency, and there is no question, from all that can be learned, that the prison is a success. It has been examined at various times by various Commissions from other States, and they nearly all unite in its praise.

The Board of Prison Commissioners of Massachusetts said:

When the New York State Reformatory was established, a new and radically different system was adopted, and has been in successful operation for several years. It is provided that sentences to the reformatory shall be merely "to the reformatory," and the Court does not fix or limit the duration, nor is it specified by the Judge; but the prisoner, under the law, may be held for the maximum term for which he might be sentenced to any other prison. Authority to release on ticket of leave is given to the "managers" of the New York Reformatory, similar to that which this Board has to release prisoners sentenced to the Massachusetts Reformatory, when it is thought that they have reformed.

Strong arguments can be made against either system. Against the system of fixed sentences these considerations may fairly be urged: Even upon the theory that penalties may be imposed in such a manner under some system as to properly punish crime, it is certain that they are not so imposed under the existing system. The Courts endeavor to ascertain the facts in each case as well as they can, but often fail entirely. The great difference in sentence, for offenses which are technically similar, has often been commented upon in a manner grossly unfair to the Courts. It is true that these differences are due partly to the different views held by different Judges as to the seriousness of certain offenses, and it often happens that two Judges, in different parts of the State, impose sentences widely different for offenses really similar, and that great injustice is done to one or the other of the offenders. It more often occurs that there are very great differences in the offenses (of which those who make comments are entirely ignorant) which not only make it proper to administer different penalties, but which would make it unjust to punish them alike. But whether the difference in sentences is just or unjust, it works greatly to the disadvantage of all efforts to secure reformation. The person receiving the longer sentence feels himself to be grossly injured, and that feeling constantly aggravates and angers, making futile all efforts to bring him under good influences. No one thing operates so disastrously against reformation as the difference in sentences for offenses technically similar.

The fixing of a sentence tends, also, to give the offender a wrong standard for measuring his offense and his relation to the community. He feels that when he has served his sentence he has "wiped out" his offense, and is entitled to return to his place in society, whether changed in character or not, and the law, by recognizing that claim and discharging him at the end of a fixed term, gives its indorsement to that theory. The sentence itself, therefore, makes no appeal whatever for penitence or reformation.

The indeterminate sentence is founded upon a different theory. Its assumption is that the character of the offender, and not the character of the offense, should determine the duration of his imprisonment. It starts also upon this other assumption, that the character of the offense does not necessarily indicate the character of the offender. The man who steals a thousand dollars is not necessarily ten times as bad as the man who steals one hundred. It therefore puts all offenders of a similar class upon the same footing when they enter the prison, assuming that in this way a fair basis is obtained for the imposition of sentences. The duration of the sentence is then made to depend upon the offender's character, to be ascertained during his imprisonment, not only by his behavior—for the most dangerous criminals are often the best behaved prisoners—but by all the means which can be adopted to ascertain the real character.

The first advantage of this system is, that it makes a strong appeal at once for the establishment of a good character. The prisoner realizes that he is imprisoned, not so much as a retribution for an offense, as because he is unfit to be at liberty, and that his return to society depends upon a demonstration that he is fit to return to it. This—perhaps not at first, but in the course of his term—impresses him, as it does every one, as a reasonable thing, and when once the idea is grasped it has of itself a strong reformatory influence.

When the average prisoner enters the prison his first thought, and the one constant thought, is of the date of his coming release, as the anxious thought before his sentence has regard to its probable length. The indeterminate sentence makes the date of release depend upon himself, and not upon the word of the Court. He must struggle for it. If he has no trade, he must learn one; if he is illiterate, he must be studious; if he has an uncontrolled temper, he must master it; if he has been lawless, he must learn to obey; if he has been shiftless, he must form habits of industry. When these things have been done, and only then, will his release come. The success of the New York Reformatory depends largely upon the fact that the indeterminate sentence makes this appeal to all who enter it. It arouses the ambition and is an incentive to the hope of every man, and by making a prisoner's future depend mainly upon himself, it secures his coöperation in the efforts made for his reformation.

There are two arguments against the system of indeterminate sentences which are entitled to attention. It is said by those who oppose it, that it commits the decision as to the length of a prisoner's sentence to a Board which may not possess or exercise good judgment, and may deal unjustly by the prisoner. We believe it to be a sufficient answer to say that, even if the offense, and not the character of the offender, is to be the basis of a sentence, a Board which can have time to get at all the facts of the case will, in most instances, be better able to reach a just conclusion than any Court can which sees the prisoner for only a few minutes, or at most a few hours. It is hard to conceive of a more difficult task than that imposed upon a Court of deciding, for instance, whether a given offense shall be punished by a sentence of twelve or eighteen or twenty-four months. Under the system of indeterminate sentences, every prisoner guilty of offenses technically similar would be sentenced to the reformatory, and might be held for the maximum term provided by law for the punishment of that offense, leaving the question of the actual duration of his sentence to be determined at a later day by his own conduct.

It is also said that no Board can ascertain a man's real character with sufficient accuracy to make his release conditional upon it. But it must be remembered that sentences are now imposed by the Courts upon precisely this basis, and a supposed general good character tends to secure a shorter sentence than would otherwise be given. It is, then, merely a question as to whether it is better, or more feasible, to ascertain the character before or after sentence. It seems clear that the authorities under whose eyes the prisoner spends every moment of his time are more likely to form a wise judgment in regard to his character than any Court can in the limited time allowed for an investigation. The Court may be able to ascertain the prisoner's reputation, but his character can hardly be known until it has been ascertained by careful study. If any mistake is made by the Board in regard to a prisoner's character, it will rarely be against him. Men rarely appear worse than they are, and there is little danger that any man will be unjustly dealt with by being kept longer than he should. It would only be upon a definite record of bad conduct, and a clear demonstration of bad character, that a prisoner would be held for the full possible term of his sentence. We can see no more reason for releasing a criminal before his reformation is probably assured, than for releasing an insane person from an asylum at the end of a definite term, regardless of his restoration to sanity.

INDIANA REFORMATORY INSTITUTION FOR WOMEN AND GIRLS.

In this connection it may be proper to say a word or two in reference to this institution, which I had the pleasure of visiting in company with Judge Jordan, President of the Reform School at Plainfield.

This institution is situated at Indianapolis, and is under the supervision of a Board of Managers consisting of three ladies. It consists of two departments—the penal and the reformatory. The Managers strongly desire to have the name of the institution changed, so as to remove any stigma that may exist upon the reformatory department, and suggest that the change should be to " The Reformatory for Girls and Woman's Prison."

The total cost for maintenance last year was $28,241 44, and the institution earned $4,041 90.

The reformatory department was created for the purpose of assuming charge of girls under fifteen years of age who might be sent to it by parents, guardians, or Courts, and who required the restraints, discipline, and guardianship of a school of this character. The period of detention is from one to three years, and the aim of this department is to teach each girl some form of industrial employment. The principal industries followed are cane seating, painting, whitewashing, plain and fancy cooking, sewing, cutting, fitting, and draping.

The Superintendent furnishes the following in regard to discipline:

Discipline in its broadest sense means to train, to develop, to chasten, to educate, and it is the regular enforcing of wholesome rules that makes good discipline.

Order cannot be maintained in any other way. Obedience is God's first law, and to its mandate all must bow.

We always give a girl a chance to tell her own story, and to defend her own case when reported for any misdemeanor, always urging her to truthfulness of statement, although she may be greatly at fault. Thus by gentleness and justice, united with firmness, we seek to win her confidence and to receive her willing and cheerful obedience.

Our punishment consists in depriving of privilege to a great extent. If a girl misbehaves in the school-room she is not allowed to enter again until she makes proper acknowledgment of her wrong-doing and promises better conduct in the future. Neither is she allowed to do any kind of work during school hours, but must remain standing idly in the hall.

If her conduct is bad in the general collection-room, or in passing down to her meals, she is deprived of the privilege of the dining-room for awhile, eating her food alone in the hall above.

Misbehavior in Sunday-school or church deprives her of those services until she thinks she can act differently. A girl who persists in quarreling or fighting, or in making disturbance of any kind throughout the house, is removed from the family to her dormitory for awhile, where she remains alone during the day, with work for working hours and books for recreation. Sometimes, as in many private families, her clothes are locked up and she must stay in bed. When these remedies all fail, then to a solitary room she must go, with no privilege save that of her own bad companionship.

The switch or small round strap is sometimes used when necessity requires, especially with the children and younger girls. The spirit and tone of the house is better even than a year ago. Fewer punishments, and these of shorter duration, are needed, while with very many girls only a word of reproof is necessary.

Forty-four girls have been received during the year; thirty have been discharged, being of age; eighteen are now out on ticket-of-leave, giving ordinary satisfaction; ten have been returned for various reasons, some doing wrong that they might come back.

While our hearts are often pained by the abandonment of some of our girls to lives of licentiousness and vice, others are doing so well as to inspire within us a song of thankfulness that we have been permitted to take them by the hand and lift them out of wrong-doing into better paths.

PART III.

State Prisons.

OHIO PENITENTIARY.

This institution is situated at Columbus, either within or adjoining the city limits, and the site consists of twenty-six acres, of which twenty-two are included within the walls. The buildings, including the shops, cell blocks, administration buildings, and others, number thirty-eight. The wall surrounding the grounds is three feet thick at the bottom, eighteen inches at the top, is twenty-two feet in height above the ground, with seven feet in foundation. The wall is surrounded with heavy dressed stone coping four inches thick and three feet in width. It has a total length of three thousand six hundred and fifty feet, and the entire cost exceeded $58,000.

The total receipts for last year were $245,559 75, and the expenditures $230,377 35, leaving the prison not only self-sustaining, but with a surplus of $15,182 40. Certainly a creditable showing.

The prison is under a management of a Board of five Managers, at least two of whom the law requires shall be practical and skilled mechanics, and not more than three of whom are to belong to the same political party. Their term of office is five years, and they are appointed by the Governor, by and with the advice and consent of the Senate. The Governor has power to remove any member at his discretion. Each member is entitled to $10 per day as compensation for his services not exceeding one hundred days in a year, and this sum includes all expenses.

In Ohio the Courts have power, if deemed proper, to sentence any person convicted of a felony, other than murder in the second degree, who has not previously been convicted of a felony and served a term in a penal institution, to a general sentence of imprisonment in the penitentiary. Such imprisonment cannot exceed the maximum term fixed by law, and cannot be less than the minimum, but may be terminated at any time between these periods by good conduct. In the case of such a sentence the clerk of the Court is required to furnish to the Warden a record containing a copy of the indictment and any special plea that may have been made, the names and addresses of the Judge presiding at the trial, the jurors, and witnesses sworn on the trial, and also a statement of any fact which the Judge may deem necessary for the comprehension of the case, with his reasons for the sentence inflicted.

When a convict is discharged, if he has passed the term of imprisonment without a breach of the rules or discipline, except such as are excused by the Board, he is restored to the rights forfeited by his conviction, and receives from the Governor a certificate, under the seal of State, of such restoration. If he is not at the time of his discharge entitled to this restoration, yet if his conduct for a year after his release has been exemplary, he may present to the Governor a certificate signed by ten or more reputable citizens of the place where he has resided for such time, certified to be such by the Probate Judge of the county, and he then becomes entitled to a restoration of his rights.

For good behavior a convict is allowed by way of commutation of sentence, for each month of the first year five days, for the second year seven days for each month, for the third year nine days for each month, and for the fourth and subsequent years ten days for each month.

The Warden is authorized to place to the credit of all prisoners, except those sentenced for life, such amount of their earnings as the Board may deem equitable, taking into consideration the character of the prisoner, the nature of the crime for which he was imprisoned, and his general deportment; but such credit cannot exceed twenty per cent of the prisoner's earnings. At least one fourth of this amount is retained for the prisoner, and paid to him at the time of his restoration to citizenship, but the balance may be paid to him or his family at such time and in such manner as the Board of Managers may deem best.

The Warden holds his office for the term of two years, unless sooner removed for cause, and is required to be a person who, from practical experience, possesses the ability and qualifications to carry on successfully the industries of the penitentiary, and the ability essential to the proper management of the officers and other employés under his jurisdiction, and to enforce and maintain proper discipline in every department. One Guard or minor officer is to be appointed from each county in the State until the necessary number is secured. The Warden's bond is $50,000, and the bond is drawn by the Attorney-General, and deposited with the Secretary of State.

If a prisoner dies, and if none of his relatives, after notice, or friends request the body for interment, the body, either before or after burial, may, on written application of the professor of anatomy in any medical college, or the President of any county medical society, be delivered to such person for the purpose of medical or surgical study or dissection.

At the time when I visited the prison it had one thousand five hundred and sixty inmates. They are classified into three grades. When a convict is received he enters the second or middle grade, and his subsequent conduct determines whether he shall be elevated to the first or lowered to the third grade. If he serves for six months in the second grade, and conducts himself in accordance with the rules, he is entitled to a place in the first grade. Those in the first grade are allowed to wear mustaches. Friends may supply a convict with underclothing, but all prisoners are required to dress in the uniform of their respective grades.

The convicts are permitted, if they so desire, to decorate their cells and to place carpet and furniture in them. Some of the cells that I inspected, occupied by criminals who before their advent into a penal colony dwelt in stately mansions, were quite elaborately furnished.

They all have the same prison fare, except that friends may once a month supply a convict with a meal when they visit him. The principal punishment is the dungeon and solitary confinement, although the shower bath is occasionally used.

Daily newspapers are strictly excluded from the prison, and while weekly papers are admitted, still all statements about criminals or the commission of crimes are cut out before the papers are delivered to the prisoners.

The convicts all eat in one large dining-room, as they do in our prisons. The prison has two thousand cells, and only one man is placed in a cell.

One of the rules of the present Warden, Mr. Coffin, which has been in force for two years, is that if six or a less number of the prisoners are reported for offenses, they are allowed to talk at dinner. The Warden states that this rule works admirably. To this prison are sent those convicted by the Federal Courts in the Territories and in the Southern States.

While walking through the prison yard I noticed two persons carefully guarded by an officer, walking up and down for exercise. They had been convicted of murder in the first degree, and were soon to be hung as the penalty of their guilt. In Ohio the death penalty is enforced only by the Warden, or in case of his death, inability, or absence, by a Deputy Warden. This punishment can be inflicted only within the walls of the prison, within an inclosure to be prepared for that purpose, under the direction of the Warden and the Board of Managers. This inclosure is to be constructed in such a manner as to hide the gallows from public view. The execution takes place on the day appointed by the Court, before the hour of sunrise, and the Warden or Deputy Warden executing the sentence receives $50 for his services as executioner. At the execution, besides the Warden and such number of Guards as he may deem necessary, there may be present the Sheriff of the county in which the prisoner was convicted, the Board of Managers and Physician of the prison, the clergyman in attendance upon the prisoner, and such other persons as the prisoner may designate, not exceeding three in number, representatives of not exceeding three newspapers in the county where the crime was committed, and one reporter for each of the daily newspapers published in Columbus. No other person is permitted to be present.

The statutes of the State provide that the Warden shall furnish each convict with a Bible, and shall permit, as often as he may think proper, regular ministers of the Gospel to preach to the convicts.

The Governor, heads of all departments, members of the Legislature, and such other persons as the Warden may think proper, are admitted as visitors within the walls of the prison free of charge. The law provides that the Board of Managers may prescribe a reasonable sum for going through the prison, and that the Warden shall procure suitable tickets, which shall be sold by the Clerk, who shall keep an account of such sales and pay the money to the Warden daily, and that the Guard at the door of the guard-room shall also keep an account of them in a book as they are received, and return them to the Warden each day before the prison is closed. The admission price fixed by the Board for general visitors is twenty-five cents.

The prisoners are not allowed to exchange a word with each other under any pretense, nor communicate any intelligence to each other in writing. They are not permitted to exchange looks, winks, or laughs at each other, or make use of any signs, except such as are necessary to convey their wants to the Guards or other officers. They are not permitted to speak to the Guards on ordinary topics, nor address them, except in relation to the work of the prision.

Each male prisoner is allowed one hat or cap, one jacket, two hickory shirts, one pair of pantaloons, and one pair of shoes. During the winter season the Warden allows sufficient underclothing to such prisoners as in his judgment may require it, and to each man a vest and two pair of socks. All other clothing found in the possession of a prisoner is taken away from him. Each prisoner may also have in his possession one handkerchief, toothpick, and toothbrush, a fine and coarse comb, photographs of his friends, a knife, the blade of which must not exceed one inch in length and be blunt at the point, and his own books. But no prisoner is allowed to have books or papers of his own except by permission of the Warden.

Mention has already been made of the division of the prison into three grades. When a prisoner is received, after undergoing the ordinary bathing and clothing, he is described in the register and medically examined. Questions are then propounded to him concerning his previous history, to ascertain as nearly as possible the causes of his crime and the best probable plan of treatment. When the examination is concluded, careful instruction is given to him in his liabilities, rights, and privileges under the law; and the prison regulations and the system of marks followed at the prison, with the conditions of promotion, degradation, and release, are fully explained to him. He enters the second grade and is assigned to a suitable industry. He may be promoted to the first grade by earning nine marks for six months successively after the minimum term of service for his crime has expired. Of the marks to be earned each month, three count for labor, three for demeanor, and three for progress in school. He may be degraded to the third class for such deliberate and continued violations of the rules and regulations as the Warden may deem sufficient cause for such degradation; for such acts of disobedience, quarreling, destruction of property, and misconduct generally as, in the judgment of the Warden, are incompatible with the the good order of the prison; for the unnecessary or wanton destruction or injury to any property, or lack of care in its preservation; or for the violation of any regulation of prison discipline; which, in the Warden's opinion, materially affects the condition of the prisoner or the grade to which he belongs. A third grade prisoner may, in the discretion of the Warden, be restored to the second grade for three months' good conduct in labor and demeanor.

Prisoners in the first grade are clothed in blue, those in the second in gray, while those in the third grade are clothed in prison stripes and march in the lock-step.

The Warden resides at the penitentiary in apartments assigned to him and furnished at the expense of the State in a plain and substantial manner. The Matron also resides at the prison, but all the other officers live in the City of Columbus. The Warden is required to examine daily into the condition of the prison, and to visit every department and see every prisoner as often as may be required for good order and proper discipline, and when not necessarily engaged in superintending general affairs and supervising his assistants in the performance of their duties, he is required to remain during working hours in the Warden's office. Every night, before retiring, he passes through the prison and satisfies himself that all is safe and that the Night Guards are properly discharging their duty.

When he is not prevented by sickness or other cause, he is required, under the rules, to attend divine service whenever it may be held in the chapel of the prison, and to inspect the moral character of the prisoners.

A prison school is maintained at this institution, which is under the charge of a Guard qualified for the place, and detailed for that purpose by the Warden, and he has charge of the illiterate and other prisoners attending the school. He assists the prisoners appointed as teachers and makes a report monthly as to the attendance of the prisoners and the progress made in their studies.

Guards are strictly enjoined to refrain from whistling, scuffling, immoderate laughter, boisterous conversation, exciting discussions on politics, religion, or other subjects, provoking witticisms or sarcasms, and all other acts calculated to disturb the harmony and good order of the prison. They are required to be men of good moral character and of temperate habits, and for consorting with lewd or vicious company they may be discharged.

No officer or employé is permitted to use ardent spirits, wines, strong beer, or ale, upon any occasions in or about the prison, nor is any person permitted to bring any intoxicating liquor within the prison walls, except for the hospital to be used for medicine, under the direction of the Warden or Physician.

In Ohio much progress has been made in prison management, and not the least important of the features of its penal system are the parole law and the law relative to habitual criminals. In 1885 the Legislature conferred upon the Board of Managers power to establish rules and regulations under which any prisoner imprisoned under a sentence other than for murder in the first or second degree, who had served the minimum term provided by law for the crime for which he was convicted, and who had not previously been convicted of a felony, might be allowed to go upon parole outside of the buildings and inclosures, but to remain, while on parole, in the legal custody and under the control of the Board and subject at any time to be taken back within the inclosure of the prison. The Legislature also conferred power upon the Board to enforce the rules and regulations made by them and to reimprison any convict upon parole. No prisoner is, however, paroled, under the rules adopted by the Board, unless he has been in the first grade continuously for a period of at least four months, nor until the Board is satisfied that the prisoner will conform to the rules and regulations of his parole, and satisfactory evidence is furnished to the Board in writing that employment has been secured for him, from some responsible person, certified to be such by the Auditor of the county where such person resides. It requires the affirmative vote of at least four members of the Board to grant a parole, and every paroled prisoner may be retaken for any reason that may be satisfactory to the Board, and at their sole discretion, and when retaken he remains in confinement until released by law.

The prisoner, when paroled, is required to proceed to the place of employment provided for him, and remain at such place, if practicable, for a period of at least six months. If he desires to change his place of employment or residence, he must first obtain the written consent of the Board. He is required to conduct himself honestly, avoid evil associations, obey the law, abstain from the use of intoxicating liquors as a beverage, and on the first day of each month until his final release, forward by mail, to the Secretary of the Board, a report of himself, stating whether he has been constantly in receipt of wages during the preceding month, and if not, stating the reason therefor; the amount of money that he has earned, the amount that he has expended, and a general statement of his surroundings and prospects.

Mr. Coffin, the Warden (in answer to a question of mine), said that this law works well and produces beneficial results. To avoid the pressure of friends to secure paroles for prisoners, the Board will hear no oral argument by attorneys or others in the interest of prisoners who have made application for parole, but all such efforts must be placed in writing and filed with the application of the prisoner to whom it refers.

Ohio also recognizes the existence of the habitual criminal, and to prevent him from preying on society, restrains him for life. A person who has been twice convicted, sentenced, and imprisoned in a penal institution for felony, whether committed in Ohio or elsewhere within the limits of the United States, and who is convicted and sentenced to the Ohio Penitentiary for felony, is deemed an habitual criminal. He is not entitled to a discharge on the expiration of the term for which he was sentenced, but, unless pardoned by the Governor, he is to be detained in prison during the term of his natural life. The Board of Managers, however, have power, after the expiration of the term for which the prisoner was sentenced, to allow him, in their discretion, to go upon parole outside of the buildings and inclosures, but to remain in the legal custody of the Board, subject at any time to be taken back.

A woolen mill is conducted at the prison, which makes an indestructible blanket for the Insane Asylums of the State. It also makes cloth for prison clothes, and the Managers desired to obtain an order to supply the California Prisons. The meat supplied to the prison costs 6½ cents a pound at Cincinnati. The salaries paid are as follows:

Warden _____$1,800 per annum.
Deputy Warden_____$1,200 per annum.
Assistant Deputy Warden_____$900 per annum.
Secretary_____$1,500 per annum.
Clerk _____$1,500 per annum.
Assistant Clerk_____$900 per annum.
Steward _____$1,200 per annum.
Storekeeper _____$900 per annum.
Physician_____$900 per annum.
Superintendent of Hospital (day)_____$780 per annum.
Superintendent of Hospital (night)_____$780 per annum.
Captain of Night Watch_____$900 per annum.
Captain of Guard-room_____$900 per annum.

The Guards receive $65 per month, without board or lodging.

The various other officers, such as Superintendent of Construction, Superintendent of State Shop, Superintendent of Subsistence, Superintendent of Gas Works, Superintendent of Yard, Superintendent of Piece Price Work, Superintendent of Woolen Mill, and Superintendent of School, each receive $65 per month. The Matron receives $50 per month and board and lodging.

The per capita expense for last year was $176 67 for the entire year, or an average of 48.296 cents per day, and was thus distributed:

Expenses for Year.		Per Capita Expense.	
		Day.	Year.
$5,000 00	Managers.	$0 00.983	$3 59$\frac{7}{10}$
22,250 51	Officers	04.376	16 00$\frac{7}{10}$
75,944 11	Guards	14.936	54 63$\frac{9}{10}$
235 65	Broom shop	00.047	16$\frac{7}{10}$
67 63	Chapel	00.013	04$\frac{7}{10}$
402 85	Female Department	00.079	28$\frac{9}{10}$
2,821 15	Flour mill	00.555	2 03
11,500 40	Fuel	02.262	8 27$\frac{3}{10}$
799 97	Halls and cells	00.157	57$\frac{3}{10}$
3,372 44	Hospital	00.663	2 42$\frac{2}{10}$
70 55	Library	00.014	05$\frac{3}{10}$
4,198 02	Miscellaneous	00.826	3 02
1,539 68	Offices and postage	00.303	1 10$\frac{9}{10}$
530 81	Photograph gallery	00.105	38$\frac{2}{10}$
1,078 70	Printing office	00.212	77$\frac{7}{10}$
319 29	School-room	00.063	23
18,399 27	State shop { Clothing	03.619	13 23$\frac{7}{10}$
5,352 83	Shoe	01.053	3 85$\frac{9}{10}$
3,370 55	Tobacco	00 663	2 42$\frac{3}{10}$
63,863 79	Subsistence	12.560	45 94$\frac{1}{10}$
2,496 74	Wash house	00.491	1 79$\frac{3}{10}$
1,958 86	Warden's house	00.385	1 40$\frac{3}{10}$
2,536 47	Woolen mill	00.499	1 82$\frac{3}{10}$
2,267 08	Yard and stable	00.446	1 63$\frac{7}{10}$
15,182 40	By balance	02.986	10 93
$245,559 75		$0 48.296	$176 67

There were at the time of my visit thirty female prisoners in the penitentiary. They are now engaged in caning chairs, but had previously been engaged in cigarmaking.

If a prisoner desires to see the Warden or a member of the Board of Managers he sends notice on a printed slip, which must be delivered to the person to whom it is addressed. Each prisoner is furnished with a number of these slips and can make this request as often as he desires, stating the reason for which he desires the interview.

The inmates are allowed two plugs of chewing tobacco each week. The plugs used are two inches wide, four inches long, and a quarter of an inch thick. No smoking is permitted except on the fourth of July, Christmas, and Thanksgiving Day. Each prisoner on these days is allowed two cigars, costing $15 per thousand. Friends are allowed to furnish a prisoner with chewing tobacco of a quality different from that supplied by the prison, but not of any larger size.

The cell-doors, instead of being made of impenetrable heavy iron, are composed of bars in the form of a grating. It is claimed by the prison officers that these doors, while they are preferable on account of allowing the sun and air to enter, are safer also, because they permit an uninterrupted view into the cells to be had at all times.

On Sunday the exercises of the day are opened by the Sunday-school, which commences at eight o'clock in the morning, and continues for an hour. A prayer meeting follows, beginning at nine o'clock and terminating at ten. At eleven o'clock the regular services commence, and every prisoner is required to attend. The services last for half an hour. In the afternoon the prisoners are locked up in their cells and remain there until Monday morning. A Catholic priest ministers to those of his faith.

The bill of fare that must satisfy the appetite of the prisoner is as follows:

Breakfast.—Coffee, bread and butter, and part of the time meat.
Dinner.—Potatoes, vegetable soup, meat, bread, one or two apples or a ripe tomato.
Supper.—Tea, molasses, and sometimes meat or sausage.

In Ohio it is recognized that protection is due to the American cow, for it is provided by a law of that State that no butter or cheese not made wholly from pure milk or cream, salt, and harmless coloring matter, shall be used in any of the charitable or penal institutions of the State.

5D

ILLINOIS STATE PENITENTIARY.

This penitentiary is situated at Joliet, Illinois, and for many years was under the superintendence of Major R. W. McClaughrey, who now has charge of the reformatory at Huntingdon, Pennsylvania.

During the year ending September 30, 1887, the total earnings of the prison were $225,328 76, and during the year ending September 30, 1888, $201,719 05.

At the time that I visited the prison the fiscal year for 1889 had not expired, so that in order to show the financial management of the prison I shall take the figures of 1887 and 1888. During the first of these years the prison earned from labor under contract, $220,536 80; from railroad dock and teaming, $2,438 58; and from the labor of female prisoners, $167 93; which, with the earnings from the State shops, amounting to $2,041 11, and the net gain from the store, make the total named. The average price paid for the labor of convicts under contract was 62.71 cents per man per day, and the average earnings per man per day, including productive and unproductive men, including working days, Sundays, and holidays, amounted to 42.31 cents.

During the year 1888 the amount realized from the earnings of convicts under contract was $194,112 32; from railroad dock and teaming, $2,318 90; from the labor of female prisoners and idle-room, $793 04; from the State shops, net gain, $1,772 05, and from the store and farm, $2,848 57. The average contract price paid for contract labor was 63.06 cents per man per day, and the average earnings per man per day, including productive and unproductive men, including working days, Sundays, and holidays, amounted to 41.72 cents.

During the year ending September 30, 1887, the average number of convicts was one thousand four hundred and fifty-nine; the total cost of maintenance during the year was $236,264 09, and the average cost for each convict per day, or the per diem, was 44.36 cents, or $161 93 for the year.

Of this maintaining cost, the sum of $102,924 10 was for salaries, board, and lodging of officers; $58,924 10 for convict subsistence; $16,-583 12 for convict clothing and bedding; $19,830 98 for convict discharge clothing and transportation; $5,786 55 for cell-houses, including rations of tobacco and writing material; $4,878 41 for incidentals, including fuel and other supplies for shops, guard boxes, solitary, armory, yard, female prison, etc.; $5,316 13 for teaming and stable department; $934 61 for hospital (special subsistence supplies); $1,920 61 for hospital (sanitary and medical supplies); $11,487 85 for motive power and steam for cooking, heating, and ventilating; $3,310 89 for gas; $5,068 85 for office and general expenses, legal and professional services; and $3,196 04 for traveling, advertising, recapturing escaped prisoners, and holiday expenses, etc.

For the year ending September 30, 1888, the total maintaining cost of the prison was $225,686 88, the average number of prisoners 1,321, and the cost per diem 46.68 cents. The details of this cost of maintenance are as follows:

DEPARTMENT OF EXPENSE.	Total During Year.	PER CONVICT.	
		Per Year.	Per Day. Cents.
Salaries, board, and lodging of officers	$102,007 00	$77 22	21.10
Convict subsistence	53,600 23	40 57	11.10
Convict clothing and bedding	14,759 95	11 17	3.05
Convict discharge clothing and transportation	15,786 48	11 95	3.26
Cell-houses, including rations of tobacco and writing material	5,741 91	4 35	1.19
Incidentals, including fuel and other supplies for shops, guard boxes, solitary, armory, yard, female prison, etc.	4,572 89	3 46	0.94
Teaming and stable department	4,116 90	3 12	0.85
Hospital (special subsistence suppiles)	1,111 71	84	0.23
Hospital (sanitary and medical supplies)	1,765 18	1 34	0.37
Motive power and steam for cooking, heating, and ventilating	12,659 89	9 58	2.62
Gas	3,190 77	2 42	0.66
Office and general expenses, legal and professional services	4,070 59	3 08	0.84
Traveling, advertising, recapturing escaped convicts, and holiday expenses, etc.	2,303 38	1 74	0.47
Totals	$225,686 88	$170 84	46.68

Average of convicts (for year) 1,321
Number of days' board (for year) 483,491

The following will show the quantities and cost of convict subsistence and the average cost per convict, for the fiscal years ending September 30, 1887, and September 30, 1888:

ARTICLES.	TOTAL, 1887.		TOTAL, 1888.	
	Quan.	Cost.	Quan.	Cost.
Fresh beef, pounds	182,770	$12,322 22	197,547	$12,249 04
Salt beef, pounds	21,732	1,345 69	22,983	1,101 10
Fresh pork, pounds	36,499	2,414 57	11,473	468 12
Salt pork and bacon, pounds	31,717	2,380 97	21,066	1,308 48
Hocks, pounds	32,650	1,379 25	....	....
Veal, mutton, and lamb, pounds	4,951	425 16	6,661	542 81
Sausage, pounds	50,544	2,913 15	49,419	3,023 52
Turkey and chickens, pounds	3,260	338 81	3,158	328 74
Shoulders, pounds	39,213	3,962 06	36,412	3,037 25
Lard, pounds	2,557	179 27	3,653	297 84
Oysters, gallons	200	200 00	100	110 00
Codfish, pounds	7,003	426 30	11,940	820 90
Eggs, dozens	1,281	152 07	1,260¾	156 21
Butter, pounds	8,880	1,645 02	5,910	1,140 23
Flour, barrels	3,101	12,407 01	2,946	11,193 87
Yeast, pounds	734	183 50	600	154 14
Milk, gallons	819	134 18	2,546	400 32

SUBSISTENCE ACCOUNT—Continued.

ARTICLES.	TOTAL, 1887.		TOTAL, 1888.	
	Quan.	Cost.	Quan.	Cost.
Cornmeal, pounds			374	$11 11
Potatoes, bushels	7,534	$5,874 80	6,555	5,075 45
Parsnips, bushels	166	64 30	42	52 12
Onions, bushels	319	189 50	394¾	421 25
Tomatoes, bushels			124	51 80
Turnips, bushels	393	161 50	171	222 10
Beets, bushels	95¼	49 00	26⅝	33 50
Cabbage, pounds	27,490	152 74	12,208	67 87
White beans, bushels	501	347 66	613⅞	1,219 94
Apples, barrels	76	166 70	166½	351 23
Pickles, barrels	17	82 48		
Sauerkraut, barrels	5	20 48		
Carrots, bushels			22	27 65
Farm vegetables		170 29		169 51
Tea, pounds	1,989	527 19	2,415	935 60
Coffee, pounds	15,957	2,229 00	12,115	2,420 54
Crackers, barrels	6	19 15	3	6 22
Sugar, pounds	730	48 74	3,895	290 97
Syrup, barrels	55	782 73	46	718 75
Ginger, pounds	373	93 05	241	61 30
Pepper, pounds	1,468	346 49	1,553	366 46
Salt, barrels	67	58 90	69	65 60
Vinegar, barrels	37	243 30	29	200 39
Mustard, pounds	245½	74 44	101	31 32
Rice, pounds	781	46 50	2,347	158 05
Hominy, pounds	24	77 65	5¼	17 38
Barley, pounds			3,676	127 48
Allspice, pounds	266	46 03	166	29 42
Cinnamon, pounds			10	4 66
Currants, pounds	1,046	70 10	810	59 68
Baking powder, pounds	156	42 32	93½	31 03
Soda, pounds			183	13 37
Soap, boxes	66	217 73	65	216 04
Ice, tons	51⅞	155 85	89½	323 95
Coal, tons	92	533 35	136	616 50
Implements and utensils		675 34		632 81
Female prison		155 71		249 30
Board of convicts in Warden house		1,460 33		1,532 58
Hospital		459 44		415 84
Repairs on implements		248 63		217 40
Totals		$58,170 17		$53,778 74
Credits for sundry sales		144 22		178 51
Net totals		$58,025 95		$53,600 23
Total number of days' board	533,526		483,491	
Daily average number of convicts	1,459		1,321	
Average cost per man { Per day—cents		10.9		11.1
Per year—dollars		$39 77		$40 57

The issues of the Clothing Department for convict clothing and bedding, the aggregate expense for the same, and the average cost per convict for the fiscal years ending September 30, 1887, and September 30, 1888, are shown by the following:

Articles.	Total, 1887. Quan.	Total, 1887. Cost.		Total, 1888. Quan.	Total, 1888. Cost.	
Clothing.						
Coats and overcoats	628	$1,444 50		693	$1,590 05	
Pants	1,821	2,822 55		2,158	3,345 35	
Vests	543	597 30		657	742 30	
Caps	64	192 00		66¼	199 25	
Straw hats	23	44 00		19	38 85	
Shoes	1,059	2,479 00		907	2,132 64	
Boots	79	243 50		68	222 50	
Rubber boots	78	239 75		21	59 75	
Hickory shirts	2,452	....		2,904	....	
Undershirts	938	....		204	....	
Woolen shirts	275	....		386	....	
Drawers	1,175	....		368	....	
Socks	300¾	1,127 06		496½	1,320 76	
Gloves and mitts	172⅛	816 23		65$\frac{10}{11}$	555 88	
Scarfs	511	....		303	....	
Suspenders	992	....		1,286	....	
Combs	65	30 44		78$\frac{4}{17}$	37 66	
Handkerchiefs	2,413	....		2,970	....	
Duck aprons	3,069	....		2,639	....	
Oversleeves	266	....		289	....	
Shop towels	1,963	....		1,376	....	
Convict slippers	....	....		57	....	
Sneak shoes	45	....		64	....	
Pants buttons	5	6 60		5	6 95	
Agate buttons	7⅞	7 41		17	15 50	
Spool cotton	105	64 75		87	75 85	
Spool linen	52	41 60		44	34 72	
Skein linen	17	23 20		15½	21 70	
Hickory	8,047½	794 21		10,394½	1,080 51	
Check flannel	1,169½	349 43		1,595½	500 54	
Cotton flannel	6,118	728 00		3,633¼	446 56	
Handkerchief muslin	1,003¼	100 12		1,048	120 00	
Duck	4,051¼	460 12		3,893½	470 94	
Crash	1,453	163 35		1,217	154 43	
Stripes	61	45 75		61¾	47 85	
Sole leather	2,543¾	813 03		2,082	464 91	
Calf patching	80	20 00		52	14 00	
Shoe thread	9	9 40		6	6 20	
Shoe oil and ink	8	12 70		8	11 85	
Shoe nails	....	13 80		....	17 04	
Shoe lace	110	57 00		42	18 80	
Sundries	....	174 32		....	168 56	
			$13,921 12			$13,921 90

REFORMATORY AND PENAL INSTITUTIONS.

CLOTHING AND BEDDING ACCOUNT—Continued.

ARTICLES.	TOTAL, 1887.		TOTAL, 1888.	
	Quan.	Cost.	Quan.	Cost.
Laundry.				
Soap	61	$206 55	74	$240 24
Potash	44	168 85	35	133 75
Tallow	2,765	138 25	2,350	117 50
Salsoda	9,943	192 66	1,490	113 27
Marking ink	6	14 79	3	13 08
Bedding.		$721 10		$617 84
Blankets	603	1,500 00		
Sheeting	3,132½	239 85	3,092¾	261 05
Ticking	1,390¾	177 82	555¼	72 37
Pillow cases	560		905	
Pillow ticks	211			
Sheets	434		810	
Straw	26₁₀₀₀¹¹	133 29	2₁₀₀₀⁹⁹	10 57
		2,050 96		343 99
Freight		17 04		4 18
Repairs on tools, etc.		53 85		56 05
Totals		$16,764 07		$14,943 96
Credit for sales of rags		180 95		184 01
Net totals		$16,583 12		$14,759 95
Total number of days	532,526		483,491	
Daily average number of convicts	1,459		1,321	
Average cost per man per day—cents		3.1		3.0
Average cost per man per year—dollars		$11 37		$11 17

The expense of discharging convicts, for discharge clothing and transportation, the average cost per prisoner discharged, and the average cost per convict per day, during the two fiscal years ending September 30, 1888, were as follows:

•

DISCHARGE CLOTHING.

Months	Number of Prisoners Discharged	Coats and Overcoats No.	Pants No.	Vests No.	Cost	Shirts Doz.	Shirts Cost	Undershirts and Drawers Doz.	Undershirts and Drawers Cost	Socks Doz.	Socks Cost	Suspenders Doz.	Suspenders Cost
1886—October	59	114	104	114	$670 50			50	$225 00	5	$5 90		
November	70	208	8	8	1,015 00					10	18 50		
December	75	131	130	130	802 75			1⅛	10 50	12	24 00		
1887—January	52	90	66	66	542 50								
February	69	34	4	4	186 50	12	$72 00	10	45 30	11½	22 67	50	$100 00
March	52	27	68	26	224 00								
April	71	113	111	111	708 50			19¾	28 21				
May	57	7	7	7	72 50								
June	64	156	156	156	945 00					9¾	9 75		
July	67	20	60	20	235 00	6	33 60						
August	56	63	75	63	470 58					6	9 00		
September	68	3	28	9	92 00								
Totals first fiscal year	760	966	817	714	$5,964 83	18	$105 60	80⅞	$308 81	54¾	$89 82	50	$100 00
1887—October	57	74	73	74	$493 00	55½	$333 00	100	$250 00	8	$14 25		
November	90	80	79	79	535 00					4	6 00		
December	57	204	28	28	1,043 50					12	24 00		
1888—January	55	12	8	8	92 00								
February	71	142	80	80	821 50	2	14 00	10	45 00				
March	58	73	92	68	508 00					6	11 00	52	$96 20
April	70	118	118	118	721 00					10¾	15 42		
May	48	7	7	7	57 00								
June	40	2	2	2	16 00			6	21 00				
July	40	124	124	124	750 50	20	130 00			10	12 50		
August	54	7	7	7	76 50								
September	82	121	121	129	736 50								
Totals second fiscal year	692	964	739	724	$5,851 00	77½	$477 00	116	$316 00	50⅝	$83 17	52	$96 20

STATEMENT SHOWING THE EXPENSE OF DISCHARGING PRISONERS—Continued.

DISCHARGE CLOTHING—Continued.

Months	Average Cost per Convict per Day—Cents.	Average Cost per Prisoner Discharged	Total Discharge Expenses	Discharge and Transportation	Total	Sundry Supplies Cost	Collars Cost	Boxes	Boots and Shoes Cost	Boots and Shoes Pairs	Hats Cost	Hats Doz.
1886—October			$1,677 06	$672 75	$1,004 30	$1 20			$105 60	66	$2 00	1
November			2,017 10	897 00	1,120 10				99 20	62	97 50	186
December			1,986 20	840 35	1,154 85				153 60	96		
1887—January			1,228 00	653 00	574 40				2 50	1	4 00	4
February			1,143 54	828 95	314 05	5 40			78 55	49	35 50	71
March			1,144 65	626 45	518 09				134 40	96		
April			1,481 56	771 15	710 50	1 52			2 00	1		
May			1,012 20	786 85	225 71				45 60	28	76 50	156
June			1,822 80	738 60	1,084 20	2 80			139 60	96		
July			1,100 20	719 85	380 35				102 00	62		
August			1,130 18	614 60	515 58				6 00	2	39 00	74
September			1,078 70	823 55	255 15				149 40	97	4 75	2
Totals first fiscal year	3.16	$22 14	$16,830 98	$8,973 70	$7,857 28	$10 92			$1,018 06	656	$259 25	494
1887—October			$1,782 75	$608 00	$1,174 75				$44 00	26	$40 50	74
November			1,301 40	676 80	624 60				69 80	48		
December			1,855 65	614 90	1,240 75				101 25	63	72 00	134
1888—January			895 30	737 20	158 10				61 60	37	2 00	2
February			1,748 81	801 05	947 76				79 80	48	54 50	101
March			1,251 85	641 85	610 00	$4 50	$5 00		36 50	24	2 50	1
April			1,625 77	763 25	962 52	1 46			127 40	84		
May			591 90	495 70	96 20				36 20	24		
June			546 65	395 25	151 40				36 40	24		
July			1,445 00	481 30	963 30		10 00		72 80	48	78 00	144
August			745 15	637 95	107 20				18 20	12		
September			1,896 25	1,038 75	857 50				114 50	75	6 50	3
Totals second fiscal year	3.26	$22 81	$15,786 48	$7,892 40	$7,894 08	$5 96	$15 00		$791 25	513	$258 50	474

The prison and buildings are heated by steam. The coal used, which is soft coal, costs $1 90 per ton. Flour costs from $4 25 to $4 50 per barrel; beef, 4¾ cents per pound, dressed, and 8 cents for hind quarters. Butterine, costing 16 cents per pound, is used instead of butter.

The tobacco furnished to the prisoners is manufactured at the prison. Each prisoner is allowed four ounces of chewing tobacco per week. Smoking is prohibited except three times during the year, on holidays, when they are allowed two cigars each, which are worth about $18 per thousand.

All the convicts are treated alike. Friends can give them fruit, to be eaten in their presence.

There are two prisons in Illinois, the other of which is known as the Southern Illinois Penitentiary. The prison at Joliet, which is the general penitentiary for the State, is under the charge of three Commissioners, appointed by the Governor, by and with the advice and consent of the Senate, and subject to removal by the Governor at his discretion. If removed, that fact, and the cause thereof, must be reported by the Governor to the next Legislature. The Warden, Chaplain, and Physician are appointed by the Commissioners, and hold their respective offices for the term of three years, unless sooner removed by the Commissioners. The Commissioners give bonds in the sum of $25,000 each for the faithful performance of their duties, and the Warden gives a like bond in the sum of $50,000.

The Warden has power, by and with the consent of the Commissioners, or a majority of them, to appoint a Deputy Warden, Clerk, and Steward, who, however, are subject to removal by the Warden.

The Commissioners prescribe the articles of food and the quantity of each kind which shall be provided for the convicts, and determine the number of hours per day during which the convicts shall be required to labor.

The law makes it the duty of the Commissioners to cause, at least once a year, a full and accurate inventory and appraisement of all the machinery, fixtures, goods, and property of every description belonging to the State in and about the penitentiary, to be made under oath by two or more competent appraisers, to be appointed for that purpose by the Commissioners, and to cause a copy of such inventory and appraisement to be filed in the office of the Auditor of Public Accounts, and another copy to be appended to their biennial report to the Governor.

It is the duty of the Commissioners to meet at the penitentiary at least as often as once in each month, and as much oftener as the proper control and superintendence of the prison may require. It is their duty also to examine and inquire into all matters connected with the government, discipline, and police of the penitentiary, the punishment and employment of the convicts, and also into any improper conduct which may be alleged to have been committed by the Warden or any other officer or employé; and for this purpose the Commissioners have power to issue subpœnas, and compel the attendance of witnesses, and the production before them of writings and papers, and examine any witnesses on oath who may appear before them.

The statutes governing the penitentiary provide that it shall be the duty of the Warden to reside in and constantly attend the penitentiary, except when absent on some necessary duty connected with his office, and that in no case shall the Warden and Deputy Warden be absent at the same time.

The Warden, among other duties, is required to examine daily into the state of the penitentiary, and into the health, condition, and safe-keeping of the convicts, and to inquire into the justice of any complaints made by any of the convicts relative to their provisions, clothing, or treatment.

Among the salaries paid per annum are:

```
Commissioners, each_____$1,500
Warden_____ 2,500
Deputy Warden_____ 1,800
Chaplain_____ 1,500
Physician_____ 1,500
```

Meal tickets are sold to visitors if they desire them. Visitors are allowed to visit the prison every day except Sundays and holidays. They are taken in charge by an usher at nine A. M., eleven A. M., two P. M., and four P. M. And if they arrive after any one of these hours they are required to wait until the next specified hour. An admission fee is charged to general visitors.

Each Guard receives twelve meal tickets free, which he may use as he pleases during the year. If he desires more he is charged at the rate of 25 cents per ticket, and if he does not use all that he is entitled to without charge, he may surrender those remaining unused and receive 25 cents for each.

This prison has a well deserved reputation throughout the United States for its discipline and government. This is largely due to its rules and regulations, and their strict and impartial enforcement. The rules now in force are these:

The Warden.

The Warden, in the performance of his duties as chief executive officer of the Illinois State Penitentiary, shall be guided by the statutes and laws providing for the management of the penitentiary, and by such rules and orders as may, from time to time, be adopted and placed on record by the Board of Penitentiary Commissioners.

Duties of the Deputy Warden.

1. The Deputy Warden is the assistant and agent of the Warden in the general government and management of the penitentiary, more particularly in matters of discipline of its officers and prisoners.

2. He shall attend daily at the prison, from the hour of unlocking in the morning until after the prisoners shall have been locked up at night.

3. In the absence of the Warden from the prison, the Deputy Warden shall perform his duties, and shall not leave the prison until the Warden returns.

4. He shall not be absent from the prison, at any time during the day, when the prisoners are out of their cells, without first obtaining leave from the Warden.

5. He shall visit the prison occasionally during the night by surprise, and personally ascertain that the prisoners are all secure; and that the officers are on duty and alert.

6. Under the orders of the Warden, he shall have special control and direction of the Keepers, Guards, Foremen, and other servants of the prison, and shall be responsible that every one performs his respective duties with intelligence, fidelity, and zeal. And it shall be his duty to report to the Warden, strictly and promptly, every neglect of duty or impropriety or misconduct on the part of any officer.

7. He shall report to the Warden the name of every officer coming upon duty under the influence of intoxicants or without being in uniform.

8. He shall not grant leave of absence to any officer for a longer period than one day without consulting the Warden, except in cases of emergency.

9. He shall enforce obedience to the prison rules and regulations, and to all orders given from time to time by the Warden, and shall maintain generally the police and discipline of the prison with the strictest exactness, for which purpose he shall frequently, during the day, but at irregular periods and without notice, visit the shops, yards, hospital, kitchen, cells, and other apartments of the prison, and the different places where work is in hand, taking every precaution for the security of the prison and prisoners, seeing that the officers are vigilant and attentive to their duties, and that they keep the prisoners under them diligently employed during their hours of labor.

10. He shall not permit any book, pamphlet, or newspaper to be read by any officer, nor to be in his possession, while on duty in or about the prison.

11. When a prisoner is received, the Deputy Warden shall see that he is properly bathed, clothed in a prison suit, and duly inspected by the prison Physician, and vaccinated. He shall then read and explain to him the rules and regulations for the government of prisoners, give

him his privilege tickets, and assign him to duty under direction of the Warden.

12. He shall at short intervals examine the locks, levers, and gratings in and about the entire prison, and see that they are in good condition.

13. He shall exercise due vigilance, to see that there is no embezzlement of the property of the penitentiary; that not only no willful waste, but also no want of economy in the necessary consumption or the use of supplies takes place, without making such known to the Warden immediately.

14. He shall consider it his duty to make himself acquainted with the social habits and conduct of every subordinate officer and employé of the prison, and particularly whether, when off duty, he is a frequenter of saloons or other houses of similar resort, or associates with idle or loose characters, and report the facts to the Warden.

15. He shall see that no material is allowed to be placed near the inclosing walls, and that nothing is accessible to prisoners which can facilitate escape. He shall especially see that ladders are properly secured.

16. He shall have a vigilant eye over every person who may have business about the prison, to see that nothing is carried in or out for a prisoner; and, so far as he can, that no communication of any description is attempted by such person with any prisoner, except by authority, and in the presence of an officer.

17. He shall, every evening, before relieving the Guards and Keepers from duty, verify by actual count the written daily count report furnished him from the office.

18. As the Penitentiary Act of 1872 affords to prisoners the privilege of earning diminution of their sentence, it will be incumbent upon all the officers of the prison to give the strictest attention to the conduct and character of every prisoner; and especially it shall be the duty of the Deputy Warden to satisfy himself as to the behavior of every prisoner, his industry, alacrity, and zeal in the execution of his work, so that the Deputy may be able to advise with the Warden, as to the diminution of sentence to be made to each convict. And for this purpose he shall communicate freely with every officer in charge of a gang, when making his rounds.

19. The Deputy Warden shall, under orders of the Warden, investigate all reports of offenses committed by prisoners, and make disposition of the same. In these investigations the Deputy Warden shall be careful in endeavoring to arrive at the truth concerning each case; in awarding punishment he shall take into consideration the age, previous conduct, habits, and disposition of the offender, so far as he may be able to ascertain the same, and in the administration of punishment he shall take special care to deprive it of all appearance of personal vindictiveness, even under great provocation, at the same time making it sufficiently severe, without cruelty, to secure the end desired. He shall make daily written report to the Warden of all prisoners reported to him, the nature of their offense, and of all punishments awarded or administered.

20. The only disciplinary punishments of prisoners allowed to be administered in this prison are:

1. Taking from prisoners one or all of their privilege tickets.

2. Solitary confinement on short rations of bread and water.

3. Handcuffing prisoner to the grated cell door at the height of his breast.

Corporal punishments of any kind are prohibited by the statute.

Duties of Assistant Deputy Warden.

1. The Assistant Deputy Warden shall attend daily at the prison from the hour of unlocking in the morning until after the prisoners have been locked up at night.

2. He shall assist the Deputy Warden in the discharge of his duties whenever called on by him; and in the absence of the Deputy Warden from the prison, he shall perform all the duties incumbent upon that officer.

3. He shall assist the Deputy Warden in maintaining and executing the rules of government of the prison, and report to him any violation of the same by either the officers or the prisoners that may come under his notice.

4. He shall keep, mornings and evenings, the time of officers on duty during the day, and report the same to the Clerk on the first of each month.

5. He shall attend the daily sick call, accompanying prisoners who are to see the Physician, from the different workshops to the hospital, and ordering them to sick cell or on duty, as the Physician may direct.

6. He shall have charge of the prison armory, assigning Guards and Keepers their arms and accouterments, and seeing that everything belonging to the armory, including the special supply of lanterns, is in good condition and serviceable at a moment's notice.

7. He shall inspect the arms and equipments of the Guards at least once a week, and report any officer whose rifle or equipments are not in good order. He shall frequently inspect all the arms and equipments not in daily use and see that they are kept in thorough repair.

Duties of Chaplain.

1. He shall conduct religious services in the penitentiary under such regulations as the Commissioners may prescribe, and attend to the spiritual wants of the prisoners.

2. He shall obtain from each prisoner, when received in the penitentiary, as complete a statement as possible, of his religious and educational antecedents, and his parental and conjugal relations, and shall make report thereof, on blanks furnished, to the Warden.

3. He shall visit the prisoners in their cells, for the purpose of giving them moral and religious instruction.

4. He shall furnish, at the expense of the State, a Bible to each prisoner.

5. He shall not have any intercourse with prisoners in the shops or while they are at work, nor shall he hold communication with them, except as may be necessary and proper in imparting to them such secular and religious instruction as is required by law and the prison regulations.

6. He shall not furnish the prisoners with any information or intelligence in relation to outside matters, except by permission of the Warden.

7. He shall visit daily the sick in the hospital and administer to their spiritual wants.

8. He shall, once a week, read to prisoners that have arrived during the preceding seven days, the rules and regulations for the government of prisoners, impressing upon them the necessity of their strict observ-ance of the same, and the benefits they may derive thereby under the good time law.

9. He shall have charge of the library, so far as to see that no im-proper books are placed in possession of the prisoners, and if such books are found, either in the cells, or in possession of prisoners, he shall take away and deliver the same to the Warden; and for the purpose of the proper discharge of these duties, he shall visit the cells in the penitentiary, and the books so taken away from prisoners shall not be returned to them without the express order of the Commissioners.

10. Sectarian doctrines in the matter of religious belief shall not be taught, nor shall any attempt be made, directly or indirectly, to prose-lyte a prisoner. If any prisoner desires communication with a minister or instructor of his particular faith, on proper application to the War-den it shall be allowed, under and in conformity with the law and the general regulations of the prison; but such minister or instructor, on such occasions, must in all things conform to the rules and regulations for the government of the Chaplain; any infringement or departure from which will debar him from future intercourse with the prisoners.

11. He shall make an annual report to the Commissioners for each year ending the first day of October, relative to the religious and moral conduct of the prisoners during such year; stating therein what services he has performed, and the fruits of his instruction, together with any other facts relative to said prisoners he may deem proper to report.

12. The Chaplain shall, when required by the Commissioners, give instruction in the useful branches of an English education to such pris-oners as, in the judgment of the Warden, may require the same and be benefited thereby, and be entitled thereto by previous good conduct; and such instruction may be given for such length of time daily as said Commissioners shall prescribe (Sunday excepted), between the hours of six and nine P. M.

13. He shall make a quarterly report to the Commissioners in case such instruction shall be given, stating the number of prisoners instructed during the quarter, the branches of education taught, the text-books used, the progress made by the convicts, and note especially any case in which unusual progress has been made by a prisoner.

Duties of the Physician.

1. He shall attend at all times to the wants of the sick prisoners, whether in the hospital or in their cells, and shall render them all necessary medical service.

2. He shall examine weekly the cells of the prisoners, for the purpose· of ascertaining whether they are kept in a proper state of cleanliness and ventilation, and report the same weekly to the Warden.

3. He shall examine, at least once a week, and oftener if he thinks proper, into the quality and condition of the provisions provided for the prisoners; and whenever he shall have reason to believe that any pro-visions are prejudicial to the health of the prisoners, he shall imme-diately make report thereof to the Warden. He shall also have power, and it shall be his duty to prescribe the diet of the sick prisoners, and

his directions in relation thereto shall be followed by the Warden and Steward.

4. He shall vaccinate every prisoner on his entering the prison, and examine him as to the condition of his heart, lungs, and chest, evidence of previous or present hereditary disease, and keep a record of such examination in a book provided for that purpose.

5. He shall visit the prison every day between the hours of seven and ten in the morning. When the state of a sick prisoner requires it, he shall visit at such hours as he may think the case demands, and if sent for at any time by the Warden or Deputy Warden, he shall immediately repair to the prison to the exclusion of all other engagements.

6. He shall keep a daily record of all admissions to the hospital, and the cases treated in the cells or elsewhere, indicating the sex, color, nativity, age, occupation, habits of life, period of entrance and discharge from the hospital, disease, and the prescription and treatment in each case.

7. He shall have full control over the patients in hospital, subject to the rules of the prison and instructions of the Commissioners, and shall leave his daily general instructions as to the government, etc., of the patients with the Hospital Steward.

8. It shall be the duty of the Physician, in case of any prisoner claiming to be unable to labor by reason of sickness, to examine such prisoner; and if, in his opinion, upon examination, said prisoner is unable to labor, he shall immediately certify the same to the Warden, and such prisoner shall thereupon be released from labor and admitted to the hospital, or placed in his cell, or elsewhere, for medical treatment, as said Physician shall direct, having a due regard for the safe-keeping of such prisoner, and such prisoner shall not be required to labor so long as in the opinion of said Physician such disability shall continue; and whenever said Physician shall certify to the Warden that such prisoner is sufficiently recovered to be able to labor, said prisoner shall be required to labor, and not before. He shall also direct the transfer, permanent or temporary, of prisoners from first to second class work, and report such transfer to the Warden.

9. He shall examine carefully every morning all prisoners in punishment in the solitary cells, and shall make written report to the Warden of their condition. He shall be particular to report to the Warden in writing any prisoner whose health he thinks is suffering or endangered by the punishment he is undergoing, and shall recommend such changes in the diet of prisoners in punishment as he may think necessary. He shall require the Hospital Steward to make a similar examination every evening, between the hours of four and five o'clock, and make a written report of the same.

10. He shall, whenever in his opinion a prisoner becomes insane, certify that fact to the Warden, giving his reasons therefor, and make, on blanks furnished him for that purpose, a brief statement of the general condition of the patient, together with his recommendation as to what disposition shall be made of him.

11. When a prisoner dies, the Physician shall record the nature of the complaint and all the circumstances connected therewith that he may deem proper and necessary, and report to the Warden.

12. When the Physician considers it necessary, or when required by the Commissioners or Warden, to make a post mortem examination of

any prisoner, he shall do so within thirty-six hours after the decease. He shall make written reports of his examination to the Warden, and of his conclusion as to the cause of death.

13. He shall keep such books and in such forms as from time to time may be indicated to him according to schedules ordered by the Commissioners; all of such books shall be open at all times to the Warden.

14. He shall make a written report daily to the Warden of the attendance at sick call in the morning, and of the disposition made of those reported sick, also of all admissions to and discharges from hospital, deaths, etc.

15. He shall, whenever requested so to do by the Commissioners or Warden, make a careful examination of any prisoner, and make written report of his physical condition.

16. He shall make report monthly to the Commissioners, of patients received into the hospital, or treated in the cells or elsewhere during the preceding month, stating their respective age, color, disease, occupation in prison, quantity and kinds of medicine administered during the month, the time they have remained in hospital, date of commencement and termination of treatment, and number of days during which such patients, in consequence of sickness, have been relieved from labor; also of all deaths and cause thereof, transfers to insane hospitals, etc.

17. He shall make a yearly report to the Commissioners of the sanitary condition of the penitentiary for the past year, in which all information in his daily and monthly reports shall be condensed. This report shall also contain nominal lists of prisoners who have died or been certified to be insane during the year.

Duties of Hospital Steward.

1. The Hospital Steward shall be the assistant to and shall act under the immediate directions of the Physician about the hospital, and in his absence shall perform the duties of his office.

2. He shall be responsible for the nurses, orderlies, and other servants, employed about the hospital, and shall see that good discipline in the hospital is at all times maintained.

3. He shall have charge of the dispensary and the hospital, for the good order and cleanliness of which, and of all its approaches and surroundings, he shall be responsible.

4. He shall have charge of the sick in the hospital, and of the convalescent prisoners, so long as they are receiving advice from the Physician, and shall strictly attend to all instructions that may be given him as to their medicine, diet, and treatment.

5. He shall also attend to the complaining prisoners not in hospital, to whom medicine is administered.

6. He shall see that every chamber in the hospital is well ventilated, the bedding and clothing cleansed and changed when necessary, the ceilings, walls, and floors cleaned and purified by frequent scrubbing and whitewashing, and that all impurities of every description are instantly removed.

7. He shall attend the Physician in his visits to the sick, make up all the prescriptions, compound all the medicines, and see that they are administered in the form and at the times ordered by the Physician.

8. Should the symptoms of any patient appear to him to become

aggravated, he shall at once report to the Warden, in order that, if necessary, the Physician may be sent for, without loss of time.

9. Should he observe the death of a prisoner approaching he shall at once notify the Warden or Deputy, in order that information may be sent to the Chaplain.

10. It shall be his duty to make a tour of the wards of the hospital frequently during the day, and especially he shall do so, as his first duty in the morning and the last duty at night.

11. He shall see that the bedclothes of patients, who are able to leave their beds, are well ventilated, while they are out of bed.

12. When a prisoner is received sick, from the cell-house during the night, the Hospital Steward shall immediately notify the Warden, if the case seems to him to be urgent.

13. He shall issue no alcoholic or intoxicating liquors to any employé or prisoner under any circumstances, except upon the written order of the Warden, or the written prescription of the Physician.

Duties of the Clerk.

1. He shall be the Warden's accountant and his assistant and agent in matters of the records and fiscal affairs of the penitentiary, and shall as such have charge, under the supervision and immediate direction of the Warden, of the following books and records.

Records:
  1. The Commissioners' Journal of Proceedings.
  2. The Warden's Record of Official Orders.
  3. The Convict Register and complete index thereto.
  4. The Discharge Register and Records.
  5. The Record of Statistics.
  6. Punishment Record.
  7. Book of Daily Counts.

Account Books:
  1. The Store, double-entry Journal and Ledger and auxiliary books, accounting for the receipts and issues of supplies. (See Storekeeper.)
  2. The State Shops' Day Book, accounting for all transactions of the State Shops, in the way of permanent improvements, repairs, furnishing of implements, fuel, etc. (See Supt. State Shops.)
  3. The Convict Money Journal and Ledger, accounting, individually, for moneys deposited by and paid to prisoners.
  4. The Consolidated Check Roll, an abstract from all the Time Check Rolls of the prison, which—in their aggregate—are daily to correspond with the evening's count.
  5. The Cash Book, with triplicate vouchers for all expenditures, and as complete a system of vouchers for receipts (by stubs, tickets, etc.) as practicable.
  These books may be consolidated and abstracted monthly, in:
  6. The General Journal; and,
  7. The General Ledger.

2. He shall be responsible for the safe-keeping and orderly arrangement of all the accounts, vouchers, bills, mittimuses, and other documents of every kind confided to him.

3. He shall make out all financial and other statements and exhibits of any kind at such times as the Warden may direct.

6D

4. He shall assist the Warden in making the annual and biennial statements and exhibits (financial and statistical) as are by law, and under the directions of the Commissioners, required of the Warden.

5. He shall collect from employés and outsiders, all the bills made against them by the Store, State Shops, Clothing Department, or other departments of the prison, give receipt for same, and report the collections to the Storekeeper or the Superintendents of the respective departments on the regular stub blanks provided for that purpose.

6. He shall give individual receipts to all prisoners from or for whom he has received money or other articles of value.

7. All vouchers for payment of supplies must be made from original bills of particulars approved by the Steward and must pass through Store books. All vouchers for payrolls and other expenses must be authorized and approved by the Warden.

8. He shall, at the end of every month, make from the Discharge Register a complete list of all prisoners to be released during the succeeding month by expiration of sentence, and furnish a copy of this list to all officers of the penitentiary whose business it is to be acquainted with it.

9. He shall, on the first of every month, make a statement to the Governor of the State, giving a nominal list of all prisoners received during the preceding month, the counties they come from, and their crimes and sentences, and also a list of all prisoners discharged, pardoned, and otherwise released during the same period.

Duties of the Assistant Clerk.

1. He shall assist the Clerk in the performance of his duties, and in his absence shall perform the duties of the office or any other clerical work required of him by the Warden.

2. He shall be a telegraphist and have charge of the prison telegraph and electric apparatus.

3. He shall take, or have taken, the photograph of every incoming male prisoner as soon as practicable after his arrival, preserve and take care of the negatives, and keep the respective photographs in orderly arrangement in a case provided for that purpose.

Duties of the Steward.

1. The Steward shall be the Warden's agent and assistant in making purchases of goods and merchandise used for the penitentiary, and generally supervising the property of the State, and shall, subject to the decision of the Warden, and under his direction, be the judge of the needs and requirements of the prison in the matter of supplies.

2. He shall have particular charge of the supply department of the penitentiary, of the kitchen, the cellars, and the other chambers where provisions are kept, and all the passages leading thereto.

3. He shall receive all the provisions directly from the party supplying the same, as well as all fuel and forage, and shall cause every article to be weighed or measured as the case may be. Immediately on receipt of goods he shall have them turned over to the store.

4. He shall not receive any article of supplies without a bill of particulars along with it, nor until after he has carefully examined the article, and ascertained that it is of good quality, and strictly according to the specifications of contract. Should the bill be correct, he shall certify

the same and transmit it to the Storekeeper without delay; if not, he shall report the facts to the Warden.

5. He shall not sell or permit the Storekeeper to sell any goods or property of the State, with the following exceptions:

Contractors are allowed to purchase such articles as they may require for shop use only. Employés may purchase, through the store, uniforms, hats, caps, cloth, and buttons. Rags, hides, tallow, lard, and bones may be sold, through the store, at market prices, to outsiders.

6. He shall see that all provisions of every kind received by him are, until used, kept in a proper place, and in proper vessels, to prevent their becoming injured. He shall take care that no provisions which have become unserviceable are cooked, and that everything unsound is taken away.

7. Should provisions be delivered by a contractor, which are found by rigid examination to be not according to contract, he shall refuse to receive them, and shall at once report the fact to the Warden, so that no delay may take place in obtaining a supply from elsewhere, if the contractor should be unable, or unwilling, to replace immediately what has been rejected.

8. He shall take special care that the utmost cleanliness prevails in the kitchen, the cellars, and in every chamber or vessel in which provisions are kept, or from which they are eaten.

9. He shall daily attend upon and see to the cooking and serving of the provisions for the prisoners, to the end that no improper food is used, that it is cooked in a proper and cleanly manner, served in clean, wholesome vessels, and equally and honestly distributed to the prisoners.

10. He shall report to the Warden from time to time the condition of the supplies and the necessities of immediate purchase thereof, and it shall be his duty, under the direction of the Commissioners and the Warden, to purchase such supplies; and at all times, when such purchases are made, to furnish the Warden proper certified bills for the same.

11. He shall have special charge of the farm, and the stock thereon, and see that everything connected with that department is managed to the best interest of the State.

Duties of Storekeeper.

1. He shall be the custodian and keeper of all supplies purchased for the use of the penitentiary by the Warden or his agent, the Steward.

2. He shall personally receive check from bills of particulars, and inspect all goods delivered to him, and report deficiencies in quantity and quality of the same to the Steward and also to the Warden, who will decide as to their receipt or rejection. He will have charge of issuing supplies to the different departments on requisitions approved by the Steward, and shall not issue anything without having such requisition therefor, or without making a memorandum bill on manifold bill book.

3. He shall, under direction and supervision of the Clerk of the penitentiary, keep accurate double-entry accounts of all transactions in the store, of receipts and issues or sales, and shall, at the end of each month, or as soon thereafter as practicable, furnish a trial balance to the Clerk, together with bills of items against contractors and such other parties

as may be permitted to purchase supplies from the store. (See duties of Steward.)

4. He shall, every three months, take inventory of all property in the store, and give a transcript of the same to the Clerk.

5. He shall, from the bill book, make individual bills for all the sales from the store to citizens (not contractors), and balance them, on stub, upon receipt of cash delivery tickets from office. These individual bills shall also be entered on his ledger.

Duties of the Warden-House Stewards.

1. The Steward of the Warden House Proper has charge of and is responsible for the good condition of the main, second, and third floors of the house, and all property therein. The house servants are accountable to him, and it is his duty to know that the rooms are in order at all times. He has charge of all rooms and will make daily (and oftener when necessary) inspection of apartments, generally supervising and directing the work of his men.

2. He shall use his best endeavors to maintain strict discipline among the men under his charge, and be particularly watchful to prevent escapes.

3. He shall see that all supplies furnished him on his daily requisitions are economically and properly used.

4. He shall assign rooms and beds for employés in such manner as to accommodate the greatest number.

5. He shall make written lists of clothes he sends to the female prison to be washed, and check them on their return.

6. He shall, on the first of every month, make a detailed report to the Steward of the Penitentiary, giving the aggregate cost of subsistence in his department and the average cost of each meal served.

7. The Steward of the Warden House Basement has charge of the basement floor of the house and its contents, receiving his instructions from the Steward of the Penitentiary.

8. He is responsible for the conduct and good discipline of the prisoners in his department, and Keepers and Guards are prohibited from interfering unless called upon; also from conversing with prisoners in basement about anything not strictly pertaining to their duties.

9. He has charge of and is accountable for all State property in his department, and shall use strict economy in the use of supplies of every kind furnished him on his requisitions.

10. He shall allow no person, not an officer of the penitentiary, unless authorized by the Warden, to take a meal in his department without a ticket procured at the Clerk's office.

11. He shall check the Clerk's office on every meal ticket sold or otherwise issued from there.

12. He shall exact and enforce strict compliance with all regulations of common decency in public eating houses.

13. He shall, on the first of every month, make a detailed report to the Steward of the Penitentiary, giving the aggregate cost of subsistence in his department and the average cost of each meal served, giving credit to the department for every commutation or single meal ticket known to him as having been sold by the Clerk.

14. The barber shop and bath-rooms are for the convenience of the

employés, and may be used by any one connected with the institution, under such restrictions as may from time to time be provided.

Duties of Convict Kitchen Steward.

1. He shall, under immediate direction of the Steward of the Penitentiary, have charge of the convict kitchen and bakery, also the flour-room, vegetable-rooms, and cellars belonging thereto, and of all State property in that department, and shall direct and supervise the labor of prisoners assigned to him, and maintain strict discipline among them.

2. He shall make his written bill of fare and requisition on the store once a week for supplies for his department during the entire succeeding week; and he shall personally inspect all supplies before cooking them, and refuse all such as may not come up to the requirement of being absolutely wholesome. He will be held responsible for cooking any article of food that is not in good and wholesome condition.

3. He shall take special care that the utmost cleanliness prevails in the kitchen, bakery, and appurtenances, and in every vessel in which provisions are kept or from which they are eaten.

4. He shall see that provisions are properly cooked and seasoned, and that the meals can be served warm, in sufficient quantity, and at the proper time.

5. He shall admit to the kitchen dining-rooms such prisoners only as have special permits to that effect from the Warden or Deputy.

6. He shall, on the first of every month, make to the Steward of the Penitentiary a detailed statement of all supplies of subsistence consumed in his department during the preceding month, the aggregate cost of such supplies, and the average cost of subsistence per man per day.

Duties of the Chief Engineer and Superintendent of State Shops.

1. He shall have charge of all property, machinery, tools, implements, and merchandise in the different departments of the State shops, of all boilers and engines belonging to the State, and of machinery and fixtures employed for the service of the State, as appearing from the annual inventory of machinery and fixtures.

2. He shall have charge of the water supply system for the prison, shall be responsible for the condition of the necessary pipes, pumps, and other appliances, and for any unnecessary waste of water.

3. He shall have supervision of the entire steam apparatus for the heating, cooking, ventilating, and mechanical purposes of the prison, and shall see that the same is kept in good condition.

4. He shall have supervision of the sewer system of the prison, and direct the construction and repairs of the same.

5. He shall have charge of the gas works, and see that waste is prevented and economy exercised.

6. He shall have charge of the fire department, take care of the chemical engines, and test their efficiency from time to time, and see that the fire buckets, grenades, etc., placed in different stations around the prison, are serviceable and in good condition. .

7. He shall have charge of the machine shop, the blacksmith, carpenter, tin, and paint shops connected with his department, together with the control and management of the prisoners therein engaged;

shall see that all work is properly done, and that skill and industry are attained and observed.

8. He shall see that all machinery, tools, implements, materials, stock, or other effects necessary for carrying on the above mentioned duties and industries are properly used, taken care of, and accounted for.

9. He shall have charge of the erection of all buildings within the prison inclosure; the plans, estimates, and specifications for the same shall be prepared by him and submitted, through the Warden, for the approval of the Board of Commissioners.

10. He shall, at the direction of the Board of Commissioners or the Warden, furnish estimates as to the cost of any proposed improvement or change in the prison buildings.

11. He shall have supervision of all improvements or repairs on the prison buildings, and see that skill, economy, and industry are exercised by those working thereon for the State.

12. He shall have general supervision of all the buildings constituting the prison, and shall see that they are kept in proper repair.

13. He shall superintend and instruct in their duties all citizens, engineers, or workmen that may from time to time, either permanently or temporarily, be employed for the service of the State.

14. He shall, in a general way, supervise the condition of the boilers and engines belonging to contractors, and shall at once make report to the Warden when, in his opinion, there is danger to life or property threatened from that source.

15. He shall furnish and charge to contractors any material or work that they may desire for their workshops and machinery.

16. He shall, under direction and supervision of the Clerk of the penitentiary, keep accurate account of his transactions in any of the branches above enumerated, in a day book, giving separately the amounts respectively charged for labor and material. A summary and abstract of this day book shall be furnished to the Clerk on the first of every month.

17. He shall from his bill book make individual bills for all work done in the State shops for citizens (not contractors), and balance them, on stub, upon receipt of corresponding cash delivery tickets from office. These individual bills shall also be entered on his day book.

Duties of Receiving and Discharging Officer (Superintendent of Clothing Department).

1. He shall receive from the office all incoming prisoners and attend personally to the bathing, washing, and clothing of the same, and take from them all money and valuables on their persons, to be turned over to the Clerk.

2. He shall, on the blanks furnished him, take a detailed personal description of every incoming prisoner, and also take his written consent to the examination of his incoming and outgoing mail by the Warden or an officer authorized by him.

3. He shall clothe and take to the office for discharge all the prisoners whose terms of sentence have expired according to monthly list furnished him from the office, or who have been pardoned or otherwise released; in so doing he shall be careful that nothing is carried out by a discharged prisoner that is not his property.

4. He is charged with the execution of all orders, special and general, relating to clothing and bedding for the use of the prisoners.

5. He shall have charge of the wash-room, bath-room, clothing-room, and repair shop, and shall keep an account of all stock received, used, and issued, and of all articles made and repaired in said shop.

6. He shall have superintendence of all work performed in the wash-room and clothing-room, and see that it is properly done.

7. He shall superintend the shaving, hair cutting, and bathing of the prisoners, and shall see that it is done at the proper time.

8. He shall, from his bill book, make individual bills for all repairs and other work done in his department for citizens, and check off and balance them, on stub, upon receipt of corresponding cash delivery tickets from office.

9. He shall, on the first of every month, make a report to the Warden of the operations under his charge, giving account of the quantities of materials used and goods issued.

Duties of Usher.

1. The Usher shall, at such hours as may from time to time be designated by the Warden, conduct visitors through the penitentiary, but to such places only as are indicated on visitors' passes and admission tickets.

2. He shall be supplied by the Clerk with admission tickets, hand to the Turnkey one for each visitor not provided with a pass, and shall, once a month, settle with the Clerk for his monthly sales of tickets.

3. He is forbidden to point out any individual prisoner to visitors.

4. He will not permit visitors to have any communication whatever with prisoners, to point at, or to speak to them, or to handle any tools, working material, or manufactured goods in shops.

5. It shall also be the duty of the Usher to closely examine all incoming and outgoing mail of prisoners, also all newspapers, parcels, and packages addressed to prisoners, and to admit and permit only such matter as is consistent with the general rules of the prison and requirements made known to him by the Warden.

6. He shall also attend to interviews between prisoners and their friends under restrictions of the general rules for the government of prisoners; shall pay close attention to their conversation, and see that no articles of contraband character pass between them.

7. He shall receive and investigate complaints of prisoners through the Keepers, of irregularities in the receipt of mail and newspapers, and remedy the defects if possible.

8. He shall turn over to the Clerk all moneys and valuables sent to prisoners by mail, or deposited with him by friends visiting them, and shall take the Clerk's receipt therefor.

Duties of Librarian.

1. He shall, under the direction of the Warden, have charge of the Prison Library, shall have the books properly covered, labeled, and shelved, and see that they are kept in good condition by prisoners or other persons entitled to the privilege of the library.

2. He shall superintend the issuing of books to prisoners under such regulations and restrictions, and in such manner as the Warden, from

time to time, may direct, and shall pay particular attention, by frequent personal inspection, that the right books are delivered to the prisoners who order them.

3. Civilians employed by or otherwise connected with the penitentiary must, before they are permitted to draw books out of the library, be provided with a written permit from the Warden to that effect, and the Librarian shall take individual receipts on blanks, furnished for that purpose, for books issued on the authority of such permits.

4. He shall examine the books when they are returned from the cell-houses, and shall report any serious mutilation or defacing of them to the Warden or Deputy.

5. He shall carefully check the bills of particulars for books bought for the library, receive the books, assort and catalogue them, and report any deficiency to the Warden.

6. He shall furnish the Warden such statements and statistics concerning the library, as may from time to time be required.

Duties of the Wagonmaster.

1. He shall have charge of the teams, conveyances, and rolling stock of the penitentiary, and all the appurtenances thereto; shall see that the horses and mules are properly cared for, and that all the State property under his charge is economically used and kept in good repair.

2. He shall, under the directions of the Warden and Deputy, supply the contractors and State department with teams in sufficient number and at the proper time.

Duties of Mail Carrier and Expressman.

1. He shall be a sworn mail carrier of the United States postal service and carry the penitentiary mail to and from the Joilet Post Office, in such manner and at such times as the Warden may direct.

2. He shall, on every mail trip to Joilet, visit the express companies for parcels directed to the institution or its employés, and do such other errands in Joilet for the service of the institution as the Warden or heads of departments may request.

3. He shall, when not on duty with his regular mail trips, assist the Usher in conducting visitors through the penitentiary.

Duties of Keepers and Guards.

1. The Keepers and Guards are the agents of the Warden in enforcing the police and discipline of the prison, and in carrying into effect the laws for the government thereof.

2. It shall be the duty of the Keepers and Guards to attend at the prison at the opening thereof, and not absent themselves therefrom, on any pretext or excuse, during prison hours, except by permission of the Warden or Deputy Warden.

3. They shall supply themselves with uniform, such as shall be prescribed by the Warden, with the approval of the Board of Commissioners, which shall be constantly worn while on duty; they shall constantly observe the utmost cleanliness in dress, person, and habits.

4. While within the prison, the Keepers and Guards shall refrain

from whistling, scuffling, immoderate laughter, boisterous conversation, exciting discussions on politics, religion, or other subjects, provoking witticisms or sarcasms, and all other acts calculated to disturb the harmony and good order of the prison.

5. In their intercourse among themselves the officers, Keepers, and Guards of the prison are at all times to treat each other with that mutual respect and kindness that become gentlemen and friends, and are required to avoid all collisions, jealousies, separate and party views and interests among themselves, and are strictly forbidden to treat each other with disrespect, or to use any ungentlemanly epithets.

6. They shall not, while on duty, hold conversation with each other, nor with the contractors or their foreman, except such as may be necessary in the discharge of their duties.

7. Neither shall they be engaged, while on duty, in reading or writing, other than making necessary entries, nor in any other employment calculated to interfere with constant care and vigilance.

8. They shall not under any circumstances allow prisoners to speak to them upon any subject not immediately connected with their duty, employments, or wants.

9. They shall keep the prisoners under their charge diligently at work at the several occupations at which they are employed, and shall make report on the check roll books of the daily attendance at work, also of all time lost by reason of sickness, punishment, or otherwise; closely following the instructions printed in front of each check roll.

10. They shall not permit prisoners to hold any conversation with each other, or with any person whatever, except those allowed by law, nor to communicate with each other by signs or signals, except in connection with their work.

11. They shall require the greatest possible cleanliness in the prisoners, their persons and clothing, and in their working and sleeping apartments.

12. They shall instruct the prisoners in all the rules of the prison necessary for their government, and admonish them on the least appearance of insubordination.

13. In all their intercourse with prisoners, they shall be careful to maintain a quiet demeanor, under any provocation, recollecting that the prisoner, however disposed to be violent or abusive, is entirely in their power.

14. They shall not punish a prisoner, nor strike him, except in self-defense, or to quell an insurrection; nor shall they use any profane or indecorous language to prisoners, or in their presence, but shall uniformly treat them in a kind and humane manner.

15. Whenever a prisoner is guilty of any infraction of prison disciplinary rules, the Keeper shall at once report the fact in writing to the Deputy, stating the nature of the offense, and keeping a copy of such report on the stub of the blank book furnished him for that purpose.

16. Discipline is the first and highest consideration in a prison, and must be maintained at all hazards, but that officer who maintains it with the lowest number of punishments deserves the highest commendation.

17. If a prisoner desires to make any complaint to or have an audience with the Governor, Commissioners, or Warden, the Keeper shall receive his application and report it in writing at once to the Warden's

office, keeping on the corresponding stub of the blank book, furnished for that purpose, a copy of such report.

18. Whenever, in the morning, a prisoner reports himself sick or desirous to see the Physician, the Keeper shall put the applicant's name and register number on the sick list book, and have both book and prisoner in readiness to go to the hospital with the Assistant Deputy Warden on his daily round for sick reports. If a prisoner is taken sick or injured during the day, the Keeper shall at once report the fact to the Deputy or his assistant.

19. It shall be the duty of Keepers to keep constant watch over prisoners in workshops, to see that, while pretending to be engaged on the work given them to do, they are not in reality at work at something else. Keepers shall not allow prisoners to leave their work without permission, nor to speak to or gaze at visitors.

20. The duties of Keepers should be understood as separate and distinct from those of foremen, and the Keepers will not interfere with or attempt to instruct the prisoners in the manner in which they shall work, or on what particular part they shall labor, or what amount they shall perform; but they shall listen to all reports the foremen may desire to make, and dispose of the cases as instructed.

21. In forming their opinions with respect to the industry of a prisoner, officers will bear in mind that as one prisoner may be able to do more work in a given time than another, so their reports on this head will have regard more to the continuous labor of the prisoner, the care bestowed upon it, and the evidence of his desire to do all he can, than the absolute quantity he does, as compared with others. An amount of work which may thus be sufficient for one man, may be quite insufficient for another, and the officers' reports will be made accordingly.

22. Keepers shall receive applications from prisoners to send or transfer money to friends or for subscription to newspapers, etc., and shall twice a month make a report to the Clerk. Transfers of money from one prisoner to another must be approved by the Warden or Deputy.

23. No officer, Keeper, or Guard shall receive from or deliver to a prisoner any article or thing whatsoever, without the knowledge or consent of the Warden or his Deputy.

24. When a prisoner is sent from one part of the prison to another, the officer sending him shall give him a pass, stating the place from which, and the place to which, or person to whom he is sent. Care shall be taken that the pass is delivered up by the prisoner, and that he is not too long away.

25. When a prisoner is obliged to retire for necessary purposes, the officer in charge shall take care that the place is so conspicuous that the prisoner cannot leave it without being fully seen; that only one is permitted to be in the place at a time, and that he is absent for a reasonable time only. Any delay in such cases should arouse suspicion at once, and the officer must immediately make certain that all is right.

26. No officer shall take the statement of one prisoner against another, on which to make a report for punishment, respecting the prisoner complained of, but shall report the facts nevertheless to the Warden or Deputy.

27. If a prisoner makes complaint to any officer of any order given him, or of any action towards him, by which he considers himself aggrieved, it shall be the duty of the officer to inform the Warden thereof

at the earliest moment convenient thereafter, and the Warden will act in the matter as he may think reason and justice may require; but the officer shall in the meantime see that the prisoner obeys the order given him.

28. As soon as the prisoners are locked up at night, each Keeper having charge of a division shall report immediately to the Deputy Warden the number he has locked up or has in charge, at the same time turning over the cell door keys to the Warden House Turnkey.

29. The Turnkey and the Gatekeepers shall permit no person, not connected with the prison as a regular employé of the State, or contractors, to enter the prison, except in company with the Governor of the State, the Commissioners, the Warden, Deputy, Assistant Deputy, or Chaplain, unless such person is provided with a pass from the office; nor shall they allow any prisoner to pass outside the walls unless he is accompanied by an officer or has written authority to pass.

30. Gatekeepers will closely examine the contents of wagons and other vehicles passing out of their gates, and must ever be vigilant in guarding against surprise or stratagem on the part of prisoners. They must never permit both of the trap gates to be opened at the same time.

31. The East Gatekeepers and West Yardkeepers shall carefully weigh all goods or merchandise in bulk, consigned to the penitentiary by railroad or teams, also all goods coming from the prison farm and slaughter house, and shall make daily report thereof in writing to the Steward and Storekeeper. The West Yardkeeper, particularly, shall keep close and accurate account of all railroad cars left on the prison tracks, and keep record of their contents, and how and where to they are disposed of, and make daily report thereof to the Steward and Storekeeper.

32. The Yardkeeper shall have general supervision of the yard, and keep it at all times in the most cleanly condition possible. He shall assist and take instructions from the Superintendent of State Shops in any work where the services of the yardmen are required on the grounds of the prison. He shall have charge of the tools and implements assigned to the yard gang, and keep them in good condition and repair.

33. The front yards and the courts of the hospital and solitary and the greenhouse shall be in charge of a special officer assigned to that duty by the Warden.

34. The Keeper of the solitary shall have charge of the punishment cells and the court solitary cells and their inmates. In regard to men in punishment, he shall strictly execute the orders given him by the Warden or Deputy, and shall at once report to them any unusual occurrence in his department. He shall carefully search each prisoner entering a solitary cell for punishment, and take from him every article found on his person, except his clothing; he shall also, at least twice a day, open every cell occupied, and look after the condition of its occupant. He will remain constantly within call of every prisoner occupying a punishment cell, except when relieved by another officer, who will assume his duties.

35. Cell-house Keepers will see that the utmost cleanliness prevails in the cells and corridors, that the houses are thoroughly ventilated and warmed when necessary, that the cells are regularly supplied with drinking and washing water, and that the distribution of food at meal times, also the regular issues of tobacco, soap, and other supplies, are properly and impartially made. They shall also carefully and promptly deliver

all letters, newspapers, etc., handed over to them by the Usher with his "permit," to their respective addresses. They are not permitted to examine or inspect either outgoing or incoming convict mail. They shall, from time to time, examine the cell doors and gratings and see that they are in good and secure condition; they also shall occasionally examine and search cells and report the presence of any contraband articles to the Warden or Deputy.

Duties of Armed Guards.

1. Guards are subject to the same rules and regulations as Keepers, in regard to their relation to officers and prisoners.

2. The first and most important duty of a Guard at all times is to maintain the safe custody of the prisoners, and to that end the rules of the institution require, and the laws of the State justify, the shooting of prisoners, when in a state of mutiny, when offering violence to officers or other prisoners, or when attempting to escape. Except in extreme cases, offenders should be once distinctly warned of the consequences before shooting is resorted to.

3. Wall and Front Guards are required to pace their beats at least half the time while on duty, with rifle in hand, and must never leave their post of duty without being relieved by proper authority.

4. Guards must keep their arms and accouterments clean and in perfect order, constantly ready for use, and neither cut, mark, nor deface them in any manner. Arms will be charged to them, and they will be required to pay for the willful or careless loss, destruction, or damage to the same.

5. The Guards will require on the part of the prisoners a strict compliance with such rules of the institution as may come within the province of their special duties to enforce, and report at the earliest practicable moment any infraction thereof.

Duties of Captain of Night Watch and Night Guards.

1. The night force shall go on duty at the sound of the evening whistle, and remain on duty until the signal is given in the morning for unlocking the cells of the prisoners.

2. The Captain shall be held responsible for the security of the prison and see that good order is maintained during the night. He shall make report to the Warden in the morning of any unusual occurrence or any violation of the rules and regulations of the prison that may have taken place during the night. It shall be his duty to call the Warden at any hour during the night that he may regard his presence necessary.

3. It shall be his duty to make a thorough inspection of the prison during the night once every two hours, and personally convince himself of the watchfulness of his subordinates in the different parts of the prison.

4. He shall require of all officers or citizens who work inside of the walls at night a strict compliance with all the rules that prevail in the daytime, and has authority to eject any citizen who does not strictly conform to them.

5. He shall not, under any circumstances, leave the prison during his time of duty, or until properly relieved, without the consent of the Warden.

6. The Warden House front door must invariably be locked at eleven o'clock P. M. The Captain and the Night Turnkey are both required to promptly report to the Warden on the following morning any person entering the prison under the influence of liquor or at an unusually late hour.

7. It shall be the duty of the Night Guards, having charge of the cellhouses, to be moving around the cells with "sneakshoes" on, in a silent manner, that they may be able to detect any unnecessary noise; and it is strictly enjoined upon them not to hold conversation with the prisoners, or to suffer the prisoners to speak to them except to make known immediate wants; they must use their utmost exertions to suppress noise of any kind, and report to the Captain of the Night Watch any violations of the rules and regulations of the penitentiary, by the prisoners, while in their cells.

8. The Night Guard in the solitary shall closely follow the instructions of the Warden and Deputy in regard to inmates of punishment cells, and shall every morning make written report to the Warden of the number of prisoners in solitary and their condition during the night, noting every unusual occurrence coming under his observation.

9. The Night Guard in the hospital shall observe the rules governing the Hospital Steward in regard to inmates of the hospital, and attend conscientiously to wants of the sick.

10. The Night Fire Watch shall make his regular rounds in the prison at short intervals, in such a way as the Warden or Captain of the Night Watch, from time to time, may direct.

Duties of Matron.

1. She shall, under the supervision of the Warden, have charge of the Female Department of the penitentiary, and of the prisoners and prison property therein. She shall conform to the general rules and regulations governing the prison.

2. She shall not introduce any change in the nature of the employment of the prisoners without the permission of the Warden.

3. She shall see that each prisoner under her charge is furnished with such clothing, food, and other articles as the prison regulations prescribe.

4. She shall see that good discipline and order are observed by all the inmates, and that the prisoners faithfully do the work required of them by direction of the Warden.

5. On the reception of a prisoner, she shall see that she is thoroughly washed, dressed in prison clothing, and examined by the Physician. Every article which a prisoner brings in with her shall be taken from her, and the same steps taken with regard to her effects as are required with those of male prisoners.

6. She shall spend the entire day visiting frequently, but irregularly and without notice, the work shop and laundry, instructing the prisoners in their work, and see that it is properly done.

7. She shall attend the sick and see that they are properly cared for.

8. Cases of sickness are to be regularly reported by her to the Physician, and any sudden case occurring during either the day or night must be reported immediately to the Warden, Deputy Warden, or Captain of the Night Watch.

9. She shall not absent herself from the penitentiary during her time of duty, without the permission of the Warden.

10. She shall attend Sunday morning services whenever held for the inmates of the female prison.

11. She shall reside at the penitentiary, in the apartments furnished for her by the State, and shall, on the first of each month, furnish a written report to the Warden of the work done in her department the previous month, and the general condition thereof.

General Rules.

1. Every man received upon the staff of the penitentiary will bear constantly in mind the nature of the institution into the service of which he enters, the peculiarity of the duties he will have to perform as an officer, and the moral obligations he is understood to assume, with reference to his own personal conduct, from the time he is engaged.

2. He must understand that the penitentiary is not only designed as a prison for the punishment of persons who have offended against the laws, but also as an institution which intends their reformation, if possible.

3. Every officer, therefore, will not only feel it his duty to see that the rules of the prison are observed by the prisoners placed under him, but will also understand that he must conduct himself, when off duty as well as when on duty, in such a way as to inspire sentiments of respect for his moral principles and character.

4. He will be accordingly expected to be circumspect in his way of life in society, careful as to the company he keeps and the places he frequents, and guarded as to the discharge of his personal obligations, debts, etc.; and the Warden will take all necessary steps to make himself acquainted with the conduct and general habits of every officer and servant of the institution, as it will be his duty to retain no man in the service whose conduct is improper.

5. It shall be the duty of every officer of the penitentiary to make himself acquainted with the provisions of the Penitentiary Act, and also with the rules and regulations of the prison, and with the orders on the bulletin board, to obey them readily himself in all points of his own duty, and to enforce strict obedience of them upon all who may come under his authority.

6. All persons entering upon or retaining any position as employés of this institution, must do so with the full understanding that they are to lead a prompt, willing, and positive obedience to the rules of the penitentiary, and the instructions of its officers, and devote their best energies and abilities industriously and faithfully to the performance of the duties to which they may be assigned; and all who cannot do so cheerfully must neither accept nor retain position here.

7. Any employé desiring to leave the service of the institution will be required to give thirty days' notice of his intention so to do, otherwise all pay due will be forfeited to the penitentiary. While the 'prison authorities are willing to give the same notice when consistent with the interests of the institution, yet they reserve the right to dismiss at any time, without notice, by paying in full for all services rendered.

8. Employés will be required to report to the Assistant Deputy Warden twice each day (morning and evening), that their time may be correctly kept, and to be promptly at their respective posts and places of business at the appointed hour.

9. No employé will be allowed to absent himself from duty under any circumstances, without permission from the Warden or Deputy. Should an employé be taken sick he must immediately send information thereof to the Warden or Deputy, so that another may be employed temporarily in his place.

10. Employés are strictly prohibited from taking newspapers, books, or other reading matter inside the walls or cell-houses, and are cautioned against leaving the same about the Warden's house within reach of the prisoners, and are absolutely prohibited from leaving any citizens' clothing inside the yard or cell-houses.

11. Employés are strictly prohibited from talking with prisoners at any time, except as the nature of their business may require, and all familiarity between employés and prisoners is absolutely prohibited.

12. Employés are prohibited from selling to or buying anything from prisoners, or giving to or receiving from them anything in the nature of a gift or present, or conveying to or from them any message, either written or verbal.

13. Employés are prohibited from replying in like terms to what they may conceive to be impudent or insulting language on the part of a prisoner. Their duty is to report such infraction of discipline.

14. Employés are prohibited from using profane, indecent, abusive, or insulting language toward prisoners, or in their presence, and are required to refrain at all times from the use of such language in or about the institution.

15. Employés will be required to pay for the willful destruction, loss, waste, or damage by them of any property of the prison.

16. All employés are prohibited from discussing, within the limits of the prison, the manner in which any officer or employé performs his duty, and from making any remarks which might tend to reflect upon the character or management of such officer or employé. They are also prohibited from discussing, in the presence of prisoners, matters relating to the discipline or management of this or other similar institutions.

17. Employés are strictly prohibited at all times from smoking inside the walls or cell-houses.

18. Intemperance will not be tolerated among employés, neither will they be allowed to keep or use intoxicating drinks in or about the institution. Frequenting saloons or disreputable places by employés will be considered as sufficient cause for their dismissal.

19. Employés will refrain from visiting the shops or yard while off duty, and from receiving visits while on duty.

20. No officer, Guard, or Keeper will be permitted, except in an emergency, to exchange duties with another or procure a substitute to discharge his duties, without first obtaining permission of the Warden or Deputy Warden.

21. Every officer of the penitentiary must understand that the Warden has the right to exact his services without extra pay in any capacity for which he may consider the officer fit.

22. Employés, who reside at the penitentiary, have to report to the Deputy Warden whenever they absent themselves from the prison in the evening or during the night. The outer doors of the prison will be locked at eleven o'clock; officers returning after that hour without special permit will be reported to the Warden.

23. Under the laws of this State the Warden of the penitentiary and

his assistants, the Guards and Keepers, shall be conservators of the peace, and, as such, have power to arrest or cause to be arrested, with or without process, upon any grounds owned or leased by the State of Illinois and used by the penitentiary, all persons who shall break the peace or be found upon said grounds violating any criminal law of this State, and take such persons before a magistrate for trial.

24. The Commissioners allow each employé of the institution, after six months' continuous service, a furlough of fourteen days each year without loss of pay, and in order to equalize this furlough among all, the commutation of the same in money to all whose salary is less than $70 per month. This commutation of furlough will be paid once a year, about the first of July, but is forfeited either by resignation or discharge. Therefore, absence from the prison for any cause whatever will be charged against the officer's payroll; the only exception being sickness, when, on producing a certificate from a physician, an officer will be allowed pay for ten days each year for absence from duty on that account.

Rules for Contractors and Foremen.

1. Contractors, their agents and foremen, shall hold no intercourse with any of the prisoners, other than those employed or superintended by them, nor upon any subject whatever, other than the business carried on by them.

2. No foreman shall be employed by contractors within the prison without first obtaining the consent of the Warden.

3. The chief duty of foremen is to instruct and direct prisoners in that particular branch of business to which they are assigned, and to do so in a mild but firm and dignified manner. In assigning tasks to prisoners the amount of each task shall be determined by the Warden, subject to revision by the Commissioners.

4. Foremen are not required for the purpose of governing or disciplining prisoners; therefore it is not necessary that they should use force or threatening language in the discharge of their duties, and the use of such is strictly prohibited, except of course in cases of self-defense, in defense of others, or to preserve the peace of the institution, and maintain the safe custody of the prisoners.

5. When prisoners willfully fail to carry out the instructions of a foreman, or use threatening, defiant, or impudent language, or commit any other act endangering the peace and good discipline of the institution, it shall be the duty of the foreman to immediately report the same to the Keeper in charge.

6. All foremen must be promptly at their respective shops at the hour fixed for prisoners to commence work, and will be required to remain there during working hours, and make a thorough examination of their premises personally, after the prisoners have left, at noon and at night.

7. Foremen are particularly prohibited from carrying in or out of the prison any mail matter for prisoners without express permission from the Warden. Offenders will invariably be summarily dealt with.

8. Contractors will not be allowed to erect any temporary wooden buildings or sheds within the prison walls.

9. All scraps, shavings, chips, sticks, and other combustible waste must be disposed of each day either for fuel or by removal from the yard.

10. Old trash and other material, not necessary to carry on the business of the contracts, must not be permitted to accumulate within the yard or shops.

WESTERN PENITENTIARY OF PENNSYLVANIA.

This institution is situated at Allegheny, Pennsylvania. In 1883 the law abolished contract labor, and this necessitated a resort to the public account system; and the management selected the manufacture of cocoa mats and matting as the main industry, for the reason that this branch of labor did not compete with any interest of the State. The work is performed almost wholly by hand, and is of such a simple character that it can be easily learned. But this industry does not give employment to all the convicts, and many are idle for want of proper employment.

The Warden receives a salary of $4,500 per annum, with a furnished house, horses, carriage, and driver, but supplies his own provisions and subsistence.

The salary of the Deputy Warden is $2,000 a year. The Chaplain receives a salary of $1,500 per year, the Physician $1,200, the Clerk $1,800, the Assistant Deputy Warden $1,000, Steward $1,000, Chief Engineer $1,300, and Assistant Engineer $1,000. The Guards or Overseers who have been in the service for less than six months receive $600 per annum; those who have been retained for two and a half years receive $700 per annum; those who have served after that time and less than five years receive $800 per annum; while those who have been in the service of the State for over five years receive $900 per annum.

At the time that I visited this institution in September, it had six hundred and seventy-one inmates. The prisoners are fed in their cells, all eating the same kind of food, and their fare is varied for different days, running through the week as follows:

Monday.

Breakfast.—Bread, coffee, and cheese; sugar or syrup once a month.
Dinner.—Fresh beef, boiled rice, and coffee, with a little sugar on top of rice.
Supper.—Bread and coffee.

Tuesday.

Breakfast.—Bread, coffee, and fried bacon.
Dinner.—Vegetables, soup, boiled beef, and potatoes.
Supper.—Bread and tea, and during the summer season a small quantity of fruit or tomatoes.

Wednesday.

Breakfast.—Bread, coffee, and fried mush.
Dinner.—Roast beef, baked beans or potatoes, coffee.
Supper.—Bread and coffee.

7D

Thursday.

Breakfast.—Bread, coffee, and "Bowery" hash. The hash is made of twelve bushels of potatoes, one hundred and fifty pounds of beef, and three bushels of onions.
Dinner.—Tomato or bean soup, boiled beef.
Supper.—Coffee and bread.

Friday.

Breakfast.—Bread, coffee, fried salmon. (Columbia River salt salmon.)
Dinner.—Stew (composed of three hundred and twenty-five pounds of mutton and beef, fifteen bushels of potatoes, and three bushels of onions).
Supper.—Bread and tea.

Saturday.

Breakfast.—Cornbread and coffee.
Dinner.—Bean soup and meat.
Supper.—Coffee and bread.

Sunday.

Breakfast.—Bread and coffee.
Dinner.—Pork, potatoes, raw onions or pickles.
Supper.—Coffee.

I made some inquiry of the officers as to what extent convicts were permitted to perform clerical work in the prison. They are allowed, I was told, to make entries in the books of the Commissary Department, but not in those of the Clerk of the prison.

The per capita cost last year was 45 cents per day, including all repairs; but excluding these, the cost was 36½ cents per capita, and of this amount a per capita cost of 12 cents was required for subsistence.

The convicts are not allowed to put furniture in their cells. They are allowed a looking-glass costing 25 cents, and all else is required to be in keeping with their surroundings.

The mode of punishment usually resorted to is incarceration in a semi-dark cell, for a period not extending over eight or nine days.

Visitors are required to have a pass from one of the Inspectors. They are received every afternoon except on Saturdays and Sundays, and the general visitor is charged an admission fee of 25 cents, and the money realized from this source is devoted to the library.

The officers all board themselves in the city. They are required to be on duty from six A. M. to six P. M. Each officer is allowed ten days leave of absence during the year without reduction of salary. If in case of sickness or other cause his absence from duty reaches a longer period, he does not receive any salary for such excess.

. Cigarette smoking is not allowed. The prisoners are allowed to smoke in their cells in the evening from six to seven o'clock. They are allowed the use of string instruments, and instruction is given to illiterate prisoners by an officer detailed for that purpose.

Convicts are allowed to write to friends or others once a month and to receive letters from them in return, and may see their friends once in three months; but these privileges may be suspended for bad conduct.

STATE PENITENTIARY FOR EASTERN DISTRICT OF PENNSYLVANIA.

The prison is situated at Philadelphia, and is unique in its character, being the only one in the United States in which the plan of the separate imprisonment of prisoners is now followed. Mr. Richard Vaux, who is President of the Board of Inspectors, and has a reputation throughout the United States and Europe as an able writer and deep thinker on prison management and penal subjects, gave me many valuable suggestions in reference to the treatment of criminals and the reformation of the young. To him I am indebted for the following information concerning the history and management of this institution.

On the seventh of February, 1776, there was formed in Philadelphia an association known as "The Philadelphia Society for Assisting Distressed Prisoners." Owing to the possession of the city by the British army, the society was able to accomplish but little.

In 1787 another society was formed under the name of "The Philadelphia Society for Alleviating the Miseries of Public Prisons." This society presented a memorial to the General Assembly of Pennsylvania, in which it was represented that punishment "by more private or even solitary labor would more successfully tend to redeem the unhappy objects." This society presented several memorials to the Legislature of the State, and several Acts were at different times passed by that body relating to prison management; and finally, in 1821, an Act was passed authorizing the erection of a State Penitentiary within the City and County of Philadelphia, to be conducted on the principle of the solitary confinement of the convicts.

The question of whether the congregate or the separate plan was the better for prison management was a topic much discussed. The separate plan had many opponents as well as friends. As showing the views that prevailed at that time among those who considered the separate plan as the more advisable, attention is called to the following extract from the answer of Roberts Vaux to the objections of an opponent of this system:

It is very evident to my mind that the true nature of the "separate confinement" which is proposed, requires explanation. I will, therefore, endeavor to describe what is intended by its friends. Previously, however, it ought to be understood that the chambers and yards provided for the prisoners are like anything but those dreary and fearful abodes which the pamphlet before me would represent them to be, "destined to contain an epitome and concentration of all human misery, of which the Bastile of France and the Inquisition of Spain were only prototypes and humble models."

The rooms of the new penitentiary at Philadelphia are fire-proof, of comfortable dimensions, with convenient courts to each, built on the surface of the ground—judiciously lighted from the roof—well ventilated and warmed, and ingeniously provided with means for affording a continual supply of excellent water, to insure the most perfect cleanliness of every prisoner and his apartment.* They are, moreover, so arranged as to be inspected and protected without a military guard, usually though unnecessarily employed in establishments of this kind in most other States.

In these chambers no individual, however humble or elevated, can be confined, so long as the public liberty shall endure, but upon conviction of a known and well defined offense, by the verdict of a jury of the country, and under the sentence of a Court for a specified time. The terms of imprisonment it is believed can be apportioned to the nature of every crime with considerable accuracy, and will no doubt be measured in that merciful degree which has uniformly characterized the modern penal legislation of Pennsylvania. Where then, allow me to inquire, is there in this system the least resemblance to that dreadful receptacle constructed in Paris during the reign of Charles the Fifth, and which at different periods through four centuries and a half was an engine of oppression and torture to thousands of innocent persons; or by what detortion can it be compared to the inquisitorial Courts and prisons that were instituted in Italy, Portugal, and Spain between the years 1251 and 1537?

With such accommodations as I have mentioned, and with the moderate duration of imprisonment contemplated on the Pennsylvania plan, I cannot admit the possibility of the consequences which thy pamphlet predicts, "that a great number of individuals will probably be put to death by the superinduction of diseases inseparable from such mode of treatment." I do not apprehend either the physical maladies, so vividly portrayed, or the mental sufferings, which with equal confidence it is promised shall "cause the mind to rush back upon itself, and drive reason from her seat." On the contrary, it is my belief that less bodily indisposition and less mortality will attend separate confinement than imprisonment upon the present method, for which some reasons might be given that it would be improper here to expose.

By "separate confinement," therefore, it is intended to punish those who will not control their wicked passions and propensities, thereby violating divine and human laws; and moreover to effect this punishment, without terminating the life of the culprit in the midst of his wickedness, or making a mockery of justice by forming such into communities of hardened and corrupting transgressors, who enjoy each other's society, and contemn the very power which thus vainly seeks their restoration, and idly calculates to afford security to the State from their outrages in future.

---

*The exact size of the chambers is eight feet by twelve feet, the highest point of the ceiling sixteen feet. The yards are eight feet by twenty feet.

In "separate confinement" every prisoner is placed beyond the possibility of being made more corrupt by his imprisonment, since the least association of convicts with each other must inevitably yield pernicious consequences in a greater or less degree.

In "separate confinement" the prisoners will not know who are undergoing punishment at the same time with themselves; and thus will be afforded one of the greatest protections to such as may happily be enabled to form resolutions to behave well when they are discharged, and be better qualified to do so, because plans of villainy are often formed in jail which the authors carry into operation when at large, not unfrequently engaging the aid of their companions, who are thereby induced to commit new and more heinous offenses, and come back to prison under the heaviest sentences of the law.

In "separate confinement" it is especially intended to furnish the criminal with every opportunity which Christian duty enjoins for promoting his restoration to the path of virtue, because seclusion is believed to be an essential ingredient in moral treatment, and with religious instruction and advice superadded, is calculated to achieve more than has ever yet been done for the miserable tenants of our penitentiaries.

In "separate confinement" a specific graduation of punishment can be obtained as surely and with as much facility as by any other system. Some prisoners may labor—some may be kept without labor—some may have the privilege of books—others may be deprived of it—some may experience total seclusion—others may enjoy such intercourse as shall comport with an entire separation of prisoners.

In "separate confinement" the same variety of discipline for offenses committed after convicts are introduced into prison, which any other mode affords, can be obtained, though irregularities must necessarily be less frequent—by denying the refractory individual the benefit of his yard, by taking from him his books or labor, and lastly, in extreme cases, by diminishing his diet to the lowest rate. By the last means the most fierce, hardened, and desperate offender can be subdued.

Hon. John Sergeant, of Philadelphia, in a letter published in 1827, in vindication of the Pennsylvania system, said:

The objection to it is that its severity would be intolerable. As it has never been fairly tested by experiment, this objection must, for the present, be somewhat conjectural. There may be individuals who will not be able to endure continued solitude for a considerable length of time. In such cases some modification in their favor may be necessary. Experience will show to what extent this ought to be made. That there are any to whom solitary confinement, even for a short time, would be fatal, or even highly injurious, may well be doubted, for we have had frequent instances of its infliction without such effects.

To return, however, to the charge of cruelty, with which it has been stigmatized in advance, and therefore gratuitously, it may be replied, in the first place, that if it be only meant that the punishment will be severe, but without injury to the health or morals of the patient, there is nothing in the objection. Punishment ought to be severe, if it is meant to operate at all. People are not sent to prison to enjoy there the comforts and luxuries of life. It may be replied, further, that admitting it to be severe, or even very severe, before it can on that account be condemned, it must be compared with any other practicable mode of punishment, and a fair comparison made of the cruelty (so called) of each. And in making this comparison we must take into account the general merits of the respective plans as they tend more or less to the welfare of society and of the unhappy subject of punishment. If there is a well grounded hope of lessening the quantity of crime, and thus promoting the general happiness and security of society, and if there is also a hope of reforming the criminal, or even deterring him from the repetition of crime, these are powerful considerations to be placed in the scale against specific objections of severity. Nor, in this estimate, must we forget that this plan of solitary confinement has one peculiar and great recommendation which no one can question. It will prevent prisoners from injuring each other by vicious instruction, a most cruel thing, it must be admitted, as it relates to those who are exposed to such a novitiate, and as it relates to society in general.

In 1828, Hon. Edward Livingston, lawyer and publicist, in a printed letter on the subject, used the following language:

But above all, do not force those whom you are obliged to imprison before trial, be they innocent or guilty, into that contaminating society from which, after they are found to be guilty, you are so anxious to keep them. Remember, that in Philadelphia, as well as in New York, more than two thousand five hundred are annually committed, of whom not one fourth are found to be guilty, and that thus you have introduced every year one thousand eight hundred persons, presumed to be inno-cent, into a school where every vice and every crime are taught by the ablest masters; and we shut our eyes to this enormous evil, and incon-sistently go on preaching the necessity of seclusion and labor and indus-try after conviction, as if penitentiaries were the only places in which the contamination of evil society were to be dreaded. Why will not Penn-sylvania take the lead in perfecting the work she began, and, instead of patchwork legislation, that can never be effectual, establish a complete system, in which all the different but mutually dependent subjects of education, pauperism, penal law, and prison discipline should be em-braced? I am preaching, I know, to the converted, when I urge the consideration of these subjects upon you; but mutual exhortation is of service even between those who think alike, and there is no cause to the success of which I would more willingly devote my feeble talents, and the exertions of my life, including, as it does, the cause of religion, humanity, and social order, than the one which forms the subject of this letter; there is none, I am sure, more interesting to you, and therefore I will mix with it no other than that of the high esteem with which I am always, my dear sir, your friend and humble servant.

The Hon. H. W. Desaussure, a member of the judiciary of South Carolina, in his views upon this subject, published in 1834, said:

I confess my own mind had imbibed some prejudices against it as a cruel punishment, and as tending to drive the mind to madness. Experience has shown, it seems, that the latter effect has not been pro-duced, and the severity of solitary confinement is entirely obviated by the prisoner being allowed to labor and to receive instruction, literary and moral, during his confinement. These seem to approximate the system as near to perfection as any human plan can be carried into effect; we must not, however, expect too much from it. If we suppose this treatment will reform all offenders, we shall be mistaken. The strongest motives are held out by human and divine laws to avoid the commission of crimes, yet men commit them daily.

In 1829, Mr. George W. Smith published a "Defense of the Pennsylvania System of Solitary Confinement of Prisoners." A second edition of this pamphlet appeared in 1833, and in it he expressed his views as follows:

The introduction of labor as an essential element of a general system of prison discipline may perhaps be justly attributed to that spirit of economy which characterizes the legislation of the Dutch. The maintenance of any class in idleness has never been intentionally practiced by this industrious and thrifty nation. Hence prisons and workhouses have been synonymous terms in Holland from a very remote period; attempts to promote reformation by the religious instruction of the prisoners appear to have been sometimes made in that country, with partial success. In no other part of Europe was this system generally pursued; in few countries was it attempted in any of their prisons; and, in Great Britain, it had not even entered into their imaginations. We think it highly probable that our illustrious founder, William Penn, observed during his travels in Holland this striking feature of their policy, and resolved to adopt the measure, when he projected the celebrated code of laws in England (1682) for the government of this province. In the tenth section it is expressly declared that "all prisons shall be workhouses for felons, vagrants, and loose and idle persons." The Great Law (1682) contains a similar enactment—the stock on which all our subsequent legislation has been grafted. The merit, therefore, of originality has been perhaps erroneously attributed to him. It is, however, sufficient praise that he had the penetration to perceive and judgment to approve and copy these useful institutions of a foreign land. His fame as a legislator for originality and humanity rests on a sure basis— the abolition of the punishment of death for all crimes but murder (which exception, however, is known to have been contrary to his opinion). From the year 1682 to 1717 labor formed an invariable portion of the punishments of those sentenced to our prisons; at this period our mild Penal Code was finally repealed by Great Britain, which had neither the humanity to adopt it, nor the magnanimity to permit its continuance. The decline of this system, until its final extinction in practice, some years before the Revolution, proves the negligence of our ancestors. At some future time we may resume this subject, but our present design will not permit us at present to discuss this interesting portion of our history.

A few years before the Revolution, the Penal Code, with its sanguinary enactments, and the abuses existing in prison discipline, began to attract the attention of some of the humane citizens of Philadelphia; they finally formed a society on the seventh of February, 1776, for the purpose of effecting their benevolent designs. This association, which was called "The Philadelphia Society for Assisting Distressed Prisoners," after a brief but not useless existence of nineteen months, was dissolved, or rather suspended, by the capture of Philadelphia in 1777. The public mind had been, however, prepared for the amelioration of the Penal Code, partly by the efforts of the members of this society; and the first Constitution of the State, in 1776, ordains in Chapter II, Section 28, that "punishments be made in some cases less sanguinary," and in Section 39, punishment by "hard labor" in the prisons is substituted. The law remained a dead letter during that memorable period; and it was not until the year 1786, after the conclusion of peace, that the subject was resumed, and hard labor enforced; but these efforts were partial and ineffectual. In the following year, May 8, 1787, some of the surviving members of the society previously mentioned, and others, reorganized the association under the name of "The Philadelphia Society for Alleviating the Miseries of Public Prisons." This useful and unassuming body is the parent of all the societies which have been since formed for similar purposes in Europe and this country. It has perhaps effected more for the permanent benefit of mankind than any of the meritorious charities of this city of benevolence. It has the enviable fame of being the first to reduce the humane and philosophic theory of preventive and reforming punishments, by the separate confinement and instruction of prisoners, to the unerring test of successful experiment.

Before we describe the actual introduction of solitary confinement, as it is perhaps erroneously styled, into our system of legislation, it may be expedient to make a few observations on the history of this interesting department of prison discipline.

As a means of more effectual seclusion from society and the prevention of further injury by prisoners during the period of incarceration, and as a mode of inflicting vindictive punishment, it has been partially practiced in almost every nation from the remotest ages. The Egyptians were accustomed to bury alive in the dark, narrow, and secluded cells of some of their vast and secure edifices, which at once served for prisons and for tombs, certain offenders against their laws. These unhappy victims, from the hour when they were immured until the tedious period when death released them from their lingering misery, never beheld the light of day, never inhaled the fresh air of heaven, and never again beheld the face of man, nor heard the consoling accents of his voice. Among the Romans, among the nations of the dark ages, among the modern Italian republics, and in yet later times, solitary confinement has been occasionally practiced as one of the most dreadful means of vindictive punishment—a confinement unmitigated, absolute, and inhuman; a confinement at the mere mention of which the philanthropist shudders with horror, and the philosophic reformer turns aside with disgust and reprobation.

The earliest cases of solitary confinement, as an intended means of reform, may be discovered in the records of ecclesiastical history. Nevertheless, it is to Catholic Rome that we owe the first great reform in penitentiary discipline. The prison in which it was introduced remained for nearly a century a solitary instance of successful benevolence, extended no further in Rome, where it originated, and unimitated in Christendom. The Hospital of St. Michael (founded in Rome, 1718) was the first "house of refuge" in Europe. Mere workhouses, in which the operatives were felons, had indeed been established in other countries; and, although in a few of them instruction had been attempted, the corrupting intercourse which was permitted day and night; the mixture of all ages, ranks, and sexes into one corrupting leavened mass of shameless iniquity, rendered the consignment of a juvenile offender to these abodes of sin a certain sentence of moral death. He who entered their gates a novice in guilt, accomplished his education in villiany; and leaving character, shame, independence, and every incentive to voluntary industry and virtue within their walls, departed an adept in crime, ignorant only of his duties, prepared to practice at the expense of society those lessons of vice which its folly had forced on his acquaintance, and almost compelled him to exercise as a profession when discharged. Such was the deplorable condition of these colleges of crime, as prisons have been too correctly denominated, when this noble institution of St. Michael was commenced; the foundations were laid on the firm basis of humanity and sound philosophy. The great evils of idleness were prevented by constant labor during the day; classification to a certain extent, and silence, as far as practicable in an assembly, were enforced; and separate dormitories, or night rooms, for each prisoner provided; appropriate moral sentiments were inscribed on conspicuous tablets, for the continual inspection of the inmates; and, above all, religious instruction was administered.

The Assembly of Pennsylvania, convinced by the arguments of the society, in the year 1789-90 effected a radical change in the discipline of the prison. The convicts were compelled to labor; the sexes were separated; the convicts were separated from the untried prisoners and debtors; suitable food and clothing were provided for them; the introduction of ardent spirits was strictly prohibited, and jail fees and garnish utterly abolished; above all, religious instruction, and as far as possible, a classification of the prisoners, were introduced; conversation was also restrained. The prisoners at that time not being numerous, these arrangements were practicable in the prison, which was, however, far too limited to test the merits of the system of improvements which the society was anxious to introduce. The Legislature was not at that time prepared to appropriate a sufficient sum of money to construct a new and perfect prison for the purpose of testing the merits of an untried experiment, however flattering might be the prospects of success. The friends of the new system were willing to test its merits with the imperfect apparatus which alone was at their disposal. These alterations, in conjunction with some others of a minor description, would alone have produced effects highly beneficial; and doubtless a portion of the reformation, which most unquestionably was produced by the new system, is attributable to them; but the great object of reform was mainly produced by the celebrated law enacted by the Legislature of Pennsylvania, April 5, 1790, by which separate and solitary confinement was first introduced. In the preamble to that Act it is declared that the previous laws for the punishment of criminals "had failed of success, from the communication with each other not being sufficiently restrained within the places of confinement, and it is hoped that the addition of unremitted solitude to laborious employment, as far as it can be effected, will contribute as much to reform as to deter." In the eighth section it is ordered that "a suitable number of cells be constructed in the yard of the jail of the said county, each of which cells shall be six feet in width, eight feet in length, and nine feet in height; and the said cells shall be separate from the common yard by a wall of such height as, without any unnecessary exclusion of air and light, will prevent all external communication, for the purpose of confining therein the more hardened and atrocious offenders," viz.: those mentioned in this and a former Act.

In section tenth, "the residue of the said jail shall be appropriated to the purposes of confining as well such male convicts sentenced to hard labor as cannot be accommodated in the said cells, as female convicts sentenced in like manner, persons convicted of capital offenses, vagrants, and disorderly persons committed as such, and persons charged with misdemeanors only; all of which persons are hereby required to be kept separate and apart from each other as much as the convenience of the building will admit," etc. In section thirteenth, "during which labor the said offenders shall be kept separate and apart from each other, if the nature of their several employments will admit thereof; and where the nature of such employment requires two or more to work together, the Keeper of the said jail, or one of his deputies, shall, if possible, be constantly present." In section twenty-first, for certain offenses committed within the prison, the Jailer is authorized to confine prisoners violating the discipline of the prison in the dark cells, on bread and water, for a short time only; but in the county prisons, the period of inflicting this punishment is unlimited.

In 1829 the Legislature of Pennsylvania enacted several reforms in the Penal Code of that State, and also prescribed the following rules for the government of the penitentiary:

SECTION 8. *And be it further enacted by the authority aforesaid,* That the following rules and regulations for the better ordering and government of said penitentiaries shall be and continue in force until altered by the Legislature, or in the manner hereinafter stated.

ARTICLE I.

Of the Inspectors and their Duties.

They shall at their first meeting, and annually thereafter, appoint out of their number a President, Secretary, and Treasurer, and keep regular minutes of their proceedings; they shall hold stated meetings once a month, and adjourned and special meetings whenever necessary; the Treasurer shall give bond with sufficient surety in such amount as the Inspectors may fix and determine, and shall receive and disburse all moneys belonging to the prison, according to the order of the Board; they shall semi-annually appoint a Warden, a Physician, and Clerk for the institution, and shall fix their salaries as well as those of the Under-keepers or Overseers, and the persons employed about the prison; they shall serve without any pecuniary compensation, and shall.be exempted from military duty, from serving on juries and arbitrations, or as guardians of the poor; they shall visit the penitentiary at least twice in every week, to see that the duties of the several officers and attendants are performed; to prevent all oppression, peculation, or other abuse or mismanagement of the said institutions; they shall have power, if they on conference find it necessary, to make such rules for the internal government of said prison, as may not be inconsistent with the principles of solitary confinement as set forth and declared by this Act.

They shall attend to the religious instruction of the prisoners and procure a suitable person for this object, who shall be the religious instructor of the prisoners; *provided*, their services shall be gratuitous.

They shall direct the manner in which all raw materials to be manufactured by the convicts in said prisons, and the provisions and other supplies for the prisons shall be purchased, and also the sale of all articles manufactured in said prisons.

They shall cause accurate accounts to be kept by the Clerk, of all expenditures and receipts in the penitentiaries, which accounts, respectively, shall be annually examined and settled by the Auditors of the county of Allegheny, and of the county of Philadelphia.

They shall on or before the first day of January in every year make a report in writing to the Legislature, of the state of the penitentiaries. The report shall contain the number of prisoners in confinement, their age, sex, place of nativity, time of commitment, term of imprisonment during the preceding year, noticing also those who have escaped or died, or who were pardoned or discharged, designating the offense for which the commitment was made, and whether for a first or repeated offense, and when and in what Court, or by whose order; and in such return the Inspectors shall make such observations as to the efficiency of the system of solitary confinement as may be the result of their experience, and give such information as they may deem expedient for making the said institution effectual in the punishment and reformation of offenders.

They shall have power to examine any person upon oath or affirmation relative to any abuse in the said places of confinement, or matter within the purview of their duties; they shall direct in what manner the rations for the subsistence of the prisoners shall be composed, in conformity with the general directions on that subject hereinafter contained.

The Inspectors in their weekly visits to the several places of confinement shall speak to each person confined therein out of the presence of any of the persons employed therein; shall' listen to any complaints that may be made of oppression or ill conduct of the persons so employed, examine into the truth thereof, and proceed therein when the complaint is well founded; and on such visits they shall have the calendar of the prisoners furnished to them by the Warden, and see by actual inspection whether all the prisoners named in the said calendar are found in the said prison, in the situation in which by the said calendar they are declared to be.

A majority of the said Inspectors shall constitute a Board, and may do any of the acts required of the said Inspectors; two of the Inspectors shall be a quorum for the weekly visitations hereby directed to be made.

The Warden shall not, nor shall any Inspector, without the direction of a majority of the Inspectors, sell any article for the use of the said penitentiaries, or either of them, or of the persons confined therein during their confinement, nor derive any emolument from such purchase or sale, nor shall he, or they, or either of them, receive, under any pretense whatever from either of the said prisoners, or from any one in his behalf, any sum of money, emolument, or reward whatever, or any article of value, as a gratuity or gift, under the penalty of five hundred dollars fine, to be recovered in the name of the Commonwealth, by an action of debt, in any Court of record thereof, having jurisdiction of sums of that amount.

108 REFORMATORY AND PENAL INSTITUTIONS.

ARTICLE II.

Of the Duties of the Warden.

The Warden shall reside in the penitentiary; he shall visit every cell and apartment, and see every prisoner under his care at least once in every day; he shall keep a journal, in which shall be regularly entered the reception, discharge, death, pardon, or escape of any prisoner, and also the complaints that are made, and the punishments that are inflicted for the breach of prison discipline, as they occur; the visits of the Inspector and the Physician, and all other occurrences of note that concern the state of the prison, except the receipts and expenditures, the account of which is to be kept in the manner hereinafter directed.

The Warden shall appoint the Underkeepers, who shall be called Overseers, and all necessary servants, and dismiss them whenever he thinks proper, or the Board of Inspectors direct him so to do.

He shall report all infractions of the rules to the Inspectors, and with the approbation of one of them, may punish the offender, in such manner as shall be directed in the rules to be enacted by the Inspectors, concerning the treatment of prisoners.

He shall not absent himself from the penitentiary for a night without permission in writing from two of the Inspectors.

He shall not be present when the Inspectors make their stated visits to the prisoners under his care, unless thereto required by the Inspectors.

ARTICLE III.

Of the Duty of the Overseers.

It shall be the duty of the Overseers to inspect the condition of each prisoner at least three times in every day, to see that his meals are regularly delivered, according to the prison allowance, and to superintend the work of the prisoners.

They shall give immediate notice to the Warden or Physician whenever any convict shall complain of such illness as to require medical aid.

Each Overseer shall have a certain number of prisoners assigned to his care.

He shall make a daily report to the Warden of the health and conduct of the prisoners, and a like report to the Inspectors when required.

No Overseer shall be present when the Warden or the Inspectors visit the prisoners under his particular care, unless thereto required by the Warden or Inspectors.

The Overseers shall obey all legal orders given by the Warden, and all rules established by the Board of Inspectors, for the government of the prison.

All orders to the Overseers must be given through or by the Warden.

The Overseers shall not absent themselves from the prison without permission from the Warden.

No Overseer shall receive from any one confined in the penitentiary, or from any one in behalf of such prisoner, any emolument or reward whatever, or the promise of any, either for services or supplies, or as a gratuity, under the penalty of one hundred dollars and imprisonment for thirty days in the county jail; and when any breach of this article shall come to the knowledge of the Warden or Inspectors, the Overseer or Overseers so offending shall be immediately discharged from his office, and prosecuted for the said offense according to law.

No Overseer who shall have been discharged for any offense whatever shall again be employed.

ARTICLE IV.

Of the Duties of the Physician.

The Physician shall visit every prisoner in the prison twice in every week, and oftener, if the state of their health require it, and shall report once in every month to the Inspectors.

He shall attend immediately on notice from the Warden that any person is sick.

He shall examine every prisoner that shall be brought into the penitentiary, before he shall be confined in his cell.

Whenever, in the opinion of the Physician, any convict in the penitentiary is so ill as to require removal, the Warden shall direct such removal to the infirmary of the institution, and the prisoner shall be kept in the infirmary until the Physican shall certify that he may be removed without injury to his health, and he shall then be removed to his cell.

He shall visit the patients in the infirmary at least once in every day, and he shall give such directions for the health and cleanliness of the prisoners, and, when necessary, as to the alteration of their diet, as he may deem expedient, which the Warden shall have executed; *provided,* they shall not be contrary to the provisions of this law, nor inconsistent with the safe custody of the said prisoners; and the directions he may give, whether complied with or not, shall be entered in the journal of the Warden, and in his own.

The Physician shall inquire into the mental as well as the bodily state of every prisoner, and when he shall have reason to believe that the mind or body is materially affected by the discipline, treatment, or diet, he shall inform the Warden thereof, and shall enter his observation in the journal hereinafter directed to be kept, which shall be an authority for the Warden for altering the discipline, treatment, or diet of any prisoner, until the next meeting of the Inspectors, who shall inquire into the case, and make orders accordingly.

The Physician shall keep a journal, in which, opposite to the name of each prisoner, shall be entered the state of his health, and if sick, whether in the infirmary or not, together with such remarks as he may deem important, which journal shall be open to the inspection of the Warden and the Inspectors, and the same, together with the return provided for in the first article in this section, shall be laid before the Inspectors once in every month, or oftener if called for.

The prisoners under the care of the Physician shall be allowed such diet as he shall direct.

No prisoner shall be discharged while laboring under a dangerous disease, although entitled to his discharge, unless by his own desire.

The infirmary shall have a suitable partition between every bed, and no two patients shall occupy the same bed; and the Physician and his attendants shall take every precaution in their power to prevent all intercourse between the convicts while in the infirmary.

ARTICLE V.

Of the Treatment of the Prisoners in the Penitentiary.—Of the Reception of the Convicts.

Every convict sentenced to imprisonment in the penitentiary shall, immediately after the sentence shall have been finally pronounced, be conveyed by the Sheriff of the county in which he was condemned to the penitentiary.

On the arrival of a convict, immediate notice shall be given to the Physician, who shall examine the state of his or her health; he or she shall then be stripped of his or her clothes, and clothed in the uniform of the prison, in the manner hereinafter provided, being first bathed and cleaned.

He or she shall then be examined by the Clerk and the Warden, in the presence of as many of the Overseers as can conveniently attend, in order to their becoming acquainted with his or her person and countenance; and his or her name, height, apparent and alleged age, place of nativity, trade, complexion, color of hair and eyes, and length of his or her feet, to be accurately measured, shall be entered in a book provided for that purpose, together with such other natural or accidental marks, or peculiarity of feature or appearance, as may serve to identify him or her, and if the convict can write, his or her signature shall be written under the said description of his or her person.

All the effects on the person of the convict, as well as his or her clothes, shall be taken from him or her, and specially mentioned and preserved under the care of the Warden, to be restored to him or her on his or her discharge.

If the convict is not in such ill health as to require being sent to the infirmary, he or she shall then be conducted to the cell assigned to him or her, numerically designated, by which he or she shall thereafter be known during his or her confinement.

ARTICLE VI.

Of the Clothing and Diet of the Convicts.

The uniform of the prison for males shall be a jacket and trousers of cloth or other warm stuff for the winter, and lighter materials for the summer; the form and color shall be determined by the Inspectors, and two changes of linen shall be furnished to each prisoner every week.

No prisoner is to receive anything but the prison allowance.

No tobacco in any form shall be used by the convicts, and any one who shall supply them with it, or with wine or spirituous or intoxicating fermented liquor, unless by order of the Physician, shall be fined ten dollars, and if an officer, be dismissed.

ARTICLE VII.

Of Visitors.

No person who is not an official visitor of the prisons, or who has not a written permission according to such rules as the Inspectors may adopt as aforesaid, shall be allowed to visit the same; the official visitors are the Governor, the Speaker and members of the Senate, the Speaker and members of the House of Representatives, the Secretary of the Commonwealth, the Judges of the Supreme Court, the Attorney-General and his Deputies, the President and Associate Judges of all the Courts in the State, the Mayor and Recorder of the Cities of Philadelphia, Lancaster, and Pittsburg, Commissioners and Sheriffs of the several counties, and the Acting Committee of the Philadelphia Society for the Alleviation of the Miseries of Public Prisons.

None but the official visitors can have any communication with the convicts, nor shall any visitor whatever be permitted to deliver to or receive from any of the convicts any letter or message whatever, or to supply them with any article of any kind, under the penalty of one hundred dollars fine, to be recovered as hereinbefore provided for other fines imposed by this Act.

Any visitor who shall discover any abuse, infraction of law, or oppression, shall immediately make the same known to the Board of Inspectors of the Commonwealth, if the Inspectors or either of them are implicated.

ARTICLE VIII.

Of the Discharge of the Convicts.

Whenever a convict shall be discharged by the expiration of the term for which he or she was condemned, or by pardon, he or she shall take off the prison uniform, and have the clothes which he or she brought to the prison restored to him or her, together with the other property, if any, that was taken from him or her on his or her commitment, that has not been otherwise disposed of.

When a prisoner is to be discharged, it shall be the duty of the Warden to obtain from him or her, as far as is practicable, his or her former history; what means of literary, moral, or religious instruction he or she enjoyed; what early temptations to crime, by wicked associations or otherwise, he or she was exposed to; his or her general habits, predominant passions, and prevailing vices, and in what part of the country he or she purposes to fix his or her residence; all of which shall be entered by the Clerk in a book to be kept for that purpose, together with his or her name, age, and time of discharge.

If the Inspectors and Warden have been satisfied with the morality, industry, and order of his conduct, they shall give him a certificate to that effect, and shall furnish the discharged convict with four dollars, to be paid by the State, whereby the temptation immediately to commit offenses against society, before employment can be obtained, may be obviated.

ARTICLE IX.

Duties of the Religious Instructor.

It shall be the duty of the Instructor to attend to the moral and religious instruction of the convicts, in such manner as to make their confinement, as far as possible, the means of their reformation, so that when restored to their liberty they may prove honest, industrious, and useful members of society; and the Inspectors and officers are enjoined to give every facility to the Instructor, in such measures as he may think necessary to produce so desirable a result, not inconsistent with the rules and discipline of the prison.

SEC. 9. *And be it further enacted by the authority aforesaid*, That the expenses of maintaining* and keeping the convicts in the said Eastern and Western Penitentiaries shall be borne by the respective counties in which they shall be convicted, and the said expense shall be paid to the said Inspectors by orders, to be drawn by them on the Treasurers of the said counties, who shall accept and pay the same; *provided*, that the said orders shall not be presented to the said Treasurers before the first Monday of May in each and every year; *and provided, also*, that the said Inspectors shall annually, on or before the first Monday of February, transmit, by the public mail, to the Commissioners of such of the counties as may have become indebted for convicts confined in said penitentiaries, an account of the expense of keeping and maintaining said convicts, which account shall be signed by the said Inspectors, and be sworn or affirmed to by them, and attested by the Clerk; and it shall be the duty of the said Commissioners, immediately on receipt of said accounts, to give notice to the Treasurers of the respective counties of the amount of said accounts, with instructions to collect and retain moneys for the payment of said orders when presented; and all salaries of the officers of the said penitentiaries shall be paid by the State, and it shall be the duty of the Inspectors to transmit to the Auditor-General the names of the persons by them appointed, and the salaries agreed to be paid to each of them under the provisions of this Act, which sums shall be paid in the usual manner, by warrants drawn by the Governor upon the Treasurer of the Commonwealth.

SEC. 10. *And be it further enacted by the authority aforesaid*, That the several Acts of Assembly of this Commonwealth, and such parts thereof, so far as the same are altered or supplied by this Act, be and the same are hereby repealed, from and after the first day of July next; *provided*, that the repeal thereof shall in no wise affect any indictment, trial, sentence, or punishment of any of the said herein mentioned crimes or offenses which have been or shall be committed before this Act shall come into operation.

SEC. 11. *And be it further enacted by the authority aforesaid*, That the Governor be and he is hereby authorized and required to issue his warrant to the State Treasurer, in favor of the Inspectors of the Western Penitentiary, for the sum of three thousand dollars, to be applied by said Inspectors to such alteration of the interior of said penitentiary, as in their opinion will best adapt the same to the provisions of this Act.

SEC. 12. *And be it further enacted by the authority aforesaid*, That, for the purpose of finishing the Eastern Penitentiary, introducing a supply of water from Fairmount Waterworks, and procuring the necessary furniture and fixtures for the accommodation and reception of the prisoners, the sum of five thousand dollars be and it is hereby appropriated for the said purposes, and the Commissioners appointed to superintend the erection of the State Penitentiary for the Eastern District of Pennsylvania are directed to carry the same into effect, and to draw the sum hereby authorized from the State Treasury, in the same manner as is by law provided.

SEC. 13. *And be it further enacted by the authority aforesaid*, That the Board of Inspectors of the Eastern Penitentiary, who shall be appointed as is hereinbefore provided, be and they hereby are authorized

* Repealed—Act of 1833.

to draw from the State Treasury, upon warrants drawn in the usual manner, any sums of money which shall not together amount to more than one thousand dollars, to enable said Inspectors to support and employ the prisoners who may be committed to said penitentiary, until so much of such sums of money as may become payable by the several counties from which convicts may be removed to said prison shall be received by said Board, as will enable them to manage the affairs of said prison without such aid, which sum so advanced by the State shall be repaid to the State Treasury by the said Board as soon as the funds of said prison will enable said Board to make such repayment.

A description of this prison can best be given in the words of those who at different times have made an exhaustive study of it. In 1823 the following description was given of this prison and its condition at that time:

The Eastern State Penitentiary is situated on one of the most elevated, airy, and healthy sites in the vicinity of Philadelphia. Large sums have been expended for the purpose of giving an unusual degree of solidity and durability to every part of this immense structure, which is the most extensive building in the United States. The ground occupied by it contains about ten acres. The material with which the edifices are built is a grayish granite, or gneiss, employed in large masses; every room is vaulted and fire-proof. The design and execution impart a grave, severe, and awful character to the external aspect of this building. The effect which it produces on the imagination of every passing spectator is peculiarly impressive, solemn, and instructive. The architecture is in keeping with the design. The broad masses, the small and well proportioned apertures, the continuity of lines, and the bold and expressive simplicity which characterize the features of the facade, are most happily and judiciously combined. The originality of the plan, the excellent arrangement and execution of the details, display the taste and ingenuity of the architect, to whom our country is indebted for some of her noblest edifices—our fellow citizen, Mr. John Haviland.

This penitentiary is the only edifice in this country which is calculated to convey to our citizens the external appearance of those magnificent and picturesque castles of the middle ages, which contribute so eminently to embellish the scenery of Europe.

A reference to the accompanying view and plan will render only a brief description necessary. The front of this building is composed of large blocks of hewn and squared granite; the walls are twelve feet thick at the base, and diminish to the top, where they are two and three quarters feet in thickness. A wall of thirty feet in height above the interior platform, incloses an area six hundred and forty feet square; at each angle of the wall is a tower for the purpose of overlooking the establishment; three other towers, which will be presently described, are situated near the gate of entrance. The facade or principal front, which is represented in the accompanying view, is six hundred and seventy feet in length, and reposes on a terrace, which, from the inequalities of the ground, varies from three to nine feet in height; the basement or belting course, which is ten feet high, is scarped, and extends uniformly the whole length. The central building is two hundred feet in length, consists of two projecting massive square towers, fifty feet high, crowned by

projecting embattled parapets, supported by pointed arches resting on
corbels or brackets. The pointed mullioned windows in these towers
contribute in a high degree to their picturesque effect. The curtain
between the towers is forty-one feet high, and is finished with a parapet
and embrasures. The pointed windows in it are very lofty and narrow.
The great gateway in the center is a very conspicuous feature; it is twenty-
seven feet high and fifteen feet wide, and is filled by a massive wrought
iron portcullis, and double oaken gates studded with projecting iron
rivets, the whole weighing several tons; nevertheless they can be opened
with the greatest facility. On each side of this entrance (which is the
most imposing in the United States) are enormous solid buttresses
diminishing in offsets and terminating in pinnacles. A lofty octangular
tower, eighty feet high, containing an alarm bell and clock, surmounts
this entrance, and forms a picturesque proportional center. On each
side of this main building (which contains the apartments of the Warden, Keepers, domestics, etc.) are screen wing walls, which appear to
constitute portions of the main edifice; they are pierced with small
blank-pointed windows, and are surmounted by a parapet; at their ex-
tremities are high octangular towers terminating in parapets pierced by
embrasures. In the center of the great court-yard is an observatory,
whence long corridors, eight in number, radiate; (three only of these
corridors, etc., are at present finished). On each side of these corridors
the cells are situated, each at right angles to them, and communicating
with them only by small openings for the purpose of supplying the prisoner with food, etc., and for the purpose of inspecting his movements
without attracting his attention; other apertures, for the admission of
cool or heated air, and for the purpose of ventilation, are provided.

Among the advocates of this system in Europe, we may refer to Howard, Paul, Eden, Mansfield, Blackstone, Paley, Liancourt, Villerme, etc.,
and in this country, to the venerable Bishop White, whose whole life
has been but one prolonged illustration of that religion which he pro-
fesses, Dr. Rush, Bradford, Vaux, Wood, Sergeant, Livingston, and many
of our most eminent citizens. The intrinsic and obvious excellence of
the plan afforded a powerful argument for its adoption upwards of forty
years since. The partial experience of its merits has been beneficially
experienced in our State and other parts of the Union, notwithstanding
the numerous disadvantages which have heretofore attended the trial.
The only failures which have occurred in other States are unquestionably attributable to the absurd and culpable manner in which the process has sometimes been conducted. The experience of several of the
European States, as well as of our own Commonwealth, incontestably
proves that this system of prison discipline is the most efficient which
the wisdom of philanthropists has heretofore devised; that, when administered in a proper manner, the reformation of the great majority of
criminals is practicable; that no injury to the health, mental or bodily,
of the convicts occur; that the severity is sufficient, not only to operate
on the inmates of the prison, but to deter others by the example of their
sufferings; and, finally, that as a means of preventing crimes it is in
fact the most economical. A superficial view of this subject has too
frequently led to erroneous conclusions in some of our sister States.

As "the Pennsylvania system of prison discipline" effects, not indeed
the extirpation, but the prevention and diminution of crime, to an
unknown and unrivaled extent, the dictates of mere economy, of sordid

self-interest, as well as of patriotism, humanity, and general religion, cry aloud for its general adoption. The prime cost of an efficient labor-saving machine is never considered by the intelligent and wealthy capitalist as a wasteful expenditure, but as a productive investment. This penitentiary will be, strictly speaking, an apparatus for the expeditious, certain, and economical eradication of vice, and the production of reformation. The State of Pennsylvania has exhibited at once her wisdom, philanthropy, and munificence, by the erection of this immense and expensive structure, which, in connection with her other noble institutions, will largely contribute to the amelioration and protection of her population.

The corner-stone of the front building of the penitentiary was laid on the twenty-second day of May, 1823, in the presence of the Commissioners, architect, Superintendent, and workmen. On this interesting occasion, Mr. Roberts Vaux said that he much regretted the unavoidable absence of the President of the Board, in whose place he had just then been unexpectedly desired to say a few words concerning the purpose for which the Commissioners were assembled.

He remarked that the occasion was calculated to awaken reflections at once painful and gratifying. Painful, because such was the erring character of man, so ungovernable were his passions, and so numerous his propensities to evil, that it was necessary society should provide means for the punishment of offenders against its laws. Gratifying, because a correct view of human nature, coupled with the indispensable exercise of Christian benevolence, had led to the melioration of punishments. Justice was now mixed with mercy, and whilst the community designed to teach offenders that the way of the transgressor is hard, it wisely and compassionately sought to secure and reform the criminal by the most strict solitary confinement. The penitentiary now to be erected was designed to accomplish these important ends, and when it shall be completed it will afford the first opportunity of putting into efficient practice the Penal Code of this State. Mr. Vaux congratulated his fellow citizens of Pennsylvania, because their legislators were the first (almost forty years ago) to abolish those cruel and vindictive penalties which are in use in the European countries from which we had descended. The pillory, the whipping-post, and the chain were not calculated to prevent crime, but to familiarize the mind with cruelty, and, consequently, to harden the hearts of those who suffered, and those who witnessed such punishments. The substitution in Pennsylvania of milder correctives had excited the notice and respect of nations abroad, as well as of our sister States; our example had, in some instances, been followed, and he had no doubt the principle would more extensively prevail.

The box deposited in the corner-stone, which you have seen laid, contains a plan and elevation of the prison, and a metal plate bearing the following inscription:

PENITENTIARY

FOR THE EASTERN DISTRICT OF THE STATE OF PENNSYLVANIA.

FOUNDED,

AGREEABLY TO AN ACT OF ASSEMBLY

Passed on the twentieth day of March, in the year of our Lord one thousand eight hundred and twenty-one.

JOSEPH HIESTER,   ANDREW GREGG,
Governor.   Secretary of the Commonwealth.

Under the direction of the following named gentlemen,

COMMISSIONERS:

Thomas Sparkes, John Bacon, Roberts Vaux, Samuel R. Wood, Coleman Sellers, James Thackara, Daniel H. Miller, William Davidson, Thomas Bradford, Jr., Caleb Carmalt, Geo. N. Baker.

JOHN HAVILAND,   JACOB SOUDER,
Architect.   Superintendent of Masonry.

It only remains for us, said Mr. Vaux, in conclusion, to express our ardent desire that this institution may fully answer the important purposes for which it was founded.

In a report to the Legislature, Mr. Thomas McElwee gave this description:

The Walnut-Street Prison was commenced in 1773, finished in 1774. It contained sixteen cells for solitary confinement—they were only used in emergency. The evils of permitting convicts to work and lodge in companies, with unrestrained intercourse with each other, were manifested at an early day to the discerning and the philanthropist.

In 1801 a memorial was presented to the Legislature by the "Philadelphia Society for Alleviating the Miseries of Public Prisons," dated Philadelphia, 12 mo., 1801, signed Wm. White, President, requesting the Legislature to devise means "to separate the convicts from all other descriptions of prisoners;" and two years afterwards the same society requested the Legislature "to adopt the mode of punishing criminals by solitary confinement at hard labor." In 1818, the society presented another petition in which they request the Legislature "to consider the propriety and expediency of erecting penitentiaries in suitable parts of the State for the more effectual employment and separation of the prisoners, and of proving the efficacy of solitude on the morals of those unhappy objects"

The chief object of the society appears to be to lessen the commission of crime by inflicting the punishment of privation, solitude, and labor for a certain time for a specified offense, not as a mere matter of restraint, but strictly as a punishment.

In 1821 another memorial was laid before the Legislature, signed by Wm. White, Roberts Vaux, and other eminent men who have labored unceasingly to promote the happiness of their fellow-beings. This petition was successful. The Legislature, by Act of March 20, 1821, authorized the construction of the Eastern Penitentiary on the principle of "separate and solitary confinement at labor," with an appropriation of $100,000, and the proceeds of the sales of certain lots of ground situate in the City and County of Philadelphia; and the interest of the Commonwealth in the Arch-Street Prison was vested in the Commissioners on condition of securing to the State the payment of $50,000 out of the proceeds of the sale of that building and the lots on which it is situated.

A lot containing thirteen acres, situate on Cherry Hill, two miles northwest of the Court House, was purchased and appropriated for this important purpose.

The corner-stone of the front building was laid on the twenty-second day of May, 1823, in the presence of the Commissioners, architect, Superintendent, and workmen; Roberts Vaux presiding over the ceremonies.

A box was deposited in the corner-stone, containing a plan and elevation of the prison, and a metal plate bearing the following inscription: [See the copy of inscription printed on page 116.]

Thus was laid the foundation of the Eastern Penitentiary of Pennsylvania.

The Eastern State Penitentiary is situated on one of the most elevated, airy, and healthy sites in the vicinity of Philadelphia. Large sums have been expended for the purpose of giving an unusual degree of solidity and durability to every part of this immense structure, which is the most extensive building in the United States. The ground occupied by it contains about ten acres. The material with which the edifices are built is a grayish granite, or gneiss, employed in large masses; every room is vaulted and fire-proof. The design and execution impart a grave, severe, and awful character to the external aspect of this building. The effect which it produces on the imagination of every passing spectator is peculiarly impressive, solemn, and instructive. The architecture is in keeping with the design. The broad masses, the small and well proportioned apertures, the continuity of lines, and the bold and expressive simplicity which characterize the features of the facade, are most happily and judiciously combined. The originality of the plan, the excellent arrangement and execution of the details, display the taste and ingenuity of the architect, who has planned some of the noblest edifices of our country.

* * * * * * * * *

In the center of the great court-yard is an observatory, whence long corridors, seven in number, radiate. On each side of those corridors the cells are situated, each at right angles to them, and communicating with them only by small openings, for the purpose of supplying the prisoner with food, and inspecting his movements without attracting his attention; other apertures for the admission of cool or heated air, and for the purpose of ventilation, are provided. The privy pipes carry off the impurities of the cell to a common sewer. Originally there was a defect in the construction of those pipes, which admitted communication between the prisoners, endangering the existence of the institution. This defect is, I understand, removed. The cells are warmed by heated air, conducted by flues through the whole range. Light is admitted by a large circular glass in the crown of the arch, which is raking, and the highest part six-teen feet six inches above the floor, which is of wood, overlying a solid foundation of stone. The walls are plastered and whitewashed; the cells are eleven feet nine inches long, and seven feet six inches wide. At the extremity of the cell, opposite to the apertures for inspection, etc., pre-viously mentioned, is the doorway, containing two doors; one a lattice work or iron grating, to admit the air, and secure the prisoner; the other composed of planks to exclude the air if required. This door leads to a yard attached to each cell on the ground floor, eighteen feet by eight, the walls of which are eleven and a half feet high. In the second story each prisoner is allowed an additional cell or bed-room. Each cell is furnished with a bedstead, clothes rail, seat, shelf, tin cup, wash basin, victuals pan, looking-glass, combs, scrubbing brush and sweeping brush, straw mattress, and one sheet, one blanket, and one coverlet.

The bedstead or bunk is so constructed that the prisoner can rear it against the wall and fasten it with a staple, which gives him more room in the cell. Each cell is provided with water by means of a stopcock. The bedstead now in use is constructed of wood. The iron bedstead and hammock were found inexpedient. There were three hundred and eleven cells completed on the first day of January, 1835; all the rest are nearly fitted for the reception of prisoners. The edifice is calculated to contain in all about six hundred and fifty convicts. The three blocks first con-structed are one story; the other four are two stories each.

The close approximation of the level of the edifice to the surface of the public reservoirs at Fairmount, has produced some difficulty in obtain-ing an ample supply of water. That difficulty has been removed by the following contrivance: A well of thirty feet in diameter, and about twenty-five feet in depth from the surface of the ground, is duly and securely walled up and arched over with bricks; contiguous to this well a building of substantial masonry has been erected of forty feet by thirty-four feet; an arched basement contains the furnaces and boilers, over which is placed a steam engine of six horse-power, by means of which the water will be drawn from the large well, and forced into a reservoir, erected also of substantial masonry, north of and adjoining the last mentioned building. This reservoir is about forty feet in diameter and ten in height above the surface of the ground, and contains about seventy-six thousand six hundred gallons of water supplied by the Fairmount Waterworks. From this reservoir the lower stories of the cell buildings and the privy pipes belonging thereto receive their supply of water.

Over this reservoir is an apartment sufficiently capacious to contain nine large cedar tanks or cisterns, filled with water from the large well by the power of the engine. From these tanks the second stories of cells and privy pipes will receive their supply of water. This contrivance, which is very excellent, will furnish an ample supply of water to the whole establishment.

An apothecary's shop is kept within the walls under the superintend-ence of the Physician. One apartment is allotted to the Inspectors and one as a hospital. Within the walls is a garden appropriated to the Warden and one to the domestics.

The food of the convicts is cooked by steam, but it is estimated that the present apparatus has not the capacity to prepare food for more than two hundred persons.

The cost of the building cannot be acurately ascertained, but the following sums are known to have been appropriated by the Legislature:

By Act of March 20, 1821	$100,000 00
By Act of March 15, 1824	80,000 00
By Act of March 1, 1825	60,000 00
By Act of March 15, 1826	89,124 09
By Act of April 9, 1827	1,000 00
By Act of April 14, 1828	4,000 00
By Act of April 23, 1829	5,000 00
By Act of April 3, 1830	4,000 00
By Act of March 28, 1831	120,000 00
By Act of February 27, 1833	130,000 00
By Act of April 15, 1834	20,000 00
By Act of April 14, 1835	60,000 00
City prison, city lots, etc.	99,476 60
Total	$772,600 69

Pennsylvania is indebted for the penitentiary system to such men as the Rt. Rev. Bishop Wm. White, R. Wells, B. Wynkoop, T. Wistar, S. P. Griffitts, J. Kaighn, Wm. Rogers, C. Marshall, T. Connelly, T. Cooper, C. Lowndes, B. Shaw, T. Harrison, Wm. Lippincott, Geo. Duffield, Roberts Vaux, N. Collin, T. Reed, etc.—men whose philanthropy knows no bounds, whose courage nothing could daunt, and whose industry in benevolence knows no resting place. Those are the men who have devised a system, and under whose auspices was commenced an institution which, in the strong language uttered by an experienced man to the writer, "had it been rightly conducted it would have been impossible to find a fault with it."

Richard Wistar led the way in alleviating the miseries of prisons in Pennsylvania. This benevolent man, before the Revolutionary War, was in the habit of causing wholesome soup, prepared at his own dwelling, to be conveyed to the prisoners and distributed among them. The jail was then situated at the southwest corner of Market and Third Streets. "The Philadelphia Society for Assisting Distressed Prisoners" was formed on the seventh of February, 1776, suspended in 1777, by reason of the presence of the British army in Philadelphia, and revived May 8, 1787, under the name of "The Philadelphia Society for Alleviating the Miseries of Public Prisons." To the efforts of this society may be attributed the construction of the Eastern State Penitentiary.

At a meeting held in March, 1872, the Board of Inspectors directed the President, Mr. Richards Vaux, to prepare a brief sketch of the origin and history of the prison for a meeting held in London to consider prison subjects, and he gives this description of the prison:

The front entrance of the penitentiary is sixteen feet wide, forty in height. It has two gates, an outer one on Coates Street, and an inside gate opening into the interior grounds. These two gates are not allowed to be opened at the same time, and when a vehicle passes in from the street the gate from the outside is closed and locked before the inner gate leading to the premises is opened. The same precaution is observed when the vehicle passes out. The Gatekeeper is always present in his room at the western side of this entrance. The eastern portion of the front buildings is for the Warden's family, and the Inspectors have their room on that side. The western is for the Resident Physician and the Clerk's office, and any other purpose for which it may be needed. The carriage and footway to the center building is thirty feet wide, and on either side of it are large plots of ground with flowers and grass.

The "center building" is forty feet in diameter. It is of an octagonal shape, and each corridor opens into it. A good idea may be had of its form by likening it to the hub of a wheel from which the spokes, representing the corridors, radiate. It is two stories high. On the top is a lantern and lookout. In the lantern or cupola are eight reflectors, twenty inches in diameter, silver-plated, and by the use of gas the light is thrown at night into all parts of the grounds. It is deemed one of the best protections. The height of these reflectors from the ground is about fifty feet. The center building stands in the exact center of the whole plot of ground, around which is a substantial stone wall, the average height of which is thirty-five feet. At the base it is twelve feet wide, and at the top two feet, with a coping overhanging inside two and one half feet. There is a tower at each corner, and the plot of ground contains about ten acres.

Escapes.

Since the opening of the penitentiary, in 1829, there have been nine escapes. Of these six were retaken.

Flour Mill.

The grist mill, situated over the cook house and boiler-room, forms an important feature in the economical arrangement of this prison, inasmuch as it furnishes the penitentiary with fresh flour, uniformly sweet and good, at a very considerably less cost than if purchased in the market.

The engine which drives the mill is one of ten horse-power, and was erected in the year 1834, for the purpose of pumping water from a large well into the reservoir at times of scarcity of water at the city waterworks, and it still performs that service when needed.

The net gain of this arrangement, for the eleven months it has been in operation, has been $1,324 46.

Carpenter Shop.

There is a building in the grounds, between the third and fourth blocks, constructed so that, in case of emergency, or if a contagious disease should manifest itself in the cells, a comfortable, well heated, and ventilated hospital could, in a few hours, be ready for use. It is fifty feet in length, twenty-five in width, and two stories in height. The use to which it is designed is a general shop for storing wood and for carpenter's work. The upper story, twelve feet in height, can be promptly made ready for a hospital, and the patients separated by temporary screens.

Reservoirs.

The water is supplied from a reservoir to all the prisoners. This reservoir is circular in form, forty-one feet six inches in diameter, twenty-five feet deep, holds two hundred and fifty-two thousand nine hundred and ninety-two gallons of water. The weight of the water, when full, is equal to one thousand five hundred tons. There were two hundred thousand bricks used on the inner wall; the outside wall is of stone. The walls are three feet thick, and bound with iron hoops, built in the wall, two feet apart. The whole is covered with a slate roof with ventilator at the top.

The kitchen, for preparing the food of the prisoners, the bake house, and the flour mill, in which all the flour is ground, are located in the buildings adjoining the reservoir. There is a well fourteen feet in diameter between the reservoir and the kitchen, out of which a supply of water is pumped by steam when the water in the basin supplied by the city waterworks is too low for general use.

Heating and Lighting.

The heating of the cells is by steam from boilers at the end of the corridors, and the refuse steam is used for the prisoners' bath house, and to heat the center building and library, which is on the second story of the center building. Five and one half miles of iron pipe are employed in conducting the steam through various parts of the premises. Steam as a means of heating has been introduced in lieu of hot water. The total number of gas burners whereby the cells are lighted is six hundred and fifty.

Wash-Room.

The wash-room is twenty-five by twenty-five feet, the drying-room twenty-five by thirty feet, and each fifteen feet high. Between these rooms is the boiler-room, twenty-five by twenty feet and twelve high, and over the boiler-room is the room for storing boots and shoes, twenty-five by twenty feet and eleven feet high. These rooms are situated at the end of the seventh block.

The drying-room is heated by steam pipes, giving a temperature of 150 to 200 degrees Fahrenheit.

The same boiler which heats this room supplies hot water in abundance for washing.

The washing is done with a machine, which is put in rapid motion by a pair of cranks or winches, turned by four men. It is found to be very effective, doing its work thoroughly. After washing, the clothes are put under a screw-press and the water forced out, leaving them nearly dry.

There are not less than two thousand eight hundred pieces of clothing washed each week.

Each article is marked with the prisoner's number, and his own clothes and bedding are always returned to him.

Receiving-Room.

On the western side of the main entrance, at a short distance beyond the inside gate, is a room properly protected for the reception of the convicts. It is so secured that no combination of prisoners to escape can be successful. They sometimes arrive, several at one time, in the night, from the counties comprising the Eastern District, when caution is necessary, as they are then unknown to the prison authorities. In this room the reception of the prisoners takes place, and all the examinations then necessary are made before they are taken to the cells. In passing from the front to the center building, and thence to their cells, they wear a cap which prevents recognition in the daytime and secures them from acquiring any topographical knowledge of the ground plan of the penitentiary. Every prisoner, on being received, is taken to a bath-room and thoroughly cleansed. He is then supplied with a clean suit of prison garments, and the clothing he wore upon admission and such articles as were found upon his person are carefully packed away, to be restored to him on his discharge. Personal cleanliness is further secured by a frequent use of the bath-room. A number is assigned to each prisoner when received, and by that number he is designated as long as he remains in the institution.

Corridors and Blocks of Cells.

The length of the "first block" is three hundred and sixty-eight feet; ten feet wide, twenty-one feet high to the top of the arch. The old cells in this block are seven feet six inches in width by twelve feet in length, and say fourteen feet in height. The new cells in this block are eight feet wide, sixteen feet long, and eleven feet high. There are twenty of these new cells, built in 1869–70. There are fifty cells in this block.

The length of the "second block" is two hundred and sixty-eight feet, including passage way from the corridor to the center building. The block is only one hundred and eighty feet in length, ten feet wide, and twenty-one feet high. There are thirty-eight cells in this block.

The size of the "third block" is same as second block. There are twenty cells in this block; eighteen "double cells," or seventeen by twelve feet, twelve feet high, and used as shops. These three blocks are one story high.

The length of the "fourth block" is two hundred and sixty-eight feet. It is two stories in height. There are fifty cells on the ground floor, and fifty cells in the second story. The size is seven feet six inches wide by fifteen feet long and eleven feet high. The cells in the second story are the same size as the others, and twelve feet high. There are one hundred and thirty-six cells in this block.

The "fifth block" is three hundred and sixty-two feet in length, ten feet wide. The corridor is thirty-three feet high and has two stories. There are sixty-eight cells on the ground floor and sixty-eight on the second floor. The size of the cells is the same as in the "fourth block."

The "sixth block" is two hundred and sixty-eight feet long, ten feet wide, two stories high. The height of the corridor is thirty-three feet, and it contains one hundred cells of the same size as in the "fourth block."

The "seventh block" is three hundred and sixty-five feet long, two stories high, fifteen feet wide on the gallery, ten feet wide on the ground floor. It is thirty-eight feet in height. The cells are seven feet six inches wide, sixteen feet long, and eleven feet high. There are one hundred and thirty-six cells in this block.

The cells on the ground floor of all the corridors have yards attached to them; the cells in the second story have no yards. Some are double cells (two cells in one), for special use.

The New Cells.

Twenty new cells have been added to the first block corridor. They are the result, in construction, of all the experience gained as to the best mode of building such apartments. These new cells are eight feet by sixteen, and twelve feet high. They are lighted by a skylight five feet by twelve inches. The means of supplying heat and ventilation and light are regarded as most complete. The heat is from steam supplied by a boiler at the end of the block, and is sufficient for this and the second block. Each cell has a yard eight by fourteen feet, and inclosed by a wall eleven feet high. The water for drinking is at the command of the prisoner. The gas is given between certain hours. A privy is in each cell, and is cleaned daily by flooding into a sewer.

The doors into the corridors slide in grooves, and the fastenings were designed by Mr. Cassidy, the principal Overseer, who had entire superintendence of the construction of the work. The cells are regarded as the most approved of any in use.

A Review of the Development of the Administration.

From the opening of this penitentiary in 1829, to the end of last year, 1871, forty-two years have elapsed. This period may be subdivided into two epochs. The first, from 1829 to 1849, should be designated as the epoch of "experiment and experience;" the latter of "development and progress." It requires neither argument nor justification to denominate the first period as one during which the system was to be studied and understood. From the earliest efforts to secure "solitude," as it was called, for the convict during his imprisonment, till the trial was so indifferently and partially made in the Walnut-Street Prison, by the separation of a few prisoners, it was the theory of separation that was mainly considered.

When the penitentiary was ready in 1829 for the reception of some occupants, it may be said that very little was really known as to the effect of the discipline on the prisoners. Indeed, the discipline of itself was a theory. For many years following 1829, it was not possible to do more than supervise the administration, and put it into working order. It required some time to settle what were the consequences of the discipline, and patient investigation was necessary to determine them. To finish all the buildings, suffer from some serious criticisms on the management, and harmonize almost irreconcilable opinions, if not feelings, among those who were first connected with the administration of the penitentiary, distracted the minds of those who were charged with the government of the institution. Therefore, from 1829 to 1835 the attention of the Inspectors was not wholly concentrated on the workings of the system which had been established for the penitentiary. From 1835 to 1849 the treatment of the prisoners was thoroughly considered, and then it was that the experience developed in the experiment of the separate system became of great importance.

From 1849 to 1871, the Inspectors were to a greater extent occupied in investigating the principles and the philosophy of the separate or individual treatment discipline, which is now in full operation in this penitentiary.

These remarks are properly prefatory to the annexed extracts from the reports of the Inspectors to the Legislature. They are also intended to present the reason for, and explain the purpose of, the statement of the results of the administration of the system of separate confinement of prisoners in the penitentiary, for the two periods to which reference has been made. This statement will give some idea of the progress made, but prominently shows the philosophic basis on which penology must rest, and the intimate relations it bears to social science.

The penitentiary went into operation, by the reception of the first prisoner, on October 25, 1829. The law organizing it was in force June 1, 1829, and S. R. Wood, the first Warden, took charge August 1, 1829. Four blocks of cells were yet unfinished, and the architect and the friends of the separate system, as well as the Inspectors, were engaged in ascertaining what improvements could be made in the details of the general plan. The State Penitentiary at Pittsburg (Allegheny), and the one at Philadelphia, constructed on the plan of separate confinement of the convicts, were both originally devised without, of course, much, if any, practical experience in their adaptation to the objects for which they were to be occupied. It is not to be presumed that experience, when obtained, did not suggest various improvements in the structure of prisons for the separation, individual treatment, and labor and instruction of the inmates.

It is but proper to note that, in 1818, there was a difference of opinion among the friends of the system as to what it really should be in its administration. Some were for solitude, as it was called in contradistinction to congregation, without labor. Others were in favor of solitude and hard labor. The first blocks of cells were erected when this subject had been settled, but it had so engaged the minds of all parties before the great results which experience has since shown were to result from separation and the individual treatment of the prisoners, that these apartments were not wholly suited to the wiser and truer discipline.

It is not now scarcely possible to explain how much of discussion and difference of opinion then existed on these subjects. The friends of the separate system had not only to educate the public mind in Pennsylvania as to its real merits, but also to combat opposition in England, New England, New York, and among various gentlemen who had some general opinions on penal jurisprudence. It is not possible to give all the views expressed from these sources. A history, even as brief as the one now presented, would not, however, be satisfactory without some reference to these interesting questions and their effects on the Pennsylvania system.

The system of Pennsylvania may now be properly described as the separate and individual treatment system of prison discipline. We believe it to be as great a success as human effort, under all the circumstances, could be expected to accomplish.

Crime and criminals should be regarded in the relation they bear to the social condition. Society, the State, or Commonwealth, demands protection against violations of those laws which are enacted for protection of the interests, happiness, security, and welfare of the people. For these violations of law, punishment is to be inflicted on the offender. Thus far the State is directly interested in the laws defining crimes, and declaring the penalties. The vindication of the law and its administration, and the infliction of the punishment, comprise the paramount interests of the State. The punishment begins its operation on the criminal, and so far as that punishment deters from crime, the State has a direct interest in the system by which it is administered. Out of the system come other benefits to the State, such as the reformation of the offender, and the protection of the State from the perils of a crime-class, created by the system of punishment.

The system by which, in penitentiary or prison, the punishment is inflicted, and by which these benefits are to be derived both by the State and the convict, is of equal importance with any other of the interests the State has directly in its jurisprudence.

This system is one to be considered and determined by applying to the principles on which it is based a scientific investigation only, for any other subordinates to the feelings and interests what should be predominant as a question of social science.

This subject, it may be remarked, is one that requires the most thorough examination before any conclusions can be safely arrived at. The questions of original cost, kind of labor, or capacity to be self-supporting, have no direct concern with the system of punishment. If the punishment by the separate and individual treatment of the convicts, secures society and protects the people; deters from crime; punishes the offender; reforms the individual; returns him to his former social relations better, or no worse, than when he was separated from them by his imprisonment; prevents the organization or augmentation of a crime-class in the community; then the principal purposes, the highest aims of punishment are obtained. It is with these that society is directly concerned. To ascertain whether these effects are the consequences of any system of punishment, requires that the system should be scientifically and practically investigated, and all other questions should be postponed till these consequences are determined.

It is claimed for the separate and individual treatment system, as now administered in the Eastern State Penitentiary at Philadelphia, that it accomplishes all these purposes. Let the contrary be demonstrated before the system is either condemned or set aside for one which yields less or none of the great objects of punishment by imprisonment of offenders. It will not suffice to condemn the separate system, because by the separation of convicts less profits are obtained from their labor than when they work, aided by machinery, in an associate or congregate prison. The State has no such paramount interest in the profits of the labor of its convicts as to abandon all the other benefits which should be derived from their punishment. The congregation or association of convicts during their punishment by imprisonment, produces evils ultimately far more expensive to the State than the loss of profits gained by working them together for the period of their imprisonment.

It is doubted if ever yet a system of penitentiary discipline, or of treatment of offenders sentenced to separation from society for crimes against it, has been adjudged the best because it is preëminently a profit-making, money-gaining system. Such a decision, based on such a principle, would, or should, shock the moral sense of mankind. It may be possible to introduce into the profit-making discipline a means of moral culture, promising the reform of those who are subjected to it. But so long as the profits are the primary purpose of the discipline, the great aim, punishment, is lost sight of, because punishment then is only incarceration in a prison, and the reformation of the prisoner is subordinate to the best method of labor.

No regard is paid to the effects of congregating in a prison large numbers of convicts working together, when these prisoners leave the institution to mix again in society. This consideration, and the reformation and individual benefits to be derived from proper instruction during punishment, are questions which, if considered, and due weight given to their importance, would involve loss of profits. A congregate prison— the system of congregating prisoners for work—unless it is profit-making, could not be regarded as defensible. Its only merit now consists in the asserted fact that it may be self-supporting. Such are the sordid influences that the system of money-making prisons begets—a system so prejudicial to the convict and society.

Remarks and Facts in Relation to Administration.

It may be said, without fear of denial, that the best system of prison discipline ever devised may utterly fail by reason of its bad administration. So, also, is it true of a bad system; it may produce good results, provided it is well administered. So much depends on administration. The most important element in all administrations is the character and capacity of the governing power, and the adaptation of the officers to their duties. It is to be remarked that the changing of the officers for any reason other than unfitness, or impropriety of conduct, is to be condemned in the strongest manner as fatal to the best interests of the institution. Political or sectarian influences should never be permitted to control the administration, nor in any way interfere with the government of a prison. It produces the worst possible condition of the administration, and destroys the independence of those who are required to be responsible for the faithful discharge of their peculiar duties, which must be systematized, rigidly supervised, and performed with exactness, and with a full understanding that direct accountability is demanded.

Very little consideration is given to the importance of these principles in prison government. It is too often the case that favoritism is made the ground for pertinacious recommendations for positions, when the want of character and fitness in the applicant is known to be positive. Appointments to positions should be in every case dependent only on integrity, character, and special qualifications for the duties to be performed, and the tenure should depend solely on good conduct. In this penitentiary all the appointments of Overseers are made by the Warden without the intervention of the Inspectors, who, however, hold the Warden responsible therefor.

It may better explain the basis of the administration of the discipline to give the following account of some of the means adopted to improve and reform the prisoners:

For the past three years, out of a total population during that period of one thousand four hundred and ninety-five persons, only ninety-six were subjected to punishment for violating the rules, for gross insubordination, or for other bad conduct. The only punishment permitted is a dark cell and bread and water.

For the same period twenty thousand three hundred lessons were given by the secular teachers, instructing those who were illiterate, or improving those who had some education.

The whole number of lessons given by the Moral Instructor was twenty-four thousand two hundred and ninety-six, besides one thousand and eighty-nine Sunday exercises on the Sundays of these years.

There were twenty-eight thousand and thirty-one newspapers, of all religious denominations, distributed.

The library contains six thousand two hundred and sixty-eight volumes, and for three years sixty-nine thousand six hundred and fifty-eight books were distributed to the prisoners, besides one hundred and twelve thousand six hundred and fifteen pages of tracts.

Every prisoner is taught a handicraft occupation, and when able to do the work he is allowed one half of the product of his labor, in excess of his task, for his own use or that of his family. All those who are received and capable of learning are taught to read, write, cipher, and a trade. When any prisoner has a decided talent for either intellectual or mechanical pursuits, he is permitted to improve himself in study or perfect himself in mechanism.

Letters to and from the prisoners are forwarded by the Warden after such examination only as to provide against infractions of the rules. Within the past three years eleven thousand two hundred and seventy-five letters were sent by prisoners, and eighteen thousand nine hundred and eleven received by them.

The influences best adapted to each individual as a reformatory treatment of his case are directly applied.

The cells are regularly cleaned, and great attention is given to this subject, and also to personal cleanliness.

The number of general visitors to the institution for the past ten years amounts to one hundred and fourteen thousand four hundred and forty. Visits to the prisoners are regulated by a general rule, but special cases are governed by the circumstances in each case.

The officers, Warden, Physician, Moral Instructors, and Teachers and Overseers in charge, have constant intercourse with the prisoners.

Two of the Inspectors are detailed each month as " Visiting Inspectors," who have the general duties of supervision imposed on them, besides such special business in regard to the administration as the Board directs.

The "Prison Society" has a visiting committee which occupies itself with visits to the prisoners, and a special officer of the society to look after discharged prisoners.

Meetings of the Board.

The regular meetings of the Board of Inspectors are held monthly, at which time a written report in detail is required from the Treasurer, Warden, Physician, Moral Instructor, and Secular Instructor. Bills are at the same time submitted by the Warden for all purchases made by him since the preceding meeting, their payment, however, not being ordered by the Board until, upon examination by a committee of the Board, they are found to be correct. The Warden is also required by law to keep a journal and enter therein daily all events happening in the penitentiary, including all cases of punishment or discipline, open to the examination of the Inspectors.

Annual Reports of the Inspectors to the Legislature.

From the first year of the opening of the penitentiary, 1829, annually, as by law required, the Inspectors have made to the Legislature of the State reports on the condition of the institution. These reports are exhaustive on all the subjects connected with the administration of the penitentiary. The views of the Inspectors as to the system of separate or individual treatment of convicts are presented, and such suggestions are from time to time made as directly relate to the cause of crime, legislation for the prevention and punishment of offenders, and also the opinions of the Inspectors on the proper means by which the effects of punishment are most surely produced. Each annual report is accompanied by statistical tables most carefully prepared from the best sources of information, in which the most thorough exposition of the relations, physical, moral, and mental, of each prisoner on admission and discharge is shown.

It is believed that no more full and complete exhibit of any institution can be found than is thus afforded.

The student of penal science, in its relations to social science, jurisprudence, systems of punishment, prison discipline, the effects of imprisonment by the separate system on all who are subjected to it, can obtain in these reports most valuable information. There are now printed and published forty-three of these reports with full tabular statistical exhibits, and in order that those who desire to learn how much has been done by the Inspectors for the past few years, for the information of those who take any interest in investigating the questions involved, it may be stated that each of the more recent annual reports contain about one hundred and fifty pages of printed matter.

Receiving Book.

The following is a copy of the "Receiving Book" which has been in use in this penitentiary for nearly forty years:

No.	
Age, Native of, Bound, Trade, Complexion, Eyes, Hair, Stature, Marks, No. of convictions, Parents, Reads, Writes, Temperate, Married, Property, Crime, Sentence, County and Court, Sentenced, Received, Remarks,	Apprenticed: and left before the end of term of apprenticeship. and served until expiration of term. Went to public school, Went to private school, Age on leaving school,

A Copy of the Medical General Record of Admissions.

Name	Date	No.	Color			Age	Sex		Bodily Health	Mental Health	Habits	Social State		Protected Against Smallpox	Hereditary Disease in the Family	No. of Convictions	Length of Sentence	Time in County Jail	Born in	Occupation
			White	Black	Mulatto		Male	Female				Married	Single							

A Copy of the Medical General Record of Discharges.

Name	Date	No.	Color			Age	Sex		Bodily Health.			Mental Health.			Health during Imprisonment.	Time in Prison.	Pardoned.	Remarks.
			White	Black	Mulatto		Male	Female	Improved	Unimproved	Impaired.	Improved	Unimproved	Impaired.				

Form of Medical Monthly Report.

Name	No.	Color			Age	Sex		Date of Admission.	Time in Prison.	Disease	Cause	Event.					Monthly Summary, Remarks, etc.
		White	Black	Mulatto		Male	Female					Cured	Relieved	Time Out.	Pardoned	Dead	

9D

Medical Department.

The health of the large number of inmates of a penitentiary is a subject of careful attention. After much experience and reflection, the Inspectors came to the conclusion that the importance of the interests involved required that a competent physician should permanently reside upon the premises, so as to be constantly at hand, by day or night, whenever an occasion should arise for his services. This has been found much more satisfactory than the system of a visiting physician from without. Medical visits, of which a daily record is kept, are constantly and systematically made by the Resident Physician to every prisoner, and each new recipient into the institution undergoes, upon his admission, a thorough and medical examination, the results of which are fully recorded. An ample assortment of medical supplies is kept in the apothecary shop of the penitentiary, which is under the charge of the Resident Physician.

The Discharge of Prisoners.

It is of great importance, where a penitentiary, located in a city, receives inmates from a distance, that they should when discharged be immediately sent to the localities whence they came, and not be exposed to the temptations of the city. In order to accomplish this beneficial object, the Inspectors have obtained authority, by an Act of Assembly of the State of Pennsylvania, to give, if it should be needed, to each prisoner, upon his discharge, a specified sum of money for the purpose of paying his traveling expenses to the county from which he came, viz.: $5 under fifty and $10 over fifty miles.

The "Prison Society" also, as a part of its benevolent operations, takes care that each prisoner, upon his discharge, shall, if his necessities require it, be supplied with such clothing as shall enable him to present a proper appearance when he rejoins his family or friends.

Rules for the Prisoner.

In each cell there is a printed copy of these rules. "You are desired strictly to observe the following rules established by the Inspectors for your government:"

First—You must keep you person, cell, and utensils clean and in order.

Second—You must obey promptly all directions given to you either by the Inspectors, Warden, or Overseers.

Third—You must not make any unnecessary noise, either by singing, whistling, or in any other manner; but in all respects preserve becoming order. You must not try to communicate with your fellow prisoners in the adjoining cells, either from your own apartment, or during the time you are exercising in your yard.

Fourth—All surplus food must be placed in the vessel provided for that purpose; and all wastage of materials, or other dirt, must be carefully collected and handed out of the cell, when called for by the Overseer.

Fifth—You must apply yourself industriously, at whatever employment is assigned you; and when your task is finished, it is recommended that your time be devoted to the proper improvement of your mind, either in reading the books provided for the purpose, or in case you cannot read, in learning to do so.

Sixth—Should you have any complaint to make against the Overseer having charge of you, make it to the Warden or Inspector; if against the Warden, to an Inspector.

Seventh—Be at all times, in your intercourse with the officers of the penitentiary, respectful and courteous, and never suffer yourself to be led astray from your duties by angry or revengeful feelings.

Eighth—Observe the Sabbath; though you are separated from the world, the day is not the less holy.

The Inspectors desire to treat every prisoner under their charge with humanity and kindness; and they hope that in return the prisoner will strictly conform to the rules adopted for his government, which are not merely advisory, but are a law to him, especially the third, any violation of which will incur proper punishment.

Special Notice.—Violations of these rules or any part of the discipline of the institution, will deprive the prisoner of the benefit of the "Commutation Law."

N. B.—Not to be defaced in any manner.

Mr. Vaux then proceeded to answer some of the popular prejudices against the separate system, and said:

The volume entitled "American Notes," by Mr. Charles Dickens, has had a large circulation in Europe and America. From his description of the Eastern Penitentiary, an impression has doubtless been made on the minds of many persons corresponding to his published idea of the institution. He thus writes in regard to it:

"In the outskirts stands a great prison called the Eastern Penitentiary, conducted on a plan peculiar to the State of Pennsylvania. The system here is rigid, strict, and hopeless solitary confinement. I believe it in its effects to be cruel and wrong. In its intention, I am well convinced that it is kind, humane, and meant for reformation; but I am persuaded that those who devised this system of prison discipline, and those benevolent gentlemen who carry it into execution, do not know what it is that they are doing. I believe that very few men are capable of estimating the immense amount of torture and agony which this dreadful punishment, prolonged for years, inflicts upon the sufferers, and in guessing at it myself, and in reasoning from what I have seen written upon their faces, and what to my certain knowledge they feel within, I am only the more convinced that there is a depth of terrible endurance in it which none but the sufferers themselves can fathom, and which no man has a right to inflict upon his fellow creature. * * * I was accompanied to this prison by two gentlemen officially connected with its management, and passed the day in going from cell to cell and talking with the inmates. Every facility was afforded me that utmost courtesy could suggest. Nothing was concealed or hidden from my view, and every piece of information that I sought was openly and frankly given. * * * In another cell there was a German sentenced to five years' imprisonment for larceny, two of which had just expired. With colors procured in the same manner, he had painted every inch of the walls and ceiling quite beautifully. He had laid out the few feet of ground behind with exquisite neatness, and had made a little bed in the center that looked, by the bye, like a grave. The taste and ingenuity he had displayed in everything were most extraordinary; and yet a more dejected, heart-broken, wretched creature it would be difficult to imagine. I never saw such a picture of forlorn affliction and distress of mind. My heart bled for him, and when the tears ran down his cheeks, and he took one of the visitors aside to ask, with trembling hands nervously clutching at his coat to detain him, whether there was no hope of his dismal sentence being commuted, the spectacle was really too painful to witness. I never saw or heard of any kind of misery that impressed me more than the wretchedness of this man."—American Notes, vol. 2, page 246, A. D. 1842.

Mr. Dickens visited at his own special request the Eastern Penitentiary. He remarked, when asking for an opportunity to examine the institution, that "the Falls of Niagara and your penitentiary are two objects I might almost say I most wish to see in America." His visit was thorough. He saw everything in the penitentiary, and all the prisoners that he chose to visit. When about to leave, he remarked to Mr. Bevan, the President of the Board, that he "never before saw a public institution in which the relation of 'father and family' was so well exemplified as in this." Not one word of criticism or objection was then or there made. He did not even express a doubt of the success of separate confinement as a system of prison discipline. How could he, for he never understood it? On his return to England, his "Notes" were published, from which the foregoing extract is taken. Mr. Dickens' recollections of his early life, and the impression then made on him by its associations and privations, perhaps gave, beyond his power of detection, the coloring to his description of the penitentiary. His delineation of character is marked by the strong contrasts which he paints in his fictions, and, therefore, his account of his visit to the "solitary prison" may be presumed to be exaggerated or untrustworthy. The case of the German prisoner, which has been given in full from the "Notes," justifies this remark.

This German prisoner, this "picture of forlorn affliction and distress of mind," this "dejected, heart-broken, wretched creature," was sentenced to this penitentiary for the first time, May 15, 1840, for five years; on June 28, 1852, he was sent to this penitentiary for one year; February 24, 1855, he was a third time committed to this prison for two years; April 4, 1861, he came again for one year; on the 12th of March, 1872, he returned to this penitentiary for two years. Thus this "picture of forlorn affliction and distress of mind" is now a living, hale, hearty man of seventy-two years of age, having served out nine years of imprisonment, under five different sentences, in this penitentiary, with all its horrors and cruelty, such as "no man has a right to inflict on his fellow man;" while the author of the "American Notes," notwithstanding his associations and journeyings, and his life in the midst of pleasure and friends, sleeps with "David Copperfield."

So much for crude and emotional criticism on an institution in which punishment is considered with the care, deliberation, and thoughtfulness devoted to any other scientific question.

Since De Tocqueville, of France, wrote his report on prison discipline, there have been several learned and eminent men who have carefully investigated the subject of individual treatment of convicts as applied under the separate system. In Italy, Belgium, and England many students of penal science, as well as those conversant practically with this subject, have published most interesting papers in defense of cellular imprisonment.

In Philadelphia there have been contributed exhaustive arguments and statistical information, derived from the actual condition of the administration of the separate system at the penitentiary in that city, both in the reports of the Inspectors to the Legislature and from other sources. Special reference is here made to William Parker Faulke's "Remarks on Cellular Separation," Philadelphia, 1871; and "Journal of Prison Discipline," Philadelphia, by the Hon. Joseph R. Chandler. The contributions by Francis Lieber, LL.D., on the Pennsylvania system are well known. In this connection it is most proper to refer to the book of the Rev. J. Field, Chaplain of the Reading (England) Gaol, entitled "Prison Discipline and the Advantages of the Separate System of Imprisonment," 2 vol., London, 1848, Longman, Brown, Green & Co., publishers.

He then gave extracts from some of the annual reports of the Inspectors to the Legislature of Pennsylvania, showing the views of the Inspectors and comparisons with other systems:

In the report of 1830 the Inspectors write:

"Believing that an accurate knowledge of the discipline established in the Western State Penitentiary, near Pittsburg (in regard to which from rumor there was some uncertainty), might be useful in estimating the operation of that in the East, the President of the Board visited that institution in June last, to ascertain from personal inspection the character of the experiment there made, and, it is trusted, the Board can in nowise be regarded as reflecting upon the highly respectable gentlemen who superintend that prison, constructed, as it confessedly was, for solitary confinement, unmitigated by labor, in the remarks here submitted. The ranges of cells being too small and not sufficiently ventilated and lighted to be used as workshops, appeared to be principally used as dormitories, and he was induced to believe that convicts could not be advantageously employed therein at solitary labor. The building being also unprovided with separate yards for the different cells, it became necessary to the health of the prisoners to allow them to associate with each other in the common yards in which the sexes only appeared to be separated. The result of this visit was a belief that no inference can be drawn from the situation of a prison thus constructed (as some unfriendly to the system appeared to think) prejudicial to the permanency of the greatly successful experiment of its operation in the Eastern Penitentiary, in which every prisoner is provided with a separate cell of ample dimensions and with sufficient light, communicating with a separate yard, for air and exercise.

"Unbiased by the speculations of enthusiastic theorists on either side, and unbending to the authority of names, whatever their repute, the Legislature of this Commonwealth, by its statute of the twenty-third of April, 1829, so far as concerned the offenses embraced in that Act, committed the ancient penitentiary system of Pennsylvania to the test of actual experiment in a building adequate to the purpose, content to abide the event before it should be abandoned or extended to the whole calendar of penitentiary offenses. That system, however imperfectly enforced heretofore, owing to the faulty construction of our prisons, this Board

considers to be briefly this: solitary confinement at labor, with instruction in labor, in morals, and in religion. . The noble structure under
the direction of the Board, so honorable to the liberality and philanthropy of the State, has, for the first time, presented the opportunity of
effectually enforcing this mode of punishing and reforming the violators
of the laws of society. In accordance with the views of the Legislature,
and in the faithful execution of the trust reposed in the Board, it is now
proposed to express a judgment founded on actual experience of the operation of solitary confinement with labor and instruction upon the moral
and physical powers of the convicts, and of the probable expense to the
counties of maintaining their prisoners.

"The evidence of the Physician, with the concurring testimony of the
Warden, whose respective reports to the Board are annexed, and the
particular observation of this Board, establish the fact that neither
insanity nor bodily infirmity has been produced by the mitigated solitude in which the prisoners are confined. Absolute solitude for years,
without labor or moral or religious instruction, probably does bear too
severely upon a social being like man, and were such the mode of punishment in this institution, the Board would feel little hesitation in
recommending its repeal, as cruel, because calculated to undermine the
moral and physical powers of the prisoner, and to disqualify him from
earning his bread at the expiration of his sentence; as impolitic, because,
when persisted in beyond a very limited time it tends to harden rather
than reform the offender, while it produces great expense to the public,
the prisoner in no way contributing by labor to his support. An opportunity of witnessing the effects of absolute solitude without labor has
occasionally been presented, when, as a punishment to a sturdy and disorderly convict, the Warden has ordered the light of his cell to be closed;.
little time has elapsed with the most hardy before the prisoner has been
found broken down in his spirit, and begging for his work and his Bible,
to beguile the tedium of absolute idleness in solitude."

From the report of the year 1834, the following extract is taken:
"The Pennsylvania system is emphatically a mild and humane system. Let us look for a moment at the condition of the majority of those
who become subject to its regulation. We find them living a hurried
and thoughtless life of hourly excitement, and shuddering at the possibility of a pause which could let in (to them) the demon reflection. We
see them wanting the ordinary comforts of clothing and cleanliness,
without home save that afforded by chance companionship. We find
them in the brothel and the ginshop, giving up to all manner of excesses,
indulging in every extreme of vice, self-degraded and brutal. We 'see
them corrupted and corrupting, initiating new candidates in the race of
misery and dragging them in their own vortex to a death of infamy and
horror. Where do we place them, and how do we treat them? They are
taken to the bath and cleansed of outward pollution, they are newly clad
in warm and comfortable garments, they are placed in an apartment
infinitely superior to what they have been accustomed, they are given
employment to enable them to live by their own industry, they are
addressed in the language of kindness, interest is shown in their present and future welfare, they are advised and urged to think of their
former course and to avoid it, they are lifted gently from their state of
humiliation; self-degradation is removed, and self-esteem inducted.
Pride of character and manliness is inculcated, and they go out of prison

unknown as convicts, determined to wrestle for a living in the path of honesty and virtue. Is not this humane? The object of all prison establishments should be to reclaim. The separation of convicts affords facilities (which would be impossible under other circumstances) to treat each individual case in a manner best adapted to that result. There are no doubt some criminals who are incorrigible, but even with these the vindictive feelings usually generated by prison discipline find no place, and they leave the establishment with sentiments of regard rather than resentment, towards those who have attempted to alter their vicious habits. We are unwilling to make any remarks which may appear invidious, but we ask that a single glance shall be taken at any of the other plans now in operation, and then let it be answered whether the Pennsylvania system does not possess distinctive features which entirely change the relationship of prisoners towards society, and whether it does not embrace an extensive plan of amelioration of their condition."

In the report for 1836, the Inspectors say:

"Although a definite labor appears to be assigned, yet inasmuch as the Inspectors may be looked upon as public agents in this particular department, it is hoped they will not be considered as stepping out of their province if they take a more enlarged view of the subject than these limits seem to prescribe. The present Inspectors stand in a peculiar relation to the Commonwealth; they were the friends and associates of the promoters of the system, and were in the habit of discussing the subject of penitentiary regulations in all its bearings. They were fully imbued with the principles and views of its advocates, and the majority of them took an active part in calling into operation the schemes of those who felt the necessity of a reform in the criminal jurisprudence of the State.

"The experiment at the time was a bold one, and was attended with difficulties at its commencement that would have dampened the courage of any set of men less persuaded of the practicability of a plan which years of deliberation had decided to be the true one. Opposed at home by a respectable number of our fellow citizens, who, with views quite as honest, held adverse opinions; its main principles questioned by a Commission of our own State especially instituted to examine the subject; assailed by the official agent of an influential and indefatigable society of a sister State, because it conflicted with his favorite system; attacked from abroad by persons of high consideration in the moral and political world, who had become endeared to America by their military and other services, the friends of the Pennsylvania system held their course unchecked, and with steadiness and perseverance worthy the cause, made their opinions public sentiment, and the State at length passed the law which will render her character for philanthropy preëminent.

"The experiment at the outset was attended with an expense which even a great nation has paused to incur, and is only to be reconciled by the prevalent humanity of the people of Pennsylvania, which yearned to ameliorate the condition of her criminals, and to substitute a moral and wholesome atmosphere in lieu of the vicious miasma which pervades great communities.

"Accustomed to look at the great results of the law, the Inspectors hold themselves excused, if in attempting to satisfy the public mind as to the wisdom of the measure, they should take a more comprehensive view of the subject than may seem to be required by the letter of the

Act of their appointment. Being called upon to attend to the operation of a system which was urged upon the State, and to test a theory by its practical results, the duty was entered upon with much anxiety and some little distrust, and the Board have hitherto delayed a positive assertion in its favor, until it is forced from them by evidence which appears to be incontestable."

The report for 1844 contains the following:

"The Inspectors believe that the following conclusions irresistibly present themselves, as the result of the above comparison of the two systems:

"1. That the separate system prevents the commission of crime.

"2. That it is preëminently calculated to induce and effect reform in the minds of the prisoners.

"3. That the health of the prisoners is equal to that of any community, and is not, in the least, injuriously affected by the system.

"4. That mortality, under the separate system, is not greater than that of any other system of prison discipline.

"5. That the discipline, and the proper administration of the system, are superior to all others.

"6. That, of the objections which have been urged against the system, none have been realized.

"It may be proper here to remark, that the term 'solitary or separate confinement' refers to the fact that each prisoner is 'alone,' in contra-distinction to the 'aggregate confinement,' or 'silent system,' where prisoners are in gangs, or together in large or small numbers. The prisoners in the separate or solitary prisons have the same intercourse with all but their fellow convicts, and an idle curiosity, as in other systems; and the idea that prisoners are shut up, and shut out, from all intercommunication with the good and the instructive, is an error—a gross error. They have that, at all times, besides almost hourly inter-course with their Overseers and other officers of the prison.

"In the last annual report of the Inspectors, they say, that 'fully impressed with the necessity of a watchful care over the moral and mental improvement of the prisoners, as constituting a fundamental principle in this, as in all penitentiary reform, we are endeavoring to effect some improvements in the present plan of such instruction, particularly as relates to the education in reading and writing, thereby to enlarge the number of those who obtain this knowledge while in confinement.'

"Within the last year the moral and rudimental instruction has been divided. The former has been left, as heretofore, under the law, together with such religious teaching as each prisoner may desire, and from whatever professional teacher he may select. The latter has been intrusted to a competent person, who acts as an Overseer when required. Ample time is thus given to both branches of learning; and thus a schoolmaster has been successfully introduced into the prison, whose chief duty it is to teach the ignorant to read and write, and practical arithmetic."

The Inspectors in their report for 1846 report as follows:

"What may be the analogy between crime and disease, so far as relates to general cause and effect in the moral and physical constitution, is not intended to be here the subject of discussion. It may, however, become the theme for serious and important inquiry and examination.

"The causes of crime as certainly exist as the causes of disease, for both are but effects in themselves. Some crimes are committed from an imperfection in the moral organization, while others are the result of sudden and exciting moral affections; the former will continue to be repeated so long as the cause remains, and the latter may never occur again, because the excitement may never reappear. The effect of punishment in these two cases would be different, and hence a primary object of punishment should be to correct the cause of the moral disturbance which has produced the crime. The separate system is peculiarly adapted to such purpose, and as the subject of prison discipline continues to receive the attention of the intelligent observer, unforeseen benefits may result from the adaptation of punishment to the correction or remedy for these moral disorders.

"The aim and end of imprisonment for crime is punishment, as the first consequence; and in considering the subject of penitentiary discipline, care should be taken not to lose sight of this primary object. The law consigns the convict to restraint of his personal liberty in a prison for a violation or infraction of its decrees, and in the prison he is to be subjected to treatment which is in unison with the object for which he was sentenced. The judgment of conviction is but a forfeiture of certain natural rights, as a recompense to society for his inability to regard and obey those regulations which have been established for the protection of the rights of individuals which constitute such community. At this point the power of the law ceases over the convict, for it has exhausted its power in the accomplishment of all its ends. By the present enlightened policy of our State Penitentiary discipline, the convict thus situated, while undergoing punishment, is sought to be improved, benefited, reformed. In this, society has a deep interest; for if the convict at the expiration of the term of imprisonment is improved in his moral character, encouraged to refrain from the commission of offenses against the law, reformed in his habits, and taught those religious or moral lessons of practical utility which will avail him on his again commingling with society—deterred by punishment from crime—the community has gained twofold by such an imprisonment; it has punished and improved a prisoner, and made an example for the warning of all who are, or may be disposed to become, enemies of social order.

"To these ends the separate system of penitentiary discipline is eminently conducive; and as they are and ever should be the prominent features of prison discipline, that system which promotes them with the most certainty and effect should be considered as the best adapted to the purposes which an enlightened people, a regenerated Penal Code, and the instincts of a just and benevolent public opinion, should seek to attain. Pennsylvania has nobly set the example; she made the experiment at a time when doubts and difficulties, impediment and hinderance, were clouding the prospect; but year after year has brought to light the wisdom of the founders of the system, and added proof upon proof of its complete success. It is now no longer an experiment; but the separate system of prison discipline speaks in the voice of experience, subjected to the test of strict trial, to the spirit of progress of this age. Its arguments are facts; and its power of convincement over the minds of the enlightened, and unbiased, and unprejudiced, is found to exist in the cumulative evidence which is adduced to maintain that all it ever promised has been more than realized.

"Irrespective of the results which are to be found in our own State and Federal Union in support of the great features of our prison reform and meliorated discipline, the testimony of France, England, and Prussia is fully sufficient to seal its success. In these countries the system has been subjected to the most scrutinizing examination, and the most able and distinguished champions of social improvement have, after long and arduous inquiry, awarded to the Pennsylvania system their support. However these lights may be sought to be kept 'hidden under a bushel,' they have nevertheless shown in the brightness of honest conviction. It is not to be supposed that improvements are not, or have not been suggested, on the plan of the administration of the separate system; this has never been asserted; but whatever these improvements may be, so long as the distinctive features of the Pennsylvania plan are adhered to, so long will that system remain in its original integrity. These features are: Separation of the prisoners from each other at all times; moral and intellectual improvement; honest and persuasive efforts to reform and reclaim the prisoners; prevention, by this constant separation from each other, of the evil of contamination and the prejudicial influence which must arise from the association of the more or less hardened offenders; the prevention, by separation, of the acquaintance and knowledge which the community of evil-minded persons obtain of each other by association in the place of punishment; the ability which is afforded, by the separation of offenders, to individualize the corrective and reformatory treatment best suited to their peculiar characters; the almost certain consequence which results from the separate system, of making those no worse who cannot be made better by the infliction of the punishment they undergo; the addition of all improvements which experience and not mere theory suggests in the improvement of the moral and physical condition of the prisoners.

" These are the principles on which the Pennsylvania system is based; these rendered it antagonistical to the congregate system. If experience has proved that one plan is better than the other, if the prisoner and the community are benefited by the operation of one rather than the other, then to the best mode the other must give place. Improve the details of administration as they require and as experience suggests, and the consequences must be that these improvements will only tend to increase the superiority of the separate system over all others."

In the forty-second report of the Inspectors to the Legislature, dated February 27, 1871, they say:

"It will be observed by the returns made by the Inspectors in this report that a large number of prisoners have been sentenced for unusually long terms of imprisonment. These were for crimes of the highest grades, and the individuals are reported to be men of dangerous character in society. When it is known that by the commutation law a ten-year sentence can, by the 'good conduct' of the prisoner, be diminished by at least twenty-three months, based on the ratio directed in the law, there is no real advantage to the public from these sentences. The words of the law are: 'One month on each of the first two years, of two months on each succeeding year to the fifth year, and of three months on each following year to the tenth year, and of four months on each remaining year of the term of their sentence.' It never has been the opinion of the Inspectors of this penitentiary that long sentences to this institution, or any penitentiary on the separate or individual treatment system, are productive of benefits to the State or the convict. The certainty of punishment is more to be regarded than its duration, so far as society is protected and crime punished by the example of convictions of offenders. Time is no true element in punishment by imprisonment. Long sentences do not reform the individual, nor protect the public security, nor produce that fear in the crime-class which prevents their committing crime. The fact that every offender is punished for his crime has the effect which is sought to be produced by penal laws.

"In the Massachusetts State Penitentiary during the year ending September 30, 1870, there was a total population of seven hundred and seventy-four convicts. Of these sixty-three were pardoned. The sentences of six of those were for life, six for ten years, two for twenty years, two for fifteen years, and the others for from one to ten years each. The better way to state it will be to say that of fifty-seven prisoners, the six for life omitted, the average sentence was seven years three months and eleven days, while the time served when they were pardoned was four years two months and eight days. It is not, therefore, a patent remedy for heinous offenses that the convict is sentenced for long terms, or even 'for life' imprisonment in that State, where, it is to be presumed, the action of the public authorities is governed by integrity, wisdom, and intelligence.

"It is stated that the Executive of the State of New York during the year 1870 issued eighty-five pardons, thirty-four commutations, and one reprieve. Of the pardons, sixteen were on account of ill health; five, insane; ten, innocent; and three for discovering plots among prisoners. Of the pardoned prisoners, two were sentenced for twenty years, five for fifteen years, nine for ten years, one for nineteen years, two for life, and three were sentenced to be hung. All but two were sentenced since 1860.

"No reference is here made of the 'commutation' for shorter periods of imprisonment than the sentence.

"During the year 1870, of the nine hundred and fifty-three total population in this penitentiary, fourteen were pardoned. Of these, thirteen were by the State of Pennsylvania, and one by the United States: for ill health, none; insane, none—all fourteen for special reasons.

"The average term of sentences was three years nine months and twenty-three days; and the average time served, one year eight months and one day.

"To a prison on the separate system the average sentences for the lesser degrees of crime, when punishment promptly follows the offense, might be fixed at two years as the maximum, while a five years' sentence in most cases might be sufficient for those offenses in the commission of which human life was not put in peril. For young offenders, for the first offense, it is very questionable if any advantage results to society or the individual by a longer imprisonment than one year, unless for exceptional cases.

"It is to be remarked that the primary object of a wise administration of penal laws, regulating the punishment by imprisonment of individuals, should be to prevent the creation of a crime-class by the association of convicts in communities after their imprisonment is terminated. The consequences resulting from such a state of things are to be feared, since by this association desperate men, each known to the other to have been a convict, conspire to commit crimes, and by this association they more easily escape arrest and defy conviction. The separate system of imprisonment, on this ground, is a protection to the public, while it presents the best opportunity for introducing to the convict's attention those reformatory agencies which it is the part of Christian benevolence ever to hold out to the just and the unjust.

"The Inspectors feel justified in calling to the attention of the Legislature the most gratifying fact that in other States some of the prominent features of the administration of the Pennsylvania system of penitentiary discipline are receiving both recognition and approval. For many years past the Inspectors, in their annual reports to your honorable bodies, have given the convictions of their judgment, from practical experience, that the government of penal institutions should be intrusted to those whose capacity, knowledge, experience, and integrity alone qualify them for such responsible duties. It has been found in this penitentiary that honesty and capability, with intelligent observation of the practical working of the system of punishment, on the part of the executive officers, were essential to secure the purposes of penitentiary discipline. Frequent change in the executive officers, or their selection on any other recommendation than fitness and fidelity, has ever been condemned as most injurious to the interests intrusted to the Inspectors to guard. Almost alone in these opinions for so long a period of time, it is now with great satisfaction the Inspectors learn that the Prison Discipline Association of the State of New York, in a public meeting, adopted a "Memorial" to the authorities of that State, which thus gives testimony in support of the Pennsylvania practice in this respect:

"'The remedy which the association proposes is a radical one, involving an entire change in the organization of the government of the prisons. Their examination has extended over the whole period of the existence of the present form of that government. They say:

"'By the Constitution, all the State Prisons are put wholly under the government of three Inspectors, who hold office for three years, and are elected one every year, and who superintend the State Prisons and appoint all the officers therein. They are called Inspectors, but are in fact governors of the prisons and controllers of the system, subject to no supervision or inspection, except such as the Legislature may direct, and that of the imperfect power given to the Prison Association. Every year one of them is thrown into the arena of party politics.'

"The 'Memorial' proposes the State Constitution to be amended so that—

"'There shall be a Board of Managers of Prisons, to be composed of five persons appointed by the Governor, with the advice and consent of the Senate, who shall hold office for ten years.

"'That Board shall have the charge and superintendence of the prisons, and have such powers and perform such duties in respect to other prisons in the State as the Legislature may prescribe.

"'They shall appoint a Secretary, who shall be removable at their pleasure, and perform such duties as the Legislature or Board may direct, and receive a salary to be determined by law.

"'The Board shall appoint the Warden, Clerk, Physician, and Chaplain of each State Prison, and shall have power to remove them for cause only, after opportunity to be heard on written charges.

"'All other officers of each prison shall be appointed by the Warden thereof, and be removable at his pleasure.

"'The Governor may remove any of the Managers for misconduct or neglect of duty, after opportunity to be heard on written charges.

"'The five Managers first appointed shall, as the Legislature may direct, be so classified that the term of one shall expire at the end of each two years during the first ten years.

"'This amendment shall go into effect on the first Monday of January next after its adoption by the people.'

"If you, gentlemen of the Legislature, will refer to the recent reports from the Inspectors of this State Penitentiary, you will observe that the 'contract system' of employing convict labor has been condemned as most injurious to society, unjust, and unworthy of an enlightened civilization.

"Under this plan of working convicts, in congregation, by contract with employers, every consideration but the benefit of the convict was absorbed in profit making out of the criminals whom the State punished for violating its laws. This profit was the claimed advantage of this plan of labor, so unworthy of a people who thus justified the brutalizing of those who were young, or convicted for a first offense, as well as those who had, it might be, some redeeming characteristics, in one common mass with the atrocious and hardened veteran in a life of crime. The Inspectors, in these reports, were the only protestants against this contract system. The experience, however, of the society alluded to has, at last, enabled it, in the 'Memorial' to which reference has been made, thus to condemn this plan of prison labor.

"Thus the 'Memorial' continues:

*   *   *   *   *   *   *   *   *   *   *   *

"'On the other side of the account this tendency to augmentation does not seem to have prevailed to the same extent. In Sing Sing, in 1847, convicts put on contracts were let at 35 cents a day; in 1869, they were let at from 30 to 40 cents a day. In Auburn they were let, in 1847, at from 30 to 50 cents a day; and in 1869, at an average of 50 cents a day. Thus while the rate of wages, inuring to the benefit of the State, increased not over 50 per cent, the expenditures, at the cost of the State, increased during the same period at the rate of 300 per cent. The contract system seeming, even to the Inspectors, to be a failure, they have attempted within the last five or six years to abandon it in a measure, and have had recourse to labor conducted under their immediate supervision, with what success the foregoing statements show. Within the past five years, from 1865 to 1869, inclusive, the deficiency of earnings to pay expenses has been $1,094,151 05; an amount larger than the deficiencies of the whole previous eighteen years; and the appropriations from the State treasury have been $4,193,760 07, being about equal in amount to the appropriations for all those previous years.'

"Again from this 'Memorial:'

"'The effort, however, during the whole of the last twenty-two years has been a failure, and is, year after year, becoming more signally and disastrously so.

"'The following is a table of the number of prisoners at the beginning and at the end of the present system:

	1848.	1869.
Auburn	473	950
Sing Sing	604	1,279
Female	84	130
Clinton	181	504
Asylum (not built until 1859)		78
Totals	1,342	2,932

Increase, 119 per cent.

Expenditures for the Same Period.

	1848.	1869.
Female	$11,790 54	$25,856 26
Sing Sing	97,221 41	351,082 57
Auburn	66,969 41	171,015 81
Clinton	41,510 16	317,309 70
Asylum		13,954 92
Totals	$217,491 52	$879,219 26

Increase, over 300 per cent.

" 'The following shows the condition of affairs from the beginning of the system to the present day:

Table of Progress from 1847 to 1869, inclusive.

YEARS.	Number of Prisoners.	Expenditures.	Earnings.	Deficits.
1847	1,421	$125,833 85	$120,860 08	$4,973 77
1848	1,366	204,091 80	110,658 94	93,432 86
1849	1,380	188,754 74	139,285 34	49,469 40
1850	1,621	208,397 74	158,422 25	50,975 49
1851	1,703	266,011 20	178,914 09	27,097 11
1852	1,852	211,751 80	193,303 11	18,448 69
1853	1,967	250,818 24	216,110 65	34,707 59
1854	2,005	272,413 03	213,178 03	59.235 00
1855	1,957	233,445 59	197,230 29	35,215 30
1856	1,910	223,477 99	197,105 13	25,372 66
1857	1,890	212,714 17	191,783 63	20,930 54
1858	2,126	250,356 02	149,173 98	101,182 04
1859	2,538	279,333 68	189,836 52	89,497 16
1860	2,729	291,744 69	238,627 56	53,117 13
1861	2,818	388,904 76	265,552 78	23,351 98
1862	2,697	294,685 57	228,481 51	66,204 06
1863	2,131	291,216 53	228,330 74	62,885 79
1864	1,915	342.794 55	255,957 81	86,836 63
1865	1,885	414,713 30	202,506 57	212,306 73
1866	2,368	463,995 46	229,413 83	234,581 63
1867	2,920	779,579 61	600,013 43	179,566 18
1868	2,881	844,373 93	601,630 05	242,734 88
1869	2,930	879,219 26	654,157 68	225,061 63
Making an aggregate deficit in twenty-three years of				$1,997,084 45

" 'The foregoing statements, though they show a result sufficiently disastrous to convince the association that the present system is finan- cially a failure, do not show the whole extent of the disaster.'

"These quotations from the 'Memorial' are made with satisfaction, because they are most important testimony in themselves, and unwillingly sustain the Inspectors of this penitentiary in their expressed opinions on the subject, and show that the time is coming when the broader and more philosophic views of penitentiary discipline which a scientific examination of so increasingly important a subject will produce, may yet become triumphant over the ignorance of bigotry, or the baser, ignoble, and narrow motives which have so long controlled the partisan management of institutions too generally considered only as public receptacles for convicted felons. It would have been worthy of those who in this 'Memorial' have so thoroughly exposed the evils against which they invoke rebuke and remedy, if they had, at least, given to Pennsylvania some credit for a consistent opposition to them. It would have been simple justice to our State, to have pointed to her as an example for the reforms which the 'Memorial' now so markedly approves and advocates in the penitentiaries of New York.

"The following extract from the 'Memorial' is so thorough a justification of the discipline, as well as the 'separate system' itself, contrasted with the 'congregate plan,' now adopted in New York, and heretofore claimed to be the best system of prison government, that it needs no comment:

"'MORAL ADMINISTRATION.—It is now about twenty-five years since a change was introduced into the moral government of our prisons. Prior to that time the prominent ideas had been punishment and earnings. This change was the introduction of rewards as well as punishments, and keeping the reformation of the prisoners in view as the main object. Appended is a brief enumeration of the measures employed, of their defective execution, and of the benefits that may result from them.

"'*The Mode of Enforcing Obedience.*—Formerly it was by means of the whip, but with occasional resorts to other means of violence. In 1830 the use of the whip was abolished among the females, and in 1849 among the males, except in cases of insurrection, revolt, and self-defense. The substitute provided for it by law was solitary confinement; and in the latter year the law directed solitary cells for that purpose to be built in all the prisons. Those cells have not yet been built, and during the succeeding twenty years other means of force were resorted to, until, in 1869, such means, so far as they assumed the form of the "shower-bath, crucifix, and yoke and buck," were forbidden. This was done without providing any substitutes, and the consequences were disastrous. As soon as the passage of the law was known, a general uneasiness in all the prisons was shown. This was followed by individual acts of violence. At Auburn a keeper was assaulted by a convict, struck down by a hammer, and his life saved only by the interposition of another convict. At Clinton a keeper was stabbed, and disabled for life; and at Sing Sing a keeper was struck down by a bar of iron, and the officers fired upon by a convict. Then ensued more general movements. At Auburn whole shops refused to work. At Sing Sing one hundred and fifty convicts, on one day, and some five hundred or six hundred the next day, refused to work; and at Clinton there was a general conspiracy to escape, which was fortunately discovered in time to be prevented. At Sing Sing twenty, at Auburn twelve, and at Clinton ten of the ringleaders were kept in irons and chained to the cells for several months, and it is believed that nothing but the action of the well-disposed among the prisoners prevented more general outbreaks, and perhaps an emptying of our prisons of the great body of their inmates. The use of blows upon the prisoners is forbidden only in our State Prisons. In all the local penitentiaries, to which many of our State prisoners have been removed, it is still allowed; and in the State Prisons it seems to be left to the discretion of the officer immediately in charge to determine what is the condition of revolt, insurrection, or self-defense, which will justify a resort to the whip. A general system of discipline to prevail alike in all the prisons, and which shall prevent the officers immediately affected by disorder from acting as complainant, Judge, and executioner, and which will cultivate the habit of self-government now so predominant among the great number of the prisoners, is a measure greatly to be desired.

"' The Introduction of Libraries.—This was begun before the adoption of our present Constitution. So thoroughly was this sanctioned by the Legislature that, during the past twenty-four years, appropriations for this purpose have been made to the amount of about $20,000, and the agents were directed to append to their annual reports a catalogue of the prison libraries. This duty has never been performed.

"' Teaching the Prisoners.—The law has provided, in this respect, that the Chaplains, besides religious services in the chapels, shall visit the convicts in their cells, and devote one hour each work-day, and the afternoon of each Sunday, to giving them religious and moral instruction. So the law has provided for ten teachers in the prisons, at an annual expense of $1,500, to instruct the unlearned in the first rudiments of education. In these respects, also, there is a great waste of the wise benevolence of the law, owing to the absence of a well digested plan of instruction; for at present the system of instruction is so conducted as to amount to a farce.

"' Overwork and Aid to Discharged Convicts.—The original allowance to convicts on their discharge was $3 to each from the prison funds. It is now increased to $10; and a practice has grown up, not yet sanctioned or organized by law, of allowing the prisoners to earn money for themselves, over and above their allotted stents. This also demands an organized system to prevent an abuse of the privilege by prisoners and contractors, to guard against unjust partiality by the officers in charge, and to accord it impartially to all.

"' Commutation of Sentence.—There is now prevailing in all our State Prisons (but not in all local ones) a measure of enabling the convicts, by their own good conduct, to shorten their terms of imprisonment. In 1863, out of one thousand one hundred and twenty-three prisoners who left during the year, only eighty-two left by expiration of sentence, while eight hundred and twenty-nine went out by commutation under the law. In this there is great danger, as well as the actual existence of partiality and injustice, which nothing can prevent so well as the creation of an intelligent and judicious tribunal.'

"Notwithstanding this is the forty-second yearly report of the Inspectors to the Legislature of this State on the practical results of the Pennsylvania system of separate treatment of prisoners, yet even now there are many, professing to be possessed of general information on penal science as applied to prison populations and systems of convict punishment, who entirely mistake the principles, and are ignorant of the practical results, which these reports exhibit of the Pennsylvania system of penitentiary convict discipline.

" It is not possible in this report to condense the statements made in the forty-one which have preceded it. But justice to this penitentiary, at least, requires that for the past year, 1870, a comparison should be made of the exhibits of one penitentiary on each system of convict treatment. The Charlestown Penitentiary of Massachusetts is taken as best managed on the congregate, and this penitentiary, on the separate system, for this purpose.

" In the Massachusetts Penitentiary the total population for 1870 is given as seven hundred and seventy-four. Out of this number there were fourteen deaths, or 1.81 per cent.

" In this penitentiary the total population for 1870 was nine hundred and fifty-three. Out of this number there were twelve deaths, or 1.26 per cent. The difference in population is as seven hundred and seventy-four is to nine hundred and fifty-three, or one hundred and seventy-nine excess in this penitentiary.

" Of the seven hundred and seventy-four in Massachusetts, sixty-three convicts were pardoned.

" Of the nine hundred and fifty-three in Pennsylvania, fourteen convicts were pardoned.

" In the Massachusetts Penitentiary two convicts were sent to the Insane Asylum.

" In this penitentiary three convicts were of unsound mind; but, by the treatment in the penitentiary, are reported by the Resident Physician, Dr. Klapp, to be ' fully restored to reason.'

"As to the discipline or government of the prisoners in the Massachusetts Penitentiary, it is stated that ' it is not to be supposed that six hundred men, some of them unquestionably bad, but more of them unfortunate; some of them receiving the just reward for crimes committed, whilst others, in their own minds, at least, are suffering unjustly, can be managed and controlled without occasional friction.'

" In this penitentiary the discipline has been maintained; for it appears that ' we have had a prison population of nine hundred and fifty-three convicts, many of whom are among the most desperate men who have ever been imprisoned within these walls. Yet quiet and good order have prevailed, and by the vigilance and active care of the officers no escape, even into the yard, has been effected, and no harsh or severe treatment has been found needful.'

" The above extracts, at least, suggest the inquiry, if congregating into one mass those convicts, the control of whom is described as producing ' occasional friction,' is the wisest plan for their proper government, or for the best interests of society.

" In Massachusetts, with seven hundred and seventy-four convicts as the total population for 1870, ' our expenses,' as given, were $122,265 72.

" In this penitentiary, with a total population for 1870 of nine hundred and fifty-three convicts, our expenses were $98,886 48.

" In the Massachusetts Prison the recommitments on seven hundred and seventy-four convicts, total population during 1870, were one hundred, or equal to 13.44 per cent.

" In this penitentiary the total recommitments on five thousand two hundred and ninety-eight convicts, the whole number liable to reconviction since 1829, were five hundred and thirty-two, or for, say, forty years, 10 per cent.

" It is shown by this comparative statement that the ' separate system '

10D

has triumphantly vindicated itself against open, as well as covert assaults, which ignorance, prejudice, or that 'little knowledge' so dangerous in scientific studies, has from time to time made against it.

"It would not be presuming too much to believe that you, gentlemen of the Legislature, will invoke the experience of this State institution before enacting into laws measures relating to convict discipline, penal jurisprudence, or crime-cause, either for prevention or punishment. Surely the knowledge of facts, and the practical working of principles or theories on penal science for a period of forty years, might be important to test either new propositions or determine the proposed benefits that the love of change always promises as the undoubted results thereby to be attained.

"The necessity for legislation presupposes an understanding of the subject-matter, and no source of information which is reliable, or experience which is respectable, or knowledge which has been carefully and intelligently acquired, should be ignored while such legislation is being perfected for its purpose. Your own experience, gentlemen of the Legislature, makes this self-evident.

"While the primary purpose of this report to the Legislature is to comply with the law directing it to be made, yet the scope of the direction that besides the specific return, 'such information' may be given as may be deemed 'expedient' for making this 'institution effectual in the punishment and reformation of offenders,' implies the expression of such suggestions as more generally relate to the subject of penal jurisprudence.

"It is believed that the statistical information contained in the tables submitted indicates the careful investigation of the case of each convict, and the confidence established between the individual and the prison authorities. This tends to create in the mind of the prisoners the impression that though convicts, human sympathy is not to be denied them, and that even in prison there is an interest felt in their welfare and improvement. To some, this is a first lesson in reformation; with others, it awakens the good impressions of childhood. The influence on all is to facilitate the acceptance of any agencies that are designed for reform.

"But, apart from these considerations, the contributions made in these reports to penal science, limited though they are to the investigation of the population of this penitentiary, it is hoped will invite the Legislature to favorably consider the great importance of authorizing by law, comprehensive reports to be obtained by a department of the State Government on those subjects which are intimately connected with unhealthful developments in the social conditions of certain classes in the whole population.

"If such information could be obtained and systematically arranged, it would enable the Legislature to understand what legislation was most necessary for the public good.

"Crime-cause would be better understood, prevention and punishment could be so adjusted as to separate the proper treatment of those who most needed either, under laws adapted to each.

"It might be then ascertained that industrial schools and reformatory institutions for the first offenses of the young offenders were more essential than neglected or ill-regulated prisons or more penitentiaries.

"From such information, the conclusions might be arrived at, that county prisons on the separate system, properly governed and administered, should be the rule for all large counties, rather than the exception in Pennsylvania.

"It could hardly be doubted that with such reports carefully made the Legislature could better determine how the money of the people might be liberally and wisely expended for the poor, the suffering, the idle, the vicious, the criminal, the ignorant, and the unfortunate. From each section of the State the real condition of these classes would be presented, and then it would be better known how to relieve, restrain, prevent, punish, and educate. It probably would indicate that for all classes a general rule was impossible. True philosophy would teach the adaptation of individual treatment to individual, or special developments of causes producing particular results.

"It would more certainly enable a judicious classification to be made of remedial, preventive, and punitive agencies, and prevent the pauperization of individuals into an idle or indigent class, or a more dreaded crime-class. If no other result was reached, it would be possible to establish by law some system by which education in handicraft skilled labor could be within the reach of those of the young who sought it, and at the same time be approved and applauded by an enlightened public opinion.

"Reference has already been made to the 'Commutation Law' by which sentences of the convicts are shortened by their 'good conduct' while under conviction. This plan has been described as a statutory recommendation to the Executive to discharge the convict before the sentence inflicted by the judicial power expires. While it is not a pardon under the exercise of the constitutional prerogative of the Governor, it is a device which, by legislation, controls the judicial and directs Executive action. How wise such legislation may be is no part of the province of the Inspectors to consider, much less to determine. It is now brought to the notice of the Legislature for the purpose of inviting attention to the precedent thus established. If the Legislature can enact a law by which a judicial sentence can be terminated before it expires by its own limitation, then it becomes a most important question to consider if this principle cannot be applied for the purpose of more effectually securing the aim of punishment by imprisonment in particular cases. It sometimes happens that the exercise of the pardoning power is subject to public criticism. There are no doubt cases in which there are grounds for this animadversion, but the Inspectors do not desire to express any opinion on cases of which they have no direct knowledge from their official relations with the prisoner.

"The comparison hereinbefore made between the pardons granted by Massachusetts, New York, and Pennsylvania, shows that in this State Executive clemency has been very sparingly exercised on convicts in this penitentiary.

"It is undoubtedly true that there are now in this institution several convicts who are fully entitled to pardon, if the purpose of their punishment was to qualify them for restoration to liberty, with benefit to themselves and advantage to society.

"To reach these cases is difficult of accomplishment under the present system. If a pardon is asked, then the Inspectors may be regarded as exceeding the line of their duty, and their action misunderstood or misconstrued; or they might be subjected to applications from unworthy persons; or the Executive might fail to appreciate their motives. Nevertheless, these cases exist; and continuing in prison those who have been brought within the effects of punishment, and over whom it has exercised all the influences designed by law and justice, is of very doubtful propriety. It is imprisonment for no purpose. The example, the prevention of crime, as they are supposed to be reached by a conviction of the guilty, has been eected by such conviction and the infliction of the punishment. The only remaining purpose of the law which this punishment proposed has been produced. Society has been protected; the example has been made; those who are intended to be warned have had their warning; and the individual who is punished is now alone to be considered. If this punishment has caused him to repent of his wickedness, and determine, in so far as he can, to reform, then his liberty is more a right than a favor, for longer incarceration is useless to him, and society gains nothing thereby. That these are the well considered opinions of the Inspectors will appear from the following extracts from their reports to the Legislature.

"From the report for the year 1852 the following extract is taken:

"'The Inspectors cannot close this report without again briefly calling the attention of the General Assembly to the subject of revising the Penal Code so as to shorten the minimum period of confinement affixed to certain crimes. The daily observation of the effects of separate and solitary confinement, with the influences connected with it in this penitentiary, have fully convinced them that a much greater degree of good would be achieved by shortening most of the sentences for first offenses, and particularly those of all young offenders. For this latter class a few months' confinement, or a year at most, would produce in general vastly more salutary effects than longer terms. The Inspectors are gratified to know that throughout the Eastern District of the State this fact has become apparent to most of the judicial tribunals, and is acted upon to the limits of the law. Should this disposition become general, and a larger discretion be given by law, it would remove, in a great measure, the necessity that is now often believed to exist for the exercise of the pardoning power.'

"The Pennsylvania system is best described as the individual treatment of convicts, as contrasted with that in other States, which is the congregate or class treatment. This distinction is important while considering the views now under discussion.

"Again, in the report for 1853 it is remarked:

"'The Inspectors have again to remark on the subject of the duration of sentences inflicted upon juvenile offenders. It is with regret the Inspectors find that, of the prisoners admitted during the year 1853, there are twenty-two under twenty-one years of age, and forty-eight under twenty-five years of age. The Inspectors are of opinion that in cases of first conviction of minors, or those of immature age, unless for crimes of the most aggravated character, a short term of imprisonment is of far greater benefit to the individual than one which is calculated to punish beyond the period when moral influences have awakened in the heart strong feelings of repentance and a desire to reform. Evil associates, bad example, and a want of proper parental care and watchfulness, admonition, and control, lead the young into crimes. When, therefore, imprisoned as a punishment, the young convict is brought to feel, probably for the first time, the truth of the proverb, that the way of the transgressor is hard, then it is that the most judicious counsel and advice induces the most decided improvement. It is believed that if in such instances the prisoner were set at liberty, a revolution would be effected in his morals and habits, and a new career would be sought after for his future life. The Inspectors make these suggestions in the hope that good may result from their careful consideration.'

"In the report for the year 1854, the Inspectors thus speak on this interesting subject:

"'The Inspectors again feel it their duty to call the attention of the Legislature to the length of sentences inflicted for first offenses, and also on young offenders. It is no longer a question that severity in punishment is no prevention of crime; neither does severity of punishment produce the desired effect upon the offender. The causes of crime should be more fully investigated after a conviction, and have a potent influence in determining the duration of the punishment. There is a period in the history of every criminal's punishment when his liberation would most benefit him, and hence society would gain, by the improvement afforded in reclaiming an offender. Those whose constant intercourse with convicts enables them to form an opinion upon the subject, will admit that such periods occur, when most decided advantage would result from the prisoner's liberation. One mode, to be sure a most imperfect one, to effect this object, is to shorten the sentence, as much as a proper regard to the interests of society would justify, in all cases of first convictions and convictions of young offenders. The Inspectors feel the force of these views, and they have ventured again to invoke legislative attention to the subject. This is not the occasion to suggest any plan to modify and improve the present laws upon this subject; but it is hoped that the time will come when the Legislature of Pennsylvania will take the important subject of the present Penal Code, as it relates to our admirable system of penitentiary punishment, into consideration. Sporadic reforms are worse than useless. Labors of those who are required to learn while they attempt to teach, are vain. The familiarity of long experience, careful and earnest devotion to the subject, and an interest in the questions involved, above and beyond an interest in self, are among the qualifications which a proper reform in penal jurisprudence will require at the hands of those who undertake the task.'

"From the report for 1860:

"'It will be observed that the Inspectors have heretofore refrained from presenting reforms in the Penal Code, in relation to young criminals. It was hoped and believed, that one of the citizens to whom the codification of the penal laws was referred, might have been selected for his interest in, and ability to understand, the subject. If such a selection had been made, it would have resulted beneficially, by the incorporation into the penal law of a provision to meet the class of cases to which the attention of the Legislature has been called.

"'The Inspectors do not feel themselves required, either by law or from their official position, to do more than make such "observations" as they deem of importance to the public, or prisoners.

"'Lest, however, it might be by some attributed to their silence that they have no practical suggestions to offer, they most respectfully submit, as the substance for amendments to the present law, the following proposition:

"'That in all cases of first conviction for crime, of minors, the term

of imprisonment shall be terminated by the Inspectors with the consent
of the President Judge of the Court in which such minor was sentenced,
when in their opinion the punishment has produced its expected results.

"'That in all cases of first conviction for crime, of persons between
twenty-one and twenty-five years of age, the term of imprisonment shall
in like manner be lessened, as a reward for good conduct, by the reduction of three days out of every thirty after the first twelve months of
imprisonment.

"'That in all cases of first conviction for crime, of minors, the jury
trying the case shall find by their verdict if the father of the minor (he
being alive and within the jurisdiction of the process of the Commonwealth) was negligent and derelict in his parental duties toward said
minor, and on so finding, the Court shall cause said father to be held to
pay the costs to the Commonwealth of said trial.

"'The Inspectors have ventured respectfully to make these suggestions,
with the view to remedy the evil which has been thus authentically
brought to the attention of the General Assembly.

"'It will not be denied that the necessity for legislation is most serious. That it is increasing, a superficial examination of the facts herein
set out cannot fail to teach the observer. That the want of parental
control is demoralizing a large and increasing number of our youths,
the consequences are manifest. The minor is ungoverned, wayward,
vagabond, vicious, contaminated, contaminating, and convict. The
moralist, as well as the Christian, must deplore such causes and consequences.

"'It is believed that the most unconcerned for the welfare of society
and its constituents would hardly agree that penitentiary discipline
should take the place of primary parental teachings and supervisory
restraint.

"'The least benevolent will fully consent to the principle, as one of
justice, that the child only should not be punished for its parent's neglect
or disregard of his duties.

"'If in either case society stands in the place of the parent, magnanimity and mercy both plead that the most reformatory and beneficent
influences should be extended to such unfortunates.'

"In the report for 1867, the Inspectors use the following language:

"'It is of vital importance that the individualities and characteristics
and surroundings of the accused should be ascertained on his trial, and
their just consideration should be taken fully into the judicial determination of the punishment. Arbitrary or merely conventional sentences, operating on classes not persons, are unphilosophical, and often
unjust, both to the individual and the community. Again, take the
crime of larceny. It should be divided into degrees. The highest, and
each in sequence to the lowest, should be determined at the trial, from
the facts and circumstances and the characteristics of the accused. To
determine beforehand, when framing the indictment, the degree of crim-
inality, before the accused can explain or defend his acts, is at war with
the principle which seeks to protect the accused till he is found beyond
the operation of the presumptions of innocence. This system adopted
as to all crimes or offenses has the advantage of placing the accused in
the exact position in which his acts place him, not that which the definition or description of a class of acts would compel him to occupy
without the explanatory benefits he alone could produce. Again, it

would not make individuals more criminal than they really are, and thus often unwisely add to the crime-class those who would else never be associated with it. The injurious effects of any system which augments the number of convicts, placing on them the distinguishing mark of enemies to public safety, becomes more and more apparent as population increases. The true principle of legislation on this branch of the subject is to make few acts of individual crimes, and as few members of society criminals as a due regard for the safety of life, rights, and property will justify. The more simple the crime code, the more it is rendered flexible in individual application; the less rigorous and unbending; the greater opportunity to take the principles of the common law as preferable to those of a statute, and the greater the responsibilities that are placed on the judiciary and taken from the law-making power—in all these respects the greater and more substantial are the benefits which society secures. It is thus that society speaks its voice, under the restraints of law, in each particular case.

"'Following this view as to the code, we come to consider the punishment of crimes. By the present practice there is really no standard. The offense too often determines the sentence, because no opportunity is permitted to investigate all the circumstances of each case; nor is any authority granted for that judicial discretion which should always be an element in the official action of the ministers of justice. The maximum and the minimum of the term of punishment are the only judicial guides, and these regulate the judgment of Judges who, from the trial of the issue of fact, are informed by the verdict of the guilt of the accused. Every offender is actuated by different motives, influenced by various causes of crime; his peculiar position as an individual in society, his lack of advantages, his associations, his mental, moral, personal disabilities, all his individualities are hid from view, because the present system only presents one fact to be ascertained. The interests of society demand that crime be punished, and crime prevented; beyond that it has no other interest, so far as a particular offense is concerned. But growing out of the determination of that fact are vastly important considerations to the very best interests of society. For what degree of crime, for what period of time the guilty is to be sentenced, the motives and causes that induced him to violate law, the effect upon the individual directly and on society indirectly, are consequences which must result to society finally, to prejudice it to a greater or less degree if the guilty has been punished without regard to these questions. There is no more dangerous element in social condition than the feeling which harshness and injustice produce in the administration of justice. The first of the dangers is the unwillingness to convict for crime, or the anxiety in the minds of juries to except the case from the operations of these influences. Vibrating between the extremes of unwillingness to convict, and the prompt conviction, in the latter case to maintain the law by sporadic firmness in the administration of justice, creates a disrespect for the law. When one is guilty of a less crime than that for which he is indicted, but escapes because of the arbitrary or fixed definition of acts, as crimes, which the trial shows the accused has not made himself technically amenable to, there is left on the public mind a feeling of insecurity and a distrust of public justice. So on either hand the present system convicts a certain portion of offenders, and society has to be satisfied that all the guilty do not escape. If, however, the system of jurisprudence was in harmony with the views expressed as to the code, these defects would probably be remedied.

"'By the judicious subdivision into degrees, and the consequent reduction of the higher grades of crime, the assimilation of the offense to the acts and motives of the accused, the certainty of, as well as a wise discrimination in the punishment, the diminution of the number of individuals united with the crime-class, the better would it be for all the great interests associated in and protected by penal legislation.'

"That some system should be made lawful by which the opinion of the Inspectors, and that of the chief officers of the penitentiary, as to the propriety of discharging prisoners deserving liberation, would be effective in producing their discharge by competent authority, is most desirable. The Inspectors respectfully call this subject to the attention of the Legislature. It may not meet with favor until a thorough investigation of the question is made, free from those objections which a first impression is most likely to suggest."

The following is the bill of fare:

Monday.

Breakfast.—Coffee and bread.
Dinner.—Stewed mutton.
Supper.—Tea and bread.

Tuesday.

Breakfast.—Coffee and bread.
Dinner.—Bologna sausage and bread.
Supper.—Tea and bread.

Wednesday.

Breakfast.—Coffee and bread.
Dinner.—Beef and soup.
Supper.—Tea and bread.

Thursday.

Breakfast.—Coffee and bread.
Dinner.—Stewed beef.
Supper.—Tea and bread.

Friday.

Breakfast.—Coffee and bread.
Dinner.—Stewed mutton.
Supper.—Tea and bread.

Saturday.

Breakfast.—Coffee and bread.
Dinner.—Mutton and mutton soup.
Supper.—Tea and coffee.

Sunday.

Breakfast.—Coffee and bread.
Dinner.—Baked potpie.
Supper.—Tea and bread.

In addition to these, vegetables when in season are supplied at dinner, but breakfast and supper remain the same during the entire year. During the winter months sauerkraut is supplied once or twice a week. No canned goods are used. In the spring, onions and tomatoes are supplied.

The Warden receives a salary of $4,500 per annum; the Clerk, $2,000; the Moral Instructor, $1,500; and the Physician, $1,500. The Overseers or Guards are paid according to their term of service, receiving for the first five years, $800 per annum; second five years, $900 per annum; third five years, $1,000 per annum; fourth five years, $1,050 per annum; fifth five years, $1,100 per annum; thirty years and over, $1,200 per annum.

MASSACHUSETTS STATE PRISON.

In Massachusetts, the Commissioners of Prisons are five in number; two of whom are required to be women. They hold office for the term of five years, and are appointed by the Governor, with the advice and consent of the Council. They receive no compensation, but are allowed their personal expenses while engaged in official duties.

They have the general supervision of the State Prison and of the reformatory prison for women, and may make all necessary rules not repugnant to law, for the direction of the officers in the discharge of their duties; the government, employment, discipline, and instruction of the convicts. They also have power to make such rules in regard to the food, clothing, and bedding of the convicts, as the health, well being, and circumstances of each convict may require. The law, however, requires that all food, clothing, beds, and bedding shall be of good quality and in sufficient quantity for the sustenance and comfort of the convicts, and the bedding shall include mattresses, blankets, and pillows. After the rules have been established, they are to be laid before the Governor and Council, who may approve, annul, or modify them. One or more of the Commissioners must visit the State Prison and reformatory prison for women at least once in each month, and a majority of the Board must visit these prisons once in three months, and oftener if they consider it to be necessary, for the purpose of inspecting their books and management, and ascertaining whether the laws and rules are duly observed, the officers competent and faithful, and the convicts properly governed and employed. The full Board are required to visit these prisons semi-annually, and make a thorough examination of them.

They must report immediately to the Governor and Council all violations of law and omissions of duty which come to their knowledge, on the part of the Warden, Chaplain, Physician of the State Prison, or on the part of the Superintendent, Chaplain, or Physician of the reformatory prison for women. Every officer of the prison who holds his office at the pleasure of the Warden and Commissioners, who is found to be unfaithful or incompetent, or who uses intoxicating liquor as a beverage, the law declares shall be immediately removed, and in the event of a disagreement between the Warden and the Commissioners relating to the removal of any officer or employé, the subject may be referred to the Governor and Council, who may make such removal.

The Warden, Chaplain, and Physician and Surgeon of the State Prison are appointed by the Governor, with the advice and consent of the Council, and hold their offices during the Executive's pleasure. The Warden appoints the Deputy Warden and all other officers, subject to the approval of the Commissioners, and they hold thir offices during the pleasure of the Warden and Commissioners. The Warden has the right to appeal to the Governor in case there is a disagreement between him and the Commissioners concerning the removal of any officer, and, after reasonable notice to the Commissioners and a hearing, the Governor and Council may make the removal.

The Warden receives an annual salary of $3,500; the Chaplain, $2,000; the Physician and Surgeon, $1,000; the Deputy Warden, $2,000; the Clerk of the Turnkeys, $1,200; each Watchman who has been in the service of the prison for less than three years, $800; each Watchman who has been in the service for three years and less than six years, $1,000; and every Watchman who has been in the service for six years, $1,200.

No officer is allowed to receive any other perquisite, reward, or emolument, except there is allowed to the Warden and Deputy Warden sufficient house-room, with fuel and lights for themselves and their families. The Warden supplies his table at his own expense.

Neither the Warden nor any officer of the prison is permitted to be employed in any business for private emolument, or which does not pertain to the duties of his office. All officers, excepting the Clerk, Physician, and Chaplain, are required to wear, while on duty, such uniform, cap, or badge as may be from time to time prescribed by the Warden and Commissioners.

The bond of the Warden is $20,000, and the Warden and Deputy Warden are compelled to reside constantly within the precincts of the prison.

The law provides that the Warden may, with the consent of the Commissioners, cause a Sabbath-school to be maintained in the prison for the instruction of the convicts in their religious duties, and permit such persons as they consider suitable to attend the school as instructors. The Warden is authorized to maintain schools for the instruction of the prisoners at such times, excepting Sunday, as he, with the approval of the Commissioners, may fix from time to time, and under such rules and regulations as the Commissioners may prescribe, and he is permitted to expend for such purposes a sum not exceeding $2,000 a year.

The laws of the State provide that convicts sentenced to the punishment of hard labor in the prison shall be constantly employed for the benefit of the State, but no convict shall be employed in engraving of any kind; that the Warden, with the consent of one or more of the Commissioners, may, for such time as may be thought necessary to produce penitence, confine to solitary labor obstinate and refractory convicts.

Contract labor is forbidden, and the law prohibits the use of new machinery other than such as may be propelled by hand or foot power.

A General Superintendent of Prisons is appointed by the Governor, and he determines, in connection with the Warden, the industries to be pursued.

The number of prisoners employed at the same time in a single industry cannot exceed one twentieth of the number of persons employed in such industry in the State of Massachusetts, according to the classification given by the last census preceding such employment, unless a number in excess of this proportion is required to produce materials to be supplied in State and county institutions.

Among the various industries carried on are brushmaking, harness-making, boot and shoe making, manufacture of tinware, and gilding.

The rations for the convicts are as follows, although varied somewhat by the Warden, who, upon holidays and at other times at his discretion, introduces articles not named herein:

Sunday.

Breakfast.—Rice and milk, white bread, and coffee.
Dinner.—Baked fish or baked meat, white bread, fruit, and tea.

Monday.

Breakfast.—Cornmeal and milk, white bread, and coffee.
Dinner.—Corned beef and vegetables.
Supper.—White bread and tea.

Tuesday.

Breakfast.—Meat hash, white bread, and coffee.
Dinner.—Baked beans and graham bread.
Supper.—Corned beef, white bread, and tea.

Wednesday.

Breakfast.—Oatmeal and milk, white bread, and coffee.
Dinner.—Beef soup, potatoes, and white bread.
Supper.—White bread and tea.

Thursday.

Breakfast.—Meat hash, white bread, and coffee.
Dinner.—Baked beans and brown bread.
Supper.—Corned beef, white bread, and tea.

Friday.

Breakfast.—Mush and milk, white bread, and coffee.
Dinner.—Fish, potatoes, and white bread.
Supper.—White bread and tea.

Saturday.

Breakfast.—Meat hash, white bread, and coffee.
Dinner.—Beef soup, potatoes, and white bread.
Supper.—Corned beef, white bread, and tea.

The hospital rations are:

Sunday.

Breakfast.—Baked beans and pancakes, bread and butter, and coffee.
Dinner.—Roast veal, mashed potatoes, bread and butter.
Supper.—Toast and tea, mush and milk.

Monday.

Breakfast.—Beefsteak, etc.
Dinner.—Roast beef or fish, potatoes, etc.
Supper.—Toast and tea, mush and milk.

Tuesday.

Breakfast.—Hot biscuit and coffee.
Dinner.—Boiled dinner, etc.
Supper.—Toast and tea, mush and milk.

Wednesday.

Breakfast.—Corned beef, mush or beans, and coffee.
Dinner.—Broiled steak, baked potatoes, pudding.
Supper.—Toast and tea, mush and milk.

Thursday.

Breakfast.—Hash, rice and milk, etc.
Dinner.—Roast beef or fried liver.
Supper.—Toast and tea, mush and milk.

Friday.

Breakfast.—Fish balls and fried pork, etc.
Dinner.—Vegetable soup, bread and butter.
Supper.—Toast and tea, mush and milk.

Saturday.

Breakfast.—Hot biscuit and coffee.
Dinner.—Beefsteak and onions, etc.
Supper.—Toast and tea, mush and milk.

The above list is subject to variations during the different seasons of the year.

CONCLUSION.

I have endeavored to convey a practical idea of the manner in which the best managed reform schools are conducted, and hope that the information submitted will be of service to the Board. I have refrained from any remarks on abstract questions, dealing only with the practical side of the management of these institutions. The portion of this report devoted to State Prisons has been made longer than perhaps was necessary, but it was deemed best to present somewhat fully what I had gleaned on this subject, in the hope that it would prove not altogether unprofitable in the superintendence of the institutions of which the Board have charge.

I was received with uniform kindness and courtesy by all whom I met, and desire to thank them one and all for the assistance they have rendered. I desire also to express my obligation to the Board for the honor they have conferred upon me in selecting me to make this investigation, and hope that the trust thus imposed has been satisfactorily discharged.

Respectfully submitted.

ROBERT T. DEVLIN,
President of the State Board of Prison Directors of California.

INDEX.

160

11D

www.ingramcontent.com/pod-product-compliance
Lightning Source LLC
Chambersburg PA
CBHW020551270326
41927CB00006B/803